HEART TO HEART

HEART
TO
HEART

Octavius Winslow's
Experimental Preaching

Tanner G. Turley

Reformation Heritage Books
Grand Rapids, Michigan

Reformation Heritage Books
2965 Leonard St. NE
Grand Rapids, MI 49525
616-977-0889 / Fax 616-285-3246
orders@heritagebooks.org
www.heritagebooks.org

Printed in the United States of America
14 15 16 17 18 19/10 9 8 7 6 5 4 3 2 1

Library of Congress Cataloging-in-Publication Data

Turley, Tanner G.
  Heart to heart : Octavius Winslow's experimental preaching / Tanner G. Turley.
     pages cm
  Includes bibliographical references.
  ISBN 978-1-60178-196-3 (pbk. : alk. paper) 1. Winslow, Octavius, -1878. 2. Preaching.
I. Title.
  BX6495.W623T87 2014
  251.0092—dc23
                        2013050593

For additional Reformed literature, request a free book list from Reformation Heritage Books at the above regular or e-mail address.

To Marsha

My wife
My love
My best friend—
"You surpass them all."

and

To the glory of

MY TRIUNE GOD

My salvation
My joy
My life—
"From You, through You,
and to You are all things."

CONTENTS

Acknowledgments

My pursuit of Octavius Winslow began with a threefold prayer for a dissertation topic that went something like this: "God, lead me to a topic that I will enjoy immensely, will have an indelible impact on my future ministry, and will be a contribution to the church and academy." Undoubtedly, the first two parts of my prayer have been answered favorably. This work is the result of God's grace and kindness, which included many encouraging friends along the journey.

My beautiful wife, Marsha, supplied constant support over the two years I absorbed Winslow. She endured countless late nights, incessant requests for coffee, and, of course, stacks of books and papers everywhere. She is godly, spunky, sweet, and my best friend. I am eternally grateful for our partnership in the gospel and for the privilege of parenting our two precious girls, Parker and Kesed, together.

Danny Akin served as my mentor and major professor throughout my time at Southeastern Seminary. More than teaching me theology and homiletics, he daily exemplified godliness, leadership, and a passion for the Great Commission. I would also like to thank Greg Heisler, who first introduced me to Winslow and has helped me grow as a homiletician. A special thanks is also in order to Joel Beeke, Jay Collier, and everyone at Reformation Heritage Books for working hard to get this book in your hands. Finally, I would like to thank Jennifer Townsend, Winslow's great-great-granddaughter, who graciously uncovered and confirmed several biographical details.

INTRODUCTION

With the opening words of his 1907 Lyman Beecher Lecture at Yale University, P. T. Forsyth prophetically warned, "It is, perhaps, an overbold beginning, but I will venture to say that with its preaching Christianity stands or falls."[1] Nearly a century later John Stott boldly stated, "Preaching is indispensable to Christianity."[2] If Forsyth and Stott are correct, the health of the church and her mission of taking the gospel to the nations are proportionately related to the health of preaching. Regrettably, many churches today are languishing from anemic homiletical convictions and practice. Walt Kaiser expressed this concern when he wrote, "One of the most depressing spectacles in the church today is her lack of power.... At the heart of this problem is an impotent pulpit."[3] If the church is to recover her missiological muscle, she should humbly learn from the faithful heralds of church history. One such pastor and preacher is Octavius Winslow (1808–1878).

Winslow served the church for nearly forty-five years as a pastor, preacher, and prolific author. He shepherded two congregations in New York City for the first five years of his ministry and spent the next forty in the English towns of Leamington Spa, Brighton, and Bath. Though he served Baptist churches most of his life, he finished his ministerial career in the Church of England. He exercised a prolific ministry, publishing more than forty books, with most being printed multiple times.[4] By all accounts, he was

---

1. P. T. Forsyth, *Positive Preaching and the Modern Mind* (London: Independent Press, 1907), 1.

2. John Stott, *Between Two Worlds: The Art of Preaching in the Twentieth Century* (Grand Rapids: Eerdmans, 1996), 15.

3. Walter C. Kaiser, *Toward an Exegetical Theology* (Grand Rapids: Baker, 1981), 235–36.

4. Joel Beeke, foreword to *Our God*, by Octavius Winslow (London: John F. Shaw, 1870; repr., Grand Rapids: Reformation Heritage Books, 2007), vii–viii.

also an excellent preacher. One historian summarized his ministry by saying, "As a writer and preacher he had few equals."[5]

Perhaps the greatest strength of Winslow's homiletic involved how he embodied the Reformers' view of preaching. They believed preaching should be the *explicatio et applicatio verbi Dei* (the explanation and application of the Word of God).[6] Winslow consistently explained the text by grounding his sermons in doctrine and centering them in Christ, but he did not stop there. He longed for people to experience the truth. That is why he followed the apostolic pattern of indicative-imperative preaching.[7] By doing so, he avoided dry, *merely doctrinal* sermons, which fill the head but shrivel the heart. At the same time, he avoided shallow, *merely applicational* sermons, which provide practical instruction devoid of real substance. Winslow believed true preaching is experimental preaching: the skillful combination of sound doctrine aimed at life application.[8] Experimental preaching presses the significance of doctrine into hearers' lives so that they experience the power of God's truth. Octavius Winslow effectively demonstrated the practice of applying doctrine to life through his experimental preaching.

Experimental Preaching: Addressing the Heart

Because this work centers on Winslow's experimental homiletic, a clear understanding of what he meant by experimental Christianity is vital. First,

---

5. T. B. Dudley, *From Chaos to the Charter: A Complete History of Royal Leamington Spa* (Royal Leamington Spa, U.K.: P. & W. E. Linaker, 1901), 246.

6. Sidney Greidanus says, "From the 17th century on, Reformed theologians had defined the sermon as *explicatio et applicatio verbi Dei*." *Sola Scriptura: Problems and Principles in Preaching Historical Texts* (Toronto: Wedge Publishing Foundation, 1970; repr., Eugene, Ore.: Wipf & Stock, 2001, 92.

7. See John Carrick, *The Imperative of Preaching: A Theology of Sacred Rhetoric* (Edinburgh: Banner of Truth, 2002). Carrick states, "The central thesis of this book is that the essential pattern or structure which God himself has utilized in the proclamation of New Testament Christianity is that of the *indicative-imperative*" (5). Carrick goes on to say: "True preaching...always involves a balance between the *indicative* and the *imperative*. True preaching always involves both *proclamation* and *appeal*. True preaching always involves *explicatio et applicatio verbi Dei*—it always involves the explication and application of the Word of God. The indicative mood is the native sphere of the explication of the Word of God and the imperative mood is the native sphere of the application of the Word of God" (145–46).

8. Joel Beeke offers the following definition of this homiletical model: "Experiential (or 'experimental') preaching addresses the vital matter of how a Christian experiences the truth of Christian doctrine in his life." "Experiential Preaching," in *Feed My Sheep: A Passionate Plea for Preaching*, 2nd ed. (Lake Mary, Fla.: Reformation Trust, 2008), 53. Note that Beeke uses the terms "experiential" and "experimental" interchangeably. John Calvin did as well (54).

it will be helpful to understand what he does *not* mean. The kind of experimental preaching Winslow practiced is completely incompatible with the kind proposed by homileticians such as John Killinger in the 1960s and 1970s. Their unconventional approach focused on experimentation with various forms of communication. Killinger explains, "The only rule is that there are no rules which may not be broken. Real communication is not static and can seldom be accomplished for very long without experimentation and innovation."[9] His primary theological assumption is that "God, in Christ, has called us out from all totalitarian superstructures, even those of mind and spirit, and it is wrong of us to obligate or enslave ourselves to them again, even in the name of religion and piety. Our first obligation now is to our own centers of freedom."[10] For Killinger, man's creativity and freedom overrule methodological practices grounded in Scripture.[11] It is not surprising that experimental preachers of Killinger's day replaced "old-fashioned" sermons with innovations such as playlets, dramatic monologues, dialogue sermons, enigmatic parables, mime shows, clown acts, and multimedia presentations.[12]

Other potential misunderstandings of experimental, or experiential, preaching remain. Experimental preaching is not simply preaching one's experience. This was a common misperception in Winslow's day.[13] Experimental preaching does not spring from experiential learning theories that promote

---

9. John Killinger, ed., *Experimental Preaching* (Nashville: Abingdon, 1973), 9.

10. Killinger, *Experimental Preaching*, 15.

11. Interestingly, Killinger takes his Christology one step further. He writes, "What has been called the *kenosis* or self-emptying of Christ finally makes it impossible for us to make any unambiguous statements about him. Who he was, what he did, what he meant by what he said, has a way of eluding us. Precisely when we think we have caught the truth in our hands and call to a neighbor to look, it evaporates and leaves us feeling silly and empty-handed. What is asked for is a spirit of constant inquiry—a pledge to follow in the way without either the hope or the despair of arriving at finalities." *Experimental Preaching*, 16.

12. John Killinger, "Experimental Preaching," *Concise Encyclopedia of Preaching*, ed. William H. Willimon and Richard Lischer (Louisville: Westminster John Knox, 1995), 150. Killinger also displays contempt for some of the most influential names who side with the historic understanding of biblical preaching. He wrote, "The secure old positions and rationales of [John] Broadus and [William E.] Sangster no longer cast their freezing shadows over neophyte preachers—the former are indeed almost unknown among the latter." *Experimental Preaching*, 17. For a deeper look at these "old positions," see Broadus's classic work on preaching. John Broadus, *A Treatise on the Preparation and Delivery of Sermons* (New York: A. C. Armstrong, 1887).

13. Nineteenth-century pastor Robert Smith said, "There is a great difference between preaching experience and preaching truth experienced. The former should be seldom indulged in; the latter should always be aimed at. Without experience of the truth proclaimed, a man conjures with mere words, or at best deals with abstractions which never

learning through "concrete participation in the daily processes of living rather than categories of information."[14] It has even less to do with the agenda of the "New Homiletic" and its narrative sermon structure, which seeks to create an experience for the listener.[15] Finally, it does not involve the experiential story-telling advocated by some today in the emerging church movement.[16]

Winslow advocated an altogether different view. Although he never provided a straightforward definition, he described experimental Christianity at length.[17] In the preface of his first major work, *The Inquirer Directed to an Experimental and Practical View of the Atonement*, Winslow presented a case for the necessity of experimental Christianity. His opening argument read, "The religion of the Lord Jesus is valuable only as its power is experienced in the heart."[18] He went on to explain:

> The man of mere taste may applaud its external beauty—the philoso-pher may admire its ethics, the orator its eloquence, and the poet its sublimity, but if the Spirit of God take not his own truth, and *impress it upon the heart, as to the great design of its revelation*, it avails nothing. What numbers there are who rest in the mere theory of Christianity. As a *practical principle* they know nothing of it. As a thing *experienced*

---

move the heart." *The Quiet Thoughts of a Quiet Thinker* (London: Oliphant Anderson & Ferrier, 1896), 101.

14. John D. Hendrix, *Nothing Never Happens: Experiential Learning and the Church* (Macon, Ga.: Smith & Helwys, 2004), 15.

15. See David Buttrick, *Homiletic: Moves and Structures* (Philadelphia: Fortress, 1987); Fred Craddock, *As One without Authority* (Nashville: Abingdon, 1979); Eugene Lowry, *The Homiletical Plot: The Sermon as Narrative Art Form* (Atlanta: John Knox, 1980); and Henry Mitchell, *Celebration and Experience in Preaching*, rev. ed. (Nashville: Abingdon, 2008).

16. See Mark Miller, *Experiential Storytelling: (Re)Discovering Narrative to Communicate God's Message* (Grand Rapids: Zondervan, 2003). Miller defines experiential storytelling as "creating an environment that allows others to participate in the telling of a story through sensory interaction" (7). In order to create a multisensory experience, this approach basically utilizes anything the mind can imagine, including Play Doh© (105).

17. Winslow wrote much about experimental Christianity. His first two major works dealt with experimental views of the atonement and the Holy Spirit. See Octavius Winslow, *The Inquirer Directed to an Experimental and Practical View of the Atonement* (London: John F. Shaw, 1856; repr., *Atonement and the Cross* [Stoke-on-Trent, U.K.: Tentmaker, 2008]); and *The Inquirer Directed to an Experimental and Practical View of the Holy Spirit* (London: John F. Shaw, 1840; repr., *The Work of the Holy Spirit: An Experimental and Practical View* [Edinburgh: Banner of Truth, 2003]). One working assumption is that Winslow's experimental homiletic can be deduced from his views concerning experimental Christianity. At the same time, a careful study of his sermons is necessary to this effort, as it is conceivable that a preacher's preaching may not match his theology.

18. Winslow, *View of the Atonement*, 7.

in the heart, it is a hidden mystery to them. They speak well of it as a religious system; believe its Divinity, and even defend its doctrines and extol its precepts; yet make no approaches *towards a personal and practical obedience to its claims*. In a word, they know nothing of *repentance toward God, and faith towards our Lord Jesus Christ*. It will surely appear to a spiritually-enlightened mind, a subject of vast and solemn moment that this delusion should be exposed—that this foundation of sand be undermined, and *the absolute necessity of experimental religion*, as necessary to an admission within the kingdom of glory, be strenuously and scripturally enforced (emphasis added).[19]

Winslow said that experimental Christianity is an "absolute necessity" and involves "a personal and practical obedience" to the truth of Scripture. In sum, it is truth "experienced in the heart." From this description, it is not difficult to deduce what he believed about experimental preaching.[20]

Another way to discern how "experimental" was understood in Winslow's day is by examining how his predecessors and contemporaries utilized the term. Reformers such as John Calvin pointed to the need for "measuring experienced knowledge against the touchstone of Scripture."[21] One of the first published works on methodology, "Of Particular and Experimental Preaching," surfaced early in the eighteenth century. John Jennings, in lectures to his students, criticized preachers who fill their sermons with doctrine but "do not sufficiently consider that holiness is the very design of Christianity; and our preaching on other topics is in order the better to enforce duty and render men like Christ."[22] He likened experimental preaching to the work of a skilled doctor who knows his patients well. Concerning the pastor's responsibility to reach the hearts of his hearers, Jennings wrote:

Now, what success can we reasonably expect if we do not take into close consideration the case of our several spiritual patients? If a man, professing to be a physician, should administer or prescribe one constant medicine for fevers, and another for consumptions, and so for other

---

19. Winslow, *View of the Atonement*, 7–8. The original wording, archaic spelling, punctuation, paragraphing, and emphases from the original works will be retained throughout.
20. See chapter 5, "Preaching to the Heart," for a detailed investigation of Winslow's understanding of experimental Christianity and preaching.
21. Beeke, "Experiential Preaching," 54.
22. John Jennings, "Of Particular and Experimental Preaching," in *The Christian Pastor's Manual: A Selection of Tracts on the Duties, Difficulties, and Encouragements of the Christian Ministry*, by John Brown (Edinburgh: David Brown, 1826; repr., Morgan, Pa.: Soli Deo Gloria, 2003), 50. Jennings clearly exposed the connection between experimental preaching and the doctrine of sanctification.

distempers, without considering the age, constitution, strength, and way of living of his patient, and not vary his method and medicines as those vary, we would hardly call this the regular practice of medicine. Nor can I think this general and undistinguishing way will be more safe or likely to answer its end in divinity than in medicine.[23]

Experimental preachers consider the condition of their hearers and address the heart accordingly. Philip Doddridge, one of Jennings's pupils, claimed that experimental preaching leads hearers into their own hearts.[24] Ultimately, the preacher's goal is to apply a remedy and restore the soul into right fellowship with God.

Like their predecessors, Winslow's contemporaries also addressed the nature of experimental preaching by distinguishing it from mere doctrinal instruction. They believed many sermons devolve into impotent lectures by neglecting the practical side of truth. Daniel Kidder spoke to this when he praised the value of experimental preaching: "How superior, in the judgment at least of the more devout, and for all the great ends of the ministry, is an experimental style of preaching to that which is merely intellectual—essay like!"[25] While experimental preaching is more than mere doctrinal divulgence, it is certainly not less.

True experimental preaching must be grounded in doctrine. That is why Daniel Moore, an Anglican contemporary of Winslow, said experimental preaching is "the Gospel of Christ laid open, in its more spiritual and subjective aspects;—shewing the relation of dogma to piety, and the direct action of a doctrinal system on the sympathies and experiences of the heart."[26] To understand experimental preaching, one must grasp the relationship between doctrine and life. Experimental preaching begins with truth, and then presses truth on the heart to lead people to respond in obedience and faith.[27]

---

23. Jennings, "Of Particular and Experimental Preaching," 61.

24. Philip Doddridge, "Extracts from Doddridge's Lectures on Preaching," in *The Preacher's Manual*, ed. Sheva (London: Richard Baynes, 1820), 137.

25. Daniel P. Kidder, *A Treatise on Homiletics: Designed to Illustrate the True Theory and Practice of Preaching the Gospel* (New York: Carlton & Porter, 1864), 278.

26. Daniel Moore, "Preaching," in *The Authorized Report of the Church Congress Held at Leeds: October 8th, 9th, 10th, & 11th, 1872* (London: John Hodges, 1872), 213.

27. Contemporary theologian David Clark insightfully says, "If a theology does not transform a Christian's heart and her church, it fails calamitously. Theology misfires if it fills a believer's head with Christian knowledge without affecting his character and demeanor." *To Know and Love God: Method for Theology* (Wheaton, Ill.: Crossway, 2003), 232.

Charles Bridges explained, "This view of the scheme of the Gospel widely differs from the dry and abstract doctrinal statement. Its life consists not in the exposition, but in the application of the doctrine to the heart for the sanctification and comfort of the sincere Christian."[28] This type of preaching served as the hallmark of Winslow's ministry.

Why Winslow?

Many preachers could be the subject of this study. So why focus on Winslow? Joel Beeke calls him "one of the most valued non-conformist ministers of the nineteenth century, largely due to the earnestness of his preaching, and the practical excellence of his prolific writings."[29] Winslow enjoyed a widely influential ministry in the nineteenth century, but little has been uncovered about his life and work.

Though he exercised a productive and thriving ministry, virtually nothing on Winslow has been published aside from brief material included in the front matter of some reprinted works and a brief dictionary article.[30] Several of his works have been reprinted, but he still remains relatively unknown among today's theologians and church historians.[31] Sadly, it seems he did not leave a diary or journal behind.[32] Winslow lacked a biographer in his day, and no one has taken up the task since he died more than 135 years ago.[33] Preaching historians have also overlooked him.[34] Considering the popularity and significance he acquired during his era, this is surprising.

---

28. Charles Bridges, *The Christian Ministry with an Inquiry into the Causes of Its Inefficiency* (London: R. B. Seely & W. Burnside, 1830; repr., Edinburgh: Banner of Truth, 2006), 260.

29. Beeke, foreword to *Our God*, vii.

30. See Joel Beeke, foreword to *Morning Thoughts*, by Octavius Winslow (London: John F. Shaw, 1857; repr., Grand Rapids: Reformation Heritage Books, 2003); J. H. Y. Briggs, "Winslow, Octavius," in *The Blackwell Dictionary of Evangelical Biography*, ed. Donald M. Lewis (Oxford: Blackwell, 1995), 1213; and Randall J. Pederson, "The Life and Writings of Octavius Winslow," in *Midnight Harmonies, or, Thoughts for the Season of Solitude and Sorrow*, by Octavius Winslow (London: John F. Shaw, 1851; repr., Grand Rapids: Ebenezer Publications, 2002).

31. I am indebted to several publishing houses that have made some of Winslow's rare works more accessible. Some of those include Reformation Heritage Books, Soli Deo Gloria, Banner of Truth, Tentmaker Publications, and Kessinger Publishing. Joel Beeke is one scholar who has worked to raise awareness concerning Winslow's ministry. He has written the forewords or introductions to several of Winslow's reprinted works.

32. Because Winslow compiled many of his mother's and son Whitmore's journal entries into books, I believe he must have also practiced this discipline. If a personal journal ever existed, there is sufficient reason to fear such a treasure of information has been destroyed.

33. The *Dictionary of National Biography* does not even include an entry on his life.

34. Winslow is omitted by the following preaching histories: Edwin Charles Dargan, *A History of Preaching*, 2 vols. (New York: Hodder and Stoughton, 1905; repr., Birmingham,

Ministerial Contributions

Winslow's gifts blessed the congregations he served and the broader evangelical world. His many important contributions can be observed in four key areas: preaching, literary production, personal reputation, and pastoral effectiveness.

Winslow exercised an influential ministry from the pulpit. Several pieces of evidence verify that he preached with great effectiveness and should be counted as one of the most prominent servants of his day. First, and perhaps most convincing, Winslow was frequently invited to fill the pulpit for special occasions at other significant and notable congregations. The most famous opportunity came when Charles Spurgeon invited him to preach at the opening of the Metropolitan Tabernacle on April 4, 1861. He preached a sermon titled "Christ's Finished Work" from John 19:30.[35] It is highly doubtful Spurgeon would have invited a mediocre preacher to his pulpit for such a momentous occasion. Winslow was also invited as a guest preacher for several different Christian denominations across the United Kingdom[36] and other

---

Ala.: Solid Ground Christian Books, 2003); O. C. Edwards, *A History of Preaching* (Nashville: Abingdon, 2004); Clyde E. Fant and William M. Pinson Jr., *A Treasury of Great Preaching*, 12 vols. (Dallas: Word, 1971); David L. Larsen, *The Company of the Preachers*, 2 vols. (Grand Rapids: Kregel, 1998); Hughes Oliphant Old, *The Reading and Preaching of the Scriptures in the Worship of the Christian Church* (Grand Rapids: Eerdmans, 1998–2010); F. W. Webber, *A History of Preaching in Britain and America: Including Many of the Biographies of Many Princes of the Pulpit and the Men Who Influenced Them*, 3 vols. (Milwaukee: Northwestern Publishing House, 1952). The sheer number of great Victorian preachers is a possible factor in historians bypassing Winslow.

35. See Charles H. Spurgeon, *The Metropolitan Tabernacle Pulpit* (Pasadena, Tex.: Pilgrim Publications, 1986), 7:243–48. In the conclusion of his sermon, Winslow spoke a prayer of blessing over Spurgeon and the ensuing gospel work: "And now, from my heart, I ask the blessing of the Triune God upon my beloved Brother, the grand substance of whose ministry I believe from my very soul is to exalt the finished work of Jesus. And I pray that this noble edifice, reared in the name and consecrated to the glory of the Triune God, may for many years echo and re-echo with his voice of melody and of power in expounding to you the glorious doctrines and precepts of Christ's one finished atonement." *Metropolitan Tabernacle Pulpit*, 7:248.

36. His *Glimpses of the Truth As It Is in Jesus* is a series of sermons that he delivered on a trip to Scotland. He wrote in the preface, "It is proper briefly to allude to the history of this work. Scotland is its birth-place. It contains the substance of a few discourses which the author delivered from the pulpit of different Christian denominations, during a recent visit to that magnificent and interesting land." Octavius Winslow, *Glimpses of the Truth As It Is in Jesus* (Philadelphia: Lindsay & Blakiston, 1856), v.

important events including conferences,[37] missionary societies,[38] church meetings,[39] and universities.[40] Second, many individual sermons were published as tracts or pamphlets, and at least five of his books are identifiable as sermon compilations.[41] His annual New Year's sermons also "enjoyed considerable popularity."[42] Third, people in his day provided glowing reviews of his preaching. He was noted as "a preacher of considerable power and ability."[43] Henry Christmas, in his book *Preachers and Preaching* (1858), wrote about the most notable preachers in England in the nineteenth century. After providing sketches of ten of England's most prominent preachers, Christmas recognized Winslow in a short list of other commendable preachers. Of the

---

37. He delivered addresses at conferences for the Evangelical Alliance and other meetings. For examples, see Octavius Winslow, *Practical Suggestions Appropriate to the Present Religious Crisis* (London: William Hunt & Co., 1868); and Evangelical Alliance, "Evangelical Alliance: The Bath Conference," *Evangelical Christendom: A Monthly Chronicle of the Churches* 7 (November 1866): 554.

38. The Baptist Missionary Society, "Anniversary Services," *The Baptist Magazine* 41 (April 1849): 248.

39. W. H. Summers, *History of the Congregational Churches in the Berks, South Oxon and South Bucks Association with Notes on the Earlier Nonconformist History of the District* (Newbury, U.K.: W. J. Blacket, 1905), 256.

40. See Octavius Winslow, *Eminent Holiness: Essential to an Efficient Ministry* (London: Houlston & Stoneman, 1843).

41. Those five works include Octavius Winslow, *Glimpses of the Truth As It Is in Jesus; The Inner Life: Its Nature, Relapse, and Recovery* (London: John F. Shaw, 1850 (these first two works include sermons from various texts); *No Condemnation in Christ Jesus: As Unfolded in the Eighth Chapter of the Epistle to the Romans* (London: John F. Shaw, 1853; repr., Edinburgh: Banner of Truth, 1991); *Patriarchal Shadows of Christ and His Church: As Exhibited in Passages Drawn from the History of Joseph and His Brethren* (London: John F. Shaw, 1863; repr., Grand Rapids: Sovereign Grace Treasures, 2005 (these sermons are from Genesis 41–47); and *Soul-Depths & Soul-Heights: Sermons on Psalm 130* (London: John F. Shaw, 1874; repr., Edinburgh: Banner of Truth, 2006). These sermons demonstrate Winslow's commitment to preaching the whole counsel of God from both the Old and New Testaments. I am convinced some of his other works are probably sermon compilations, though they lack explicit evidence supporting such a view. Some of those include *Christ and the Christian in Temptation: Counsel and Consolation for the Tempted* (London, 1878); *Emmanuel, or, Titles of Christ: Their Teaching and Consolations* (London: John F. Shaw, 1869); *The Foot of the Cross and the Blessings Found There* (New York: Robert Carter, 1868; repr., *Atonement and the Cross* [Stoke-on-Trent, U.K.: Tentmaker, 2008]); *Pisgah Views, or, The Negative Aspects of Heaven* (London: John F. Shaw, 1873); and Octavius Winslow, *The Tree of Life: Its Shade, Fruit, and Repose* (London: John F. Shaw, 1868).

42. Lucius E. Smith, ed. "Editorial Notices," *The Baptist Quarterly* 1 (1867): 380. Several of these New Year addresses were collected in book form. See Octavius Winslow, *Divine Realities, or, Spiritual Reflections for the Saint and Sinner* (London: John F. Shaw, 1860).

43. Judy Middleton, *The Encyclopaedia of Hove and Portslade D to E* (self-published, 2002), 4:74.

nonconformists, he had the most to say about Winslow. He described him as "a most admirable preacher, and a highly educated and high-minded Christian gentleman."[44] Finally, one can discern his homiletical gifts by noting with whom he preached on some special occasions. The fact that Winslow preached with the likes of Spurgeon and R. W. Dale speaks well of his preaching credentials.[45] Winslow fulfilled his calling as a herald with great force and fruitfulness.

His massive literary output serves as another feature of his valuable ministry. He was considered one of the "best religious writers in Europe" and was mentioned with the eminent Scottish divine Thomas Guthrie and the heralded German pastor F. W. Krummacher as "stars of magnitude which have been long above the horizon."[46] He averaged publishing more than one book per year after his first work hit the press in 1838.[47] His writings reached a multitude of readers through multiple printings. One of his contemporaries said he was "one of the most widely and deeply influential writers of the present day."[48]

Another indication of Winslow's influence involves his reputation among other evangelicals. He was regarded as "an eminent Nonconformist."[49] One reviewer called him an "eminent minister of Christ."[50] He also served as a reviewer of other books and wrote a recommendation or introduction to several books during his ministry.[51] Aside from his involvement in the

---

44. Henry Christmas, *Preachers and Preaching* (London: William Lay, 1858), 116. Powerful preachers such as Charles Spurgeon, Robert Hall, Thomas Chalmers, and R. W. Dale demonstrate the quality of Christmas's observations. That Winslow was listed after these greats is significant.

45. Baptist Missionary Society, "Recognition and Ordination Services," *The Baptist Magazine* 49 (1857): 504.

46. The American and Foreign Christian Union, "Book Notices," *Christian World: A Magazine of the American and Foreign Christian Union* 14 (March 1863): 95.

47. See Octavius Winslow, *The Inquirer Directed to an Experimental and Practical View of the Atonement* (New York: M. W. Dodd, 1838).

48. George Cole, *Euthanasia: Sermons and Poems in Memory of Departed Friends* (London: William MacIntosh, 1868), 303.

49. Catherine Marsh, *The Life of the Rev. William Marsh, D.D.* (London: James Nisbet & Co., 1867), 179.

50. "Notices of Books," *The Christian Observer and Advocate Conducted by Members of the Church of England for the Year 1875* (February 1875): 157.

51. See Octavius Winslow, introductory preface to *The Spirit of Holiness*, by James Harington Evans (New York: J. S. Taylor, 1837); Octavius Winslow, introductory preface to *Sermons on the First Epistle of Peter*, by Hermann Friedrich Kohlbrügge (London: Patridge & Oakley, 1853); and Octavius Winslow, preface to *The Nature and Evidences of Regeneration*, by George Townshend Fox (London: William Hunt, 1872).

Evangelical Alliance, one other evidence of his esteemed reputation was the respect paid by those who differed with Winslow theologically.[52]

Finally, Winslow's effectiveness as a pastor confirms his ministerial worth. As will be noted later, Winslow demonstrated an ability to be used by God to grow churches. Both Warwick Street and Emmanuel Chapel enjoyed great success under his ministry. The latter witnessed 1,300 congregants sitting under his preaching weekly.[53] Most importantly, Winslow was loved by his people. All of these aspects reveal his valuable contributions as a gospel minister.

The primary concern of this work deals with identifying Winslow's homiletic theology and methodology. The absence of a specific work on preaching by Winslow himself presents a challenge for pinning down his homiletic. Thankfully that challenge is alleviated by the amount of ink he devoted to preaching and related topics in his abundant writing ministry.[54] Additionally, his sermon compilations provide a great treasure for analyzing the prominent elements of his homiletic.

Chapter 1 provides a biographical sketch of Winslow's life and ministry. After tracing his birth, heritage, and early life, it presents a summary of his conversion, education, and ordination. Then an investigation of his ministerial career addresses the historical context in which he ministered, noting the Puritan influence on his ministry as well as the golden age of preaching in Victorian England. It also unfolds his view of ministry before describing his five pastorates in New York, Leamington Spa, Bath, and Brighton. Notable events are highlighted, such as the controversy with Spurgeon over baptismal regeneration and his decision to leave the Baptist church in order to complete his ministry in the Anglican church. The chapter concludes by providing an account of his death and legacy.

Chapter 2 outlines Winslow's theology and methodology of preaching. It argues his theology of preaching provided the impetus for his pulpit practice. First, an examination of his convictions concerning the nature of preaching

---

52. See "Review," *The General Baptist Repository and Missionary Observer* 4 (1842): 21. The reviewer wrote, "The...work is by an esteemed living author, who though he is decidedly Calvinistic in his views, and occasionally takes up a position from which we dissent, has so much of the savour of deep piety, and holy spirituality, as commend him to our love, and his work to the perusal of all who desire to 'grow in grace.' While meditating on the most impressive passages, we could not avoid reflecting, how little, both practically and experimentally, true Christians differ from each other" (21).

53. "Death of the Rev. Dr. Winslow," *Brighton Gazette*, March 7, 1878.

54. I am greatly appreciative of the people at www.grace-ebooks.com who have made thirty-four of Winslow's books available electronically in searchable PDF format.

is offered. Winslow believed speaking God's words was both weighty and a delight. His theology of the Holy Spirit and preaching is covered next. He believed the Spirit is essential for the work of regeneration, illumination, anointing, and sanctification. This chapter also covers Winslow's methodology of preaching by analyzing the influence of Jesus and the Puritans on his homiletic. In the end, it presents a case that Winslow's methodology should be described as experimental. The two foundational pillars of Winslow's experimental homiletic are explained in the next two chapters.

Chapter 3 analyzes Winslow's doctrinal preaching. His doctrinal preaching was grounded in Scripture. Because he viewed the Bible as inspired by God, he staked his preaching on the trustworthiness and effectual power of God's Word. Winslow's understanding of the gospel and the importance of doctrinal precision is also covered. The last major section demonstrates how Winslow preached the doctrines of grace, addressing their content and the results that accompany proclaiming them.

Chapter 4 expounds on the previous chapter by highlighting the dominant doctrine of Winslow's preaching: Jesus Christ. Winslow's writings, preaching, and ministry were thoroughly Christ centered. An examination of his hermeneutic is offered before moving to his preaching practice. It then discusses his convictions concerning Christ-centered preaching and analyzes Winslow's sermons from various genres of Scripture. Additionally, it argues that Winslow's Christ-centered preaching was motivated by his Trinitarian theology. He believed the work of redemptive history focuses on the person of Christ because it is Jesus who reveals the Father, and the Spirit who reveals the Son.

Chapter 5 describes how Winslow preached to the heart. His theory of experimental preaching is explained at the onset of the chapter. It then examines the goal of experimental preaching by highlighting Winslow's doctrine of progressive sanctification and the preacher's responsibility to preach for holistic change. An analysis of the key experimental elements in Winslow's preaching, including its applicatory, discriminating, interrogating, illustrating, exhortative, and persuasive qualities closes the chapter.

Chapter 6 considers what Winslow has to say to today's church with several constructive proposals for today's preachers. It concludes that Winslow's homiletic has much to teach contemporary preachers regarding a theology of preaching and experimentally declaring the relevance of doctrine for one's life in a Christ-centered manner. Finally, two of Winslow's sermon manuscripts are included as samples in appendixes 1 and 2 covering an Old

Testament and New Testament text, respectively. Following the appendixes is an annotated bibliography of Winslow's works.

It is necessary to begin with the man himself, because true experimental preaching begins with a heart constantly being changed by God's grace. It is illegitimate for preachers to declare a gospel they fail to experience. Winslow was a man who first preached from the heart before he sought to preach to the heart.

1

~

OCTAVIUS WINSLOW'S LIFE
AND MINISTRY

Octavius Winslow was born August 1, 1808, on Queen's Row in Pentonville, a district of London.[1] As his name suggests, Octavius was the eighth son of Thomas and Mary Winslow.[2] Thomas was a native of Boston, Massachusetts, but moved to England at the age of four.[3] He enjoyed an enviable pedigree, being a lineal descendant of Edward Winslow, a *Mayflower* pilgrim and one of the first governors of Plymouth Colony.[4] Thomas served as a captain in the 47th Regiment of Foot in the British Army.[5] While stationed in Bermuda, he met Mary Forbes. Although Mary's mother had discouraged the pursuit of her daughter by military men, the two were soon married in St. George's,

---

1. Jennifer Townsend, e-mail message to the author, November 17, 2009. Jennifer is Winslow's great-great-granddaughter. Her great-grandfather was Octavius Winslow Jr. She resides in Brighton, England, and was immensely kind in sharing some rare family information. I am very grateful for her generous help. Because Winslow did not have a biographer and did not leave behind a journal, the material in this chapter has been gathered from the memoirs he penned about his mother, Mary, and his son John Whitmore, as well as other primary and secondary sources.

2. The family Bible of Robert Forbes Winslow, one of Octavius's older brothers, provides a list of his siblings. The following list details those who shared the gift of life with Octavius during his childhood years: Thomas Forbes (b. 1795); Isaac Deblois (b. 1799); Edward (b. 1801); George Erving (b. 1804); Henry James (b. 1806); Robert Forbes (b. 1807); Forbes (b. 1810); Emma (b. 1813); and Mary (b. 1814). Sadly, Thomas and Mary had three other children who died before their first birthday: Mary (b. 1797); Robert Deblois (b. 1798); and Mary Elizabeth (b. 1803). "The Robert Forbes Family Bible," http://winslowtree.com/robert.htm.

3. Parker M. Reed, *The Bench and Bar of Wisconsin: History and Biography, with Portrait Illustrations* (Milwaukee: P. M. Reed, 1882), 439; and Molly Whittington-Egan, *Doctor Forbes Winslow: Defender of the Insane* (Foley Terrace, U.K.: Cappella Archive, 2000), 17.

4. James Deetz and Patricia Scott Deetz, *The Times of Their Lives: Life, Love, and Death in Plymouth Colony* (New York: W. H. Freeman, 2000), 245. For evidence on the family lineage, see Douglas Kenelm Winslow, *Mayflower Heritage: A Family Record of the Growth of Anglo-American Partnership* (New York: Funk & Wagnalls Co., 1957), 188.

5. Sidney Lee, ed., "Winslow, Thomas," *Dictionary of National Biography, Whichcord–Zuylestein* (New York: MacMillan, 1900), 21:674.

Bermuda, on September 6, 1791.[6] Neither of Winslow's parents were Christians when they wed.

Several years later, shortly before Octavius's birth, Mary was converted.[7] She trusted Christ just a short time before Octavius's birth. In a letter to him she wrote, "A few months before your birth, the Lord met with my soul, and most blessedly drew me to Himself, making Himself known to me as my Saviour and my God. I bore you during this sweet season of my espousal to Christ."[8] Mary quickly became the spiritual leader of her home.

One of Mary's inaugural acts of faith involved leading her family in worship. Octavius later reflected on the courage she exercised during these moments:

> As a follower of Christ, she stood alone in her family. She felt her responsibility and resolved to act. Her first step in carrying out this her solemn resolution to serve the Lord was the erection of what until now had no place in her domestic circle—a family altar to God. The accomplishment of her purpose demanded no little moral courage, wisdom, and firmness. The proposal was submitted to her husband, and though kindly, was yet strongly opposed. But the conviction of duty was too deep to be overcome. The energy of will, and the remarkable grace which in after years confronted and vanquished difficulties in the way of duty more formidable, and which bore her through trials yet more severe, crowned this her first work and testimony for God with the most pleasing success. Consent was at length given; the effort was made in God's strength, and God blessed it. The family and household were convened for what to them was a novel yet impressive service. Her husband, at first declining to be present, was there. She conducted the service, read a portion of God's word, and then all but one of that circle knelt

---

6. Octavius Winslow, *Life in Jesus: A Memoir of Mrs. Mary Winslow Arranged from Her Correspondence, Diary, and Thoughts* (London: John F. Shaw, 1890; repr., Grand Rapids: Reformation Heritage Books, 2013), 8. D. Winslow added an extra detail to the story: "There was a most romantic courtship which Mary's mother tried to end when she found young Thomas up a ladder carrying on his wooing at Mary's bedroom window." *Mayflower Heritage*, 146.

7. Mary testified, "I had been in vain trying to work out my own salvation, but my work always fell short, and left me as poor and miserable as ever. Now was held out to me the hope that I might be saved by the work of another—the work of Jesus Christ." Winslow, *Life in Jesus*, 16.

8. Winslow, *Life in Jesus*, 71. In the same letter, Mary reflected on the tumultuous experience of Octavius's birth. She added, "After your birth, I was brought to the verge of eternity; for nearly twenty-four hours there was hardly a hair's-breadth between me and death. The physicians concealed my danger; but God did for me what no human skill could do, and I was spared,—snatched as from the grave."

while she offered solemn prayer,—the father of that worshipping family alone stood. But when again they assembled, that heart was subdued, its hostility disarmed, and side by side with his wife and little ones he bent the knee before their Father in heaven. From this moment the fire enkindled on that domestic altar never went out. Whether at home or abroad, journeying on the land, or voyaging upon the sea, family prayer was never omitted. "As for me and my house, we will serve the Lord," was a holy resolve with which no other engagements ever were allowed to interfere.[9]

Mary also prioritized corporate worship. When Octavius was a child, the family worshiped at Pentonville Chapel under the pastoral ministry of Rev. Thomas Sheppard.[10]

Mary's devotion did not relieve her family from a host of trials, and little Octavius was not exempt from this season of hardship. Early in his childhood he suffered from what seemed to be a life-threatening illness. During a stay in Twickenham, just outside of London, Mary wrote a letter to her mother describing her "sweet little sufferer":

My dearest Mother,

Yours was forwarded to me at this place, where I am for a week, with my dear little suffering O[ctavius], in the hope, with God's blessing, the change of air may be of service. The Lord only knows whether I shall ever rear him. The physician in town pronounces him in a decline, but that the change of air may be of service. He is very dear and precious to me; but I desire to resign him into His hand, who is able to rescue him even from the grave; and if it be His blessed will to take him, I have a humble hope that He will give me grace to say, *Thy will be done!* But oh, my dear mother, you know my heart is wrapped up in my children; and this sweet little sufferer is particularly dear to me, because he has been almost all his life afflicted; and I believe, if every hair of his head were numbered, I have had a tear, a sigh, a groan for each one. I am often

---

9. Winslow, *Life in Jesus*, 21–22. Mary's greatest mentor in the early days of her Christian walk was her favorite author, John Newton. Speaking of the days following her conversion she wrote, "At this time I became acquainted with the writings of the Rev. John Newton. I read them with great delight; and if he had been alive I would have walked miles to have conversed with him" (18).

10. In a letter to Octavius, Mary wrote, "On Sunday evening I worshipped in Pentonville Chapel, and heard Mr. Sheppard. As soon as I was seated, I felt such an inexpressible love to God for His great and wonderful goodness to me in all my weary pilgrimage, from the time I used to worship there with your dear father and all you little ones, that I wept." Winslow, *Life in Jesus*, 92. Rev. Sheppard should not be confused with seventeenth-century Puritan pastor Thomas Shepard (1605–1649).

afraid the Lord is chastening me for my too anxious concern about my children. But I know that all He does will eventually be for my good and His glory.[11]

Octavius nearly died while in Twickenham. Due to a nurse's mistake, Mary administered the wrong medicine, and the doctors said it should have killed ten men. Mary's faith sustained her through this traumatic event. She wrote, "The physicians said that you must die. The Lord said, 'He shall not die, but live.' He answered prayer, and gave you back to me. They afterwards said it was a miracle."[12] God's merciful kindness rested on Winslow as a child. He was blessed to have a mother who loved him deeply and trusted in God's sovereignty. Sadly, these early events only served as a precursor to more difficult suffering that loomed ahead.

Several years after Thomas retired from the army, he squandered much of his fortune through a series of "ill-advised and disastrous investments" in the stock market.[13] This prompted the family to seek refuge in the United States. In June 1815, Mary and the children embarked for New York to prepare a home for Thomas, who planned to follow a few months later. Tragically, the shores of America greeted them with their most difficult calamity. Octavius described the woeful scene: "[Mary] had scarcely become settled in her new and pleasant home ere death invaded it. The infant daughter she had borne across the Atlantic sickened and died. This was the first draught from sorrow's cup. That cup was now to be brimmed. While the corpse of her babe lay yet unentombed, the woeful intelligence reached her that she was a widow!"[14] Mary lost her baby girl, then her husband in the blink of an eye. The sorrowing family experienced this bitter providence when Octavius was seven years old. Thankfully, God provided them a reason to grieve with hope. During the final days of his life, Thomas gave evidence he had become a Christian.[15]

Naturally, without Captain Winslow, the family struggled. Family historian D. Kenelm Winslow recorded their plight: "[Mary] had the youngsters out on the streets of New York selling matches and newspapers as soon as

---

11. Winslow, *Life in Jesus*, 40–41. Octavius sought to preserve some level of anonymity by typically using only the first initial of a person's name.

12. Winslow, *Life in Jesus*, 72.

13. Winslow, *Life in Jesus*, 44. See also D. Winslow, *Mayflower Heritage*, 154.

14. Winslow, *Life in Jesus*, 47.

15. Mary confidently clung to this hope until her dying days. Shortly before her death, she wrote in her journal, "So shall I behold Him who loved me with an everlasting love and landed me at last in the kingdom of glory. Then I shall meet my beloved husband, his little faith at the eleventh hour saving him for ever." Winslow, *Life in Jesus*, 321.

they were old enough for such tasks. She set them to any job they could tackle, gathering them round her at night for Scripture-reading, followed by a good sound evangelical harangue and prayers."[16] Growing up without a father was perhaps Octavius's most difficult trial during his childhood. With only a faith-filled mother in his formative years, it is not surprising he possessed such reverence for her throughout his life.

Mary and the children lived in New York City until 1820. Following a four-month visit to England, she returned to America and took her family to rural Sing Sing, New York, where she rented a small estate on the banks of the Hudson for "four years of congenial repose."[17] The family moved back to New York City in 1824 and experienced a season of revival. Octavius and two of his brothers were converted. In addition, Octavius, George, and Issac became convinced God was calling them to Christian ministry.

Octavius and his brothers were recipients of Mary's love and godly instruction. An example of her wise counsel is observed in a letter she penned to them. She wrote, "Keep close to Jesus. Forget not my old exhortation. Pray without ceasing. Go to Him for all you need; lean upon Him. There is a fulness in Christ, treasured up for you, that the highest angel in heaven cannot fathom. Tell Him all that is in your heart. Lay your case before Him as if He did not already know it."[18] Her wisdom was filled with experimental truth that would guide them in paths of righteousness.

Winslow possessed great love for his mother. He displayed his affection and gratitude on the dedicatory page of his first major work, *An Experimental and Practical View of the Atonement*. He wrote, "This volume is respectfully and gratefully inscribed to my beloved and revered mother, through whose early instructions and prayers, I am indebted under God, for my first acquaintance with, and for many of my maturer views of, the great doctrine, which it is an humble attempt to unfold, by her affectionate and dutiful son, the author."[19] He also dedicated *The Inquirer Directed to an Experimental*

---

16. D. Winslow, *Mayflower Heritage*, 155. She also sought the support of other family members throughout America and Canada (154).

17. Winslow, *Life in Jesus*, 65. Although the only dated letter was sent from Mt. Pleasant, they probably resided in Sing Sing, now known as Ossining. See J. Thomas Scharf, *History of Westchester County, New York, including Morrisania, Kings Bridge and West Farms Which Have Been Annexed to New York City* (Philadelphia: L.E. Preston & Co., 1886), 1:322.

18. Winslow, *Life in Jesus*, 74.

19. Winslow, *The Inquirer Directed to an Experimental and Practical View of the Atonement* (London: John F. Shaw, 1856; repr., *Atonement and the Cross*, Stoke-on-Trent, U.K.: Tentmaker, 2008), 5.

and Practical View of the Holy Spirit and *The Glory of the Redeemer in His Person and Work* to his mother.[20] Reflecting on his mother's influence, Winslow wrote:

> How powerful and deathless is the influence of a holy mother! That influence, employed in planting the first seedlings of thought, in shaping the first actions of childhood, still lives to instruct, admonish, and cheer in manhood's riper years. Honoured and privileged are they, around whose toilsome path yet lingers a spell so sacred, a power so gentle, and a charm so holy and persuasive.[21]

Mary's piety and holy influence made a remarkable impact on Winslow in his early years. In order to know him well, it is necessary to know his godly mother. He later memorialized her in a book titled *Life in Jesus*.[22]

Preparation for Ministry
The godly instruction Winslow received as a youth yielded great fruit as he entered manhood. Between 1827 and 1833, Winslow confessed his faith in Christ, experienced the call to ministry, pursued theological education, and was ordained. These formative years provided the foundation and prepared him for future ministry.

Conversion
Winslow was saved under the ministry of Samuel Eastman, who served as the pastor of the Stanton Street Baptist Church in New York City.[23] While Eastman presumably played an important role in Winslow's conversion, it is likely that his mother was the most influential gospel witness in his life. As

---

20. On the dedicatory page of *The Inquirer Directed to an Experimental and Practical View of the Holy Spirit*, 4th ed. (Philadelphia: Lindsay & Blakiston, 1856), iii. In a similar vein, *The Glory of the Redeemer in His Person and Work* dedication: "To my mother, who first directed my eye to the glory of the Redeemer, this volume, with the deepest filial affection and gratitude, is inscribed." 8th ed. (London: John F. Shaw, 1865; repr., Pittsburgh: Soli Deo Gloria, 1997), vi.

21. Winslow, *Life in Jesus*, 127.

22. He also compiled other selections of her personal correspondence into another book titled *Heaven Opened: A Selection from the Correspondence of Mrs. Mary Winslow* (London: John F. Shaw, 1864; repr., Grand Rapids: Reformation Heritage Books, 2001).

23. Geoffrey R. Breed, *Calvinism and Communion in Victorian England: Studies in Nineteenth-Century Strict-Communion Baptist Ecclesiology Comprising the Minutes of the London Association of Strict Baptist Ministers and Churches, 1846–1855 and the Ramsgate Chapel Case, 1862* (Springfield, Mo.: Particular Baptist Press, 2008), 605n16.

noted, it was Mary who introduced him to the work of the Spirit, the glory of Christ, and His atoning work.

On Wednesday, April 11, 1827, Winslow shared his testimony and professed his faith before the members of Stanton Street.[24] He was then baptized in the Hudson River on Sunday, May 6, at 4:00 p.m.[25] Great joy filled Mary's soul when God saved her son. More than a year later, August 2, 1828, she wrote in her journal:

> Yesterday was dear [Octavius's] birthday. I felt happy at the birth of my son, but that happiness was trifling, although all that a fond mother could feel, in comparison of what my heart experienced at the hour of his spiritual birth. I truly did travail with him a second time, that Christ might be revealed within him the hope of glory. Oh, the gladness of that interesting moment! Angels united in a mother's joy. The church below, the church above,—all, all rejoiced; and Christ was well pleased to see the travail of His soul. May He who then made Himself known to him as his Redeemer, be graciously pleased to pour into his heart the rich blessing of His grace, and fit and qualify him for great usefulness in His blessed cause. Give him, Lord, humbleness of spirit, and stamp Thine image deep within his inmost soul.[26]

Though young in his faith, Winslow was serious about leading others to Christ. During this time, Mary penned a letter to her former pastor in England detailing the evangelistic fervor of Octavius and his brothers. She wrote: "My children are earnestly engaged in bringing sinners where the Holy Ghost is displaying His mighty power. They visit from house to house, dealing faithfully with all they meet who know not God."[27]

Though Winslow planned to enter the medical profession, shortly after his conversion the Lord called him to preach the gospel.[28] He understood

---

24. Stanton Street Baptist Church, *A History of Stanton Street Baptist Church in the City of New York; With a Sketch of Its Pastors, and a Register of the Entire Membership* (New York: Sheldon & Co., 1860), 26. While Breed (*Calvinism and Communion*, 605n16) dates Winslow's public profession on April 10, 1827, the *History of Stanton Street* identifies the date as being April 11: "The good work went forward, so that on the first of April the pastor baptized six persons more in the same place. Ten days afterward, the church listened to the experiences of seven converts—among whom were James Cowan, Octavius Winslow, Mrs. Margaret Wallace and Mary Cox; the last two are still members with us, after a lapse of nearly one-third of a century" (26).

25. Stanton, *History of Stanton*, 26.

26. Winslow, *Life in Jesus*, 79.

27. Winslow, *Life in Jesus*, 112.

28. T. B. Dudley, *From Chaos to the Charter: A Complete History of Royal Leamington Spa* (Royal Leamington Spa: P. & W. E. Linaker, 1901), 246.

the necessity of the new birth for ministers: "Thus, to be able and successful preachers of the word, we must have Christ in our hearts."[29] Winslow was licensed to preach by Stanton Street in October of 1827 at the age of nineteen. His license was then forwarded to London, where he pursued his studies.[30]

Education

Just as Winslow knew the necessity of a transformed heart, he also recognized the value of theological education. He was blessed to have a mother who spent family resources judiciously so that she could provide an education for her sons.[31] Several of Octavius's brothers enjoyed significant professional success. Edward served as the private secretary of Lord Lyndhurst while he was chancellor of England and later as a master in Lunancy.[32] Both Issac Deblois and George served as vicars in the Church of England.[33] Robert Forbes labored as an accomplished lawyer in New York, Wisconsin, and Illinois.[34] Forbes Benignus became "a supreme authority" on mental illnesses and, like Octavius, was a prolific writer.[35] Needless to say, Mary's wise sacrifices paid great dividends for her boys.[36]

---

29. Octavius Winslow, *Eminent Holiness: Essential to an Efficient Ministry* (London: Houlston & Stoneman, 1843), 41.

30. Stanton, *History of Stanton*, 27. See also Breed, *Calvinism and Communion*, 605n16.

31. Octavius and his brothers studied in England beneath the eye of Thomas, their oldest brother. Winslow, *Life in Jesus*, 56–57.

32. Reed, *Bench and Bar*, 440.

33. Winslow, *Life in Jesus*, 114–15, 263.

34. Reed, *Bench and Bar*, 439–43. Robert Forbes was also one of the pioneers of Wisconsin and even served as a colonel in the militia. Interestingly, at the request of the war department, he drilled and trained a regiment of infantry for the Civil War in Bureau County, Illinois. The following description was given of his life in 1882 when Robert was seventy-five years old: "He is a member of the second Baptist church, in Chicago. He is a gentleman of the old school, clothed with becoming dignity, without vanity; courteous and gentle, conscientious and unswerving in his fidelity to truth and uprightness; is a faithful and reliable attorney and counselor; systematic, accurate and methodical in preparing his cases, and has few equals in point of ability in presenting them to court or jury; is true to his clients, and esteemed by the members of his profession; held in high regard by all who know him as a citizen and gentleman. His life has been one of beneficent activity" (443).

35. George Edward Rines, ed., "Forbes Benignus Winslow," *The Encyclopedia Americana: A Library of Universal Knowledge in Thirty Volumes* (New York: The Encyclopedia Americana Corporation, 1920), 29:400. See also "Forbes Benignus Winslow," *Dictionary of National Biography*, ed. Leslie Stephen and Sidney Lee (London: Oxford, 1922), 21:674–75.

36. Molly Whittington-Egan wrote of them, "The Winslows were a clubbable clan, busy men of affairs, fitting in the writing of their lengthy tomes by what ardours of lucubration." *Dr. Forbes Winslow*, 31.

Winslow attended Stepney College in London, which was founded by Particular Baptists in 1811.[37] The annual report for 1829 reveals that ill health prevented him from graduating at Stepney.[38] Nevertheless, his relationship with the school remained strong. In 1843, Winslow was invited to address the students and faculty at their opening convocation.[39] Upon completing his time at Stepney, Winslow returned to New York and discovered that Rev. Eastman had resigned as pastor of Stanton Street. In November of 1830, the church chose him to moderate various church meetings for the next five months until the new pastor was selected.[40]

Winslow viewed the college years as a time of maturation, saying that an undergraduate should "feel that the great work for which he is now to employ every moment and task every energy is, self-development."[41] He believed this development should be intellectual and spiritual. He declared, "Let there be learning, let the mind be furnished with ancient and modern lore, let the intellectual powers be cultivated to their utmost extent, but let *personal piety* be the groundwork, and in the advance of all."[42] For those training for ministry, these must be combined, because unsanctified learning is "a bane to the church, and a curse to the world."[43] Winslow deplored the danger of intellectual pride.

Winslow twice had the privilege of receiving honorary degrees. The first was an honorary master of arts (M.A.) conferred by the University of the City

---

37. R. E. Cooper, *From Stepney to St. Giles: The Story of Regent's Park College 1810–1960* (London: Carey Kingsgate Press, 1960). The college moved to Oxford in 1856, where it was renamed Regent's Park College at Oxford (58).

38. The College Annual Report for Stepney College 1829 reads: "During the past year, nineteen Students have enjoyed the patronage of this Society.... Mr. O. Winslow has been obliged, by ill health, to discontinue his studies." Jennifer Townsend, e-mail message to the author, February 11, 2010. This contradicts the research of T. B. Dudley, who said Winslow "passed in divinity at Stepney." *From Chaos to Charter*, 246.

39. This address was later published. See Winslow, *Eminent Holiness*. He dedicated this work to Rev. William H. Murch with these words: "To the Rev. William H. Murch, D.D., President of Stepney College, This Work, as a small testimony of respect to his personal worth; as a grateful momento [*sic*] of the many expressions of his friendship; and as a public acknowledgement of the advantages derived from his theological instructions, is dedicated, with sentiments of affection and esteem, by the author" (iii).

40. Breed, *Calvinism and Communion*, 605n16. See also Stanton, *History of Stanton*, 35.

41. Octavius Winslow, *Hidden Life: Memorials of John Whitmore Winslow* (London: John F. Shaw, 1872), 94.

42. Winslow, *Hidden Life*, 96.

43. Winslow, *Eminent Holiness*, 78.

of New York (NYU) in 1836.[44] Then, in 1851, Columbia College in New York City conferred upon him the honorary degree of doctor of divinity (D.D.).[45] Of the latter, T. B. Dudley wrote, "This was in acknowledgement of his contribution to theological literature, and was a distinction very rarely granted to ministers outside the pale of the Episcopal Church."[46] The benefit gained from these years of training is confirmed by his literary output and theological acumen displayed throughout his ministry.

Ordination

Winslow insisted one's calling must possess a divine stamp. Concerning the inward call of God he declared, "He who is truly and properly called to the work of the Christian ministry is called, as Aaron was, of God. He cannot be self-moved nor self-commissioned. The 'will of man' cannot breathe in his soul an inspiration for the work, nor can the power of man clothe him with gifts and authority for its discharge."[47] At the same time, he believed in the external affirmation of God's people.[48] He experienced this during his own ordination on July 21, 1833, at the Oliver Street Baptist Church in New York City.[49] During his ordination, "deep solemnity pervaded a crowded audience."[50] His mother provided an eyewitness account:

---

44. New York University Alumni Association, *Biographical Catalogue of the Chancellors, Professors and Graduates of the Department of Arts and Science of the University of the City of New York* (New York: Alumni Association, 1894), 208.

45. Joseph Foulkes Winks, ed., "Intelligence: Baptist," *The Baptist Reporter and Missionary Intelligencer* 25 (November 1851): 433.

46. Dudley, *From Chaos to Charter*, 246.

47. Winslow, *Eminent Holiness*, 6.

48. See M. E. Agnus, *Henry Dunckley M.A., LL.D.* (Manchester, U.K., 1896; repr. Charleston, S.C.: BiblioBazaar, 2009), 5–7. Angus tells the story of how Dunkley joined Winslow's church after Winslow convinced him of his need for believer's baptism at the age of sixteen. Dunkley was then invited to preach a trial sermon in front of Winslow and the deacons so that his giftedness for ministry could be assessed. Winslow then recommended him for admission to Stepney College.

49. It appears that his ordination was conducted at the Oliver Street Baptist Church. Although the Stanton Street records show he was already licensed to preach, Oliver Street probably ordained and sent him out for this new work. See Jonathan Greenleaf, *A History of the Churches, of All Denominations, in the City of New York, from the First Settlement to the Year 1846* (New York: E. French, 1846), 260. Several dates have been given for Winslow's ordination; I am following the correspondence of Mary Winslow. Winslow, *Life in Jesus*, 108.

50. See "Ordinations," *The Baptist Magazine* (November 1833): 516. The charge was given by the Rev. S. H. Cone and the address to the newly formed church was supplied by the Rev. J. Gowing, D.D. (516).

Last evening dear O[ctavius] was ordained. It was a most interesting service. You may suppose what I felt when I saw my son kneeling, while the hands of the Presbytery were laid upon his head, and prayer was offered that God would fit him for the great work to which he was solemnly being set apart. When I saw the hands of the ministers resting upon him, my prayer was, "Now, Lord, lay Thy hand, Thy blessed hand upon him, and fill him with the Holy Ghost, that he may do Thy work from the heart, and be kept humbly sitting at Thy feet."[51]

That prayer would serve him well as he travelled the pastoral road over the next forty-five years. A few weeks later, eight people were baptized and joined the church.[52]

Winslow took the call to ministry with great seriousness. Addressing the students at Stepney College, he proposed that every prospective minister should assess his readiness for ministry with a series of piercing questions:

Has the Great Head of the church endued me with intellectual gifts and spiritual graces, peculiar and appropriate to the work of the Christian ministry? Have I a sincere and earnest desire to be engaged in the work? Is it the one all-absorbing, all-engaging impulse of my mind, pressing me into the holy strait of the apostle, when he exclaimed, "Woe is unto me if I preach not the gospel?" Have I narrowly scrutinized my motives and aim in desiring the work; and are they such as involve a deep concern for the glory of God? Am I willing to forego all the allurements of human ambition, and prospects of earthly glory and temporal advantage, and become a humble, self-denying, self-sacrificing, holy, and laborious minister of Jesus? Does the love of Christ constrain me? Do I pant to preach him in the glory of his person, in the perfection of his work, in the depth of his love, in the fullness of his grace to dying sinners? Do I long for the conversion of souls, and is it my heart's desire and prayer to God that his spiritual Israel be saved?[53]

This high view of calling transferred into a high view of the pastoral office. His conversion, education, and ordination prepared him for his future ministry assignments.

The Pastoral Ministry of Octavius Winslow

After his ordination, Winslow never wavered from his pastoral call. In order to better understand his five pastorates, it is important to examine those who

---

51. Winslow, *Life in Jesus*, 108.
52. "Ordinations," *The Baptist Magazine*, 516.
53. Winslow, *Eminent Holiness*, 9–10.

influenced him, the religious scene of Victorian England, and his view of pastoral ministry. But before looking at his immediate context, it is necessary to assess Winslow's greatest influencers, the Puritans.

The Puritan Influence on His Ministry

Winslow loved the experimental Christianity of the old divines. Their "sound theology, depth of thought, and elevated spirituality" drew him to their works.[54] Early in his ministry, his mother exhorted him: "I perceive you have forgotten 'Rutherford's Letters.' I wish you had taken them. Keep to the old divines. Modern divinity is very shallow—has very little of Christ and experience."[55] He did not forget his mother's instruction.

Although there were times he leaned on early church fathers such as Tertullian and Chrysostom and Reformers such as Martin Luther, Hugh Latimer, John Knox, and John Calvin, and even those who came just before him such as John Newton, Robert Hall, Robert Murray McCheyne, and Thomas Chalmers, it was the Puritans who most influenced him. Throughout his works, Winslow quotes and references Samuel Rutherford, Thomas Goodwin, Thomas Brooks, Richard Baxter, John Owen, William Gurnall, John Flavel, John Bunyan, Stephen Charnock, Robert Traill, Cotton Mather, Philip Doddridge, Jonathan Edwards, and more.[56] He obviously spent hours studying their works.

His contemporaries noticed this influence. In the preface to the American edition of *Personal Declension and Revival of Religion in the Soul*, Thomas De Witt, pastor of the Dutch Reformed Collegiate Church in New York City, wrote, "Very few modern writers remind me more of the marrow of sound doctrine and rich experience in the old Puritan Divines, than the author of this volume."[57] The editors of *The Biblical Repertory & Princeton Review* observed these same qualities. Concerning his *An Experimental View of the Holy Spirit* they wrote, "The address is affectionate and winning, yet closely practical. It strongly reminds one of the manner of Flavel and

---

54. Winslow, *Life in Jesus*, 266.

55. Winslow, *Life in Jesus*, 96.

56. For a couple of representative examples, see Octavius Winslow, *The Sympathy of Christ with Man: Its Teaching and Its Consolation* (New York: Robert Carter & Brothers; repr., Harrisonburg, Va.: Sprinkle, 1994), 72, 153, 332; and Octavius Winslow, *Soul-Depths & Soul-Heights: Sermons on Psalm 130* (London: John F. Shaw, 1874; repr., Edinburgh: Banner of Truth, 2006), 33–34, 58, 107.

57. Thomas De Witt, recommendation for *Personal Declension and Revival of Religion in the Soul*, by Octavius Winslow (New York: Robert Carter, 1847), vi.

Doddridge, and others of the olden time. The discriminations of character are close and happy: and the whole book evinces a deep knowledge of the heart, and a familiar, practical, and divinely illumined acquaintance with the Scriptures."[58] In both style and content, Winslow wrote, preached, and ministered in a manner reflecting the voice of the Puritans.

Victorian England and the Golden Age of Preaching
Queen Victoria ascended her throne in 1837 and reigned until 1901. After Winslow spent his first five years as a pastor in America (1833–1838), he served the next forty in England during her reign (1839–1878). Victorian England was deeply religious. The amount of literature devoted to the sacred exceeded other interests of the day. This created an excitement that pervaded the religious scene.[59] As Robert Ensor said, "No one will ever understand Victorian England who does not appreciate that among the highly civilized, in contradistinction to more primitive, countries it was one of the most religious that the world has ever known."[60] Perhaps the Victorian pulpit provides the greatest evidence of England's religious fervor.

The Victorian era has been dubbed "The Golden Age of Preaching."[61] People not only flocked to hear great preaching but also to buy printed sermons. Robert Ellison explains, "Many Victorians' interest in preaching was not confined to the one, two, or even three services they attended each Sunday; their 'sermon tasting' also involved purchasing printed discourses and reading them during the week."[62] Men such as Charles Haddon Spurgeon,

---

58. See the back advertisements in W. Suddards, *The British Pulpit: Consisting of Discourses by the Most Eminent Living Divines, in England, Scotland, and Ireland,* vol. 2 (New York: Robert Carter, 1845).

59. Asa Briggs, *Victorian People: Some Reassessments of People, Institutions, Ideas, and Events, 1851–1867* (London: Odhams Press, 1954), 24.

60. Robert Charles Kirkwood Ensor, *England, 1870–1914* (Oxford, U.K.: The Clarendon Press, 1936), 137. See also Owen Chadwick, *The Victorian Church: An Ecclesiastical History of England, Part I* (New York: Oxford University Press, 1966).

61. See Edwin Charles Dargan, *A History of Preaching,* 2 vols. (New York: Hodder and Stoughton, 1905; repr., Birmingham, Ala.: Solid Ground Christian Books, 2003); Robert T. Henry, *The Golden Age of Preaching: Men Who Moved the Masses* (New York: iUniverse, 2005); and F. W. Webber, *A History of Preaching in Britain and America: Including Many of the Biographies of Many Princes of the Pulpit and the Men Who Influenced Them,* 3 vols. (Milwaukee: Northwestern Publishing House, 1952).

62. Robert Ellison, *The Victorian Pulpit: Spoken and Written Sermons in Nineteenth-Century Britain* (London: Associate University Presses, 1998), 46.

Joseph Parker, Alexander Maclaren, and R. W. Dale wooed the masses with their eloquent exposition.[63]

Even though Victorian England was feverishly religious, Winslow believed it lacked true revival. Across the years of his ministry, he pleaded for an outpouring of the Holy Spirit. In 1841 he wrote, "Oh never did the Church of God more need the baptism of the Spirit than now.... Popery is increasing—infidelity is triumphing—formalism is abounding—God-dishonouring, Christ-denying, Bible-rejecting, and soul-destroying doctrines in rank and rampant growth, are springing forth on every side."[64] In another work he called English churches to seek revival like the ones witnessed in America.[65]

Winslow's View of Pastoral Ministry

Winslow's understanding of pastoral ministry can be summarized in one word: *holiness*. First, his high view of the office demanded a rigorous pursuit of Christlike character. In turn, he believed the pastor's personal holiness should be transferred to his people in word and deed. Finally, as the pastor works for the sanctification of his people, he must do so with holy motives and a heart sanctified by grace.

The Pastor's Task: A Great Work

Winslow held a high view of the pastoral office. He did not treat the minister's vast responsibility to serve Christ and His church with the slightest levity. He declared:

> A work of greater magnitude, and on whose issues more tremendous consequences were suspended, never was intrusted to mere human hands. It is the office of the Christian minister to treat on the great matters of eternity between God and the soul of man. Before this view of its transcendent greatness and corresponding solemnity, all the pomp and circumstance of human glory melts into thin air.[66]

He believed pastoral ministry demands a humble and serious approach. He added, "Their office is holy and honorable; their responsibility, tremendous and solemn; their duties, arduous and trying; their anxieties many, and their

---

63. See Clyde E. Fant and William M. Pinson Jr., *A Treasury of Great Preaching*, vols. 4 and 5 (Dallas: Word, 1995).

64. Winslow, *Glory of the Redeemer*, 290.

65. Octavius Winslow, *"Is the Spirit of the Lord Straitened?" A Plea for a National Baptism of the Holy Ghost with Incidents of American Revival* (London: John F. Shaw, 1858).

66. Winslow, *Eminent Holiness*, 11.

trials sore; and they are to be 'esteemed very highly in love for their works' sake.'"[67] In short, pastors engage in a great work.

He was particularly concerned with how the office relates to Christ and His church. Reflecting on 1 Peter 5, he described ministers as "under-shepherds" who are "infinitely subordinate, and solemnly accountable to Him, the 'Chief Shepherd and Bishop' of His Church, in the administrative authority which they wield, in the divine gifts which they possess, and in the spiritual functions which they perform."[68] Moreover, pastors should pattern their ministry after the apostles. They should emulate the apostles' holiness, devotion to God's mission, and Christ-exalting preaching.[69]

At the same time, Winslow believed the menial tasks of ministry reveal the pastor's heart. He wrote:

> Let the pastor be seen in his appropriate sphere; let him descend from the scene of excited feeling, pass from the midst of an admiring people, and wend his solitary way to the house of mourning, and ascend the darkened chamber of sickness and solitude;—then will he be seen as he really is; and his true spirituality of mind, the native feeling, delicacy, and tenderness of heart and address, will shine forth in their own beautiful and unveiled reality.[70]

Though Winslow declared the riches of Christ to thousands of people, he knew a minister's true character is displayed in moments where the audience is often very small.

The Pastor's Need: Personal Holiness

For Winslow, pastors should serve as a channel of blessing to God's people, and they do this as they walk in holiness. The ministry of the Spirit is essential in this process. Winslow announced, "We shall be *blessings* to them, in proportion as we are *blessed* with the anointing of the Holy Ghost. And we shall be a hindrance to their soul's progress in holiness, stumbling-blocks in the way of their advance towards heaven, as our heads lack ointment, and our souls are not constantly thirsting for God."[71] Winslow sought the Spirit's

---

67. Octavius Winslow, *The Nightingale Song of David: A Spiritual and Practical Exposition of the Twenty-Third Psalm* (London: John F. Shaw, n.d.), 4. He signed the preface November 1876, so the publication date should be 1876 or 1877.

68. Winslow, *Nightingale Song*, 4.

69. Winslow, *Eminent Holiness*, vii.

70. Winslow, *Eminent Holiness*, 21.

71. Winslow, *Eminent Holiness*, 69.

anointing by prioritizing his devotional life. Jesus' example in the Gospels of
withdrawing from the disciples in order to commune with the Father provided sufficient motivation for his pursuit.[72] The life-giving grace of God's
Word and earnest prayer were the resources that kept his soul thriving.[73] He
knew intimacy with God produces personal holiness.

Winslow recognized that the consequences of a holy walk are serious.
Speaking to the students of Stepney, he declared:

> The man who combines intellectual gifts, properly and thoroughly
> trained,—a mind ample in its intellectual resources, and capable of
> combating with error and of elucidating truth,—with a soul deeply
> baptized in the Spirit of holiness, and a heart enveloped in one heaven-
> ascending flame of love to Christ and men, will be the best expounder of
> the truth, and the most successful in winning souls to Christ.[74]

A pastor must also strive for personal holiness so that he will not succumb
to temptation. Winslow wisely warned others, "Oh, let us not be deceived!
Because we are ministers we are not the less men; and because we are by habit
and profession necessarily and constantly occupied in the contemplation of
divine and heavenly things…we are not the less exposed to the deadening
influence of the things that are carnal."[75] He knew this applied especially in
the most holy of tasks:

> That we can speak of God's amazing love, and taste so little of its
> sweetness; that we can descant on the glories of Christ, and be so little
> enamoured of his loveliness; that we can dilate upon the beauties of
> holiness, and approximate so little in conformity to the divine image;
> that we can administer the most solemn ordinances, and be engaged
> in the most spiritual services, with the spirit of inward transforming
> holiness at so low an ebb, with the springs of sanctity and vigour so dry,

---

72. See Octavius Winslow, *Evening Thoughts, or, Daily Walking with God: A Portion
for Each Evening in the Year* (London: John F. Shaw, 1859; repr., Grand Rapids: Reformation
Heritage Books, 2005), 248–49.

73. See Octavius Winslow, *The Lights and Shadows of Spiritual Life* (London: John F.
Shaw, 1876; repr. as *Spiritual Life* [Stoke-on-Trent, U.K.: Tentmaker, 1998]), 69–72. Of the
latter Winslow wrote, "Prayer is the spiritual pulse of the renewed soul; its beat indicates
the healthy or unhealthy state of the believer." Octavius Winslow, *Personal Declension and
Revival of Religion in the Soul* (London: John F. Shaw, 1841; repr., Edinburgh: Banner of
Truth, 2000, 94).

74. Winslow, *Eminent Holiness*, 81–82.

75. Winslow, *Eminent Holiness*, 30.

with the anointings of the Holy One so far evaporated, is a fact almost too fearful to entertain, and yet too real to doubt![76]

With these warnings, Winslow explained the danger of attaching any "mysterious sanctity" to the pastoral office.[77]

He identified pride as one of the minister's greatest temptations. Because of pride's varied manifestations, he decried it as "a Protean evil."[78] He believed it could reveal itself in any ministry task. Thus, he warned against the pride of office, the pride of knowledge, the pride of influence, the pride of eloquence, the pride of denomination, and the pride of applause. With these strong words he warned his fellow ministers:

> There is no soil so holy in which its root will not strike;—there is no employment so sacred on which it will not engraft itself. It will even make the cross of Christ a pedestal on which to erect its deformed visage. Yea, while exalting Jesus, we may be found but exalting ourselves; and while exclaiming, 'Behold the Lamb of God!' we may be but veiling his true glory behind our insignificant persons; virtually exclaiming, 'Behold my talents, my eloquence, and my zeal!' Is there not in us, my brethren, a manifest deficiency of the lowly, self-annihilating spirit of the Divine Master whom we serve, and whom it should be our aim and glory to resemble?[79]

Though pride is not the only work of the flesh with which pastors must contend, it is one of the most pervasive and destructive. Winslow understood that immense consequences attach themselves to the pastor's pursuit of God. Without holiness, ministers bring great shame to the church and great delight to Satan.[80]

---

76. Winslow, *Eminent Holiness*, 26.
77. Winslow, *Eminent Holiness*, 30.
78. Winslow, *Eminent Holiness*, 55.
79. Winslow, *Eminent Holiness*, 55.
80. Winslow provided another stern warning against ministerial immorality: "Who stands upon an elevation so conspicuous, or occupies a position so perilous, or sustains responsibilities so tremendous, or is exposed to temptations so many, so varied, and so powerful; at whose halting such serious consequences would ensue, or over whose fall hell's loud laugh would more exultingly and triumphantly ascend,—who, save the minister of Christ? It has been said that death loves a shining mark—so does Satan. And if there is singled out from among the 'sacramental host of God's elect' one more exposed to the fiery darts of the adversary than another, it is the standard-bearer, beneath whose convoy that host is conducted to glory. If *he* falls, what consternation, what dismay, strike into the very heart of the camp." *Eminent Holiness*, 27.

The Pastor's Pursuit: Corporate Holiness

A pastor should not simply pursue holiness as an end in itself. Everything the pastor does should promote the sanctification of his flock. This is the great purpose of pastoral ministry. According to Winslow, the church should be a people who hunger and thirst for divine conformity.[81] He also understood that a pastor's personal holiness, for better or worse, has a proportionate effect on his people, and he insightfully declared, "Let us ever remember how close is the relation of a pastor and his people; that, as he is, so, in a great degree, will they be; that he will impart to their souls the complexion of his piety, will impress upon their minds the spiritual character of his own, and will share with them the blessing he himself has received of God."[82] Because of this he maintained that a church will rarely rise above the piety and deeds of their pastor. He declared, "But it is not often that, in the intensity of benevolent action, or in the vigour and purity of Christian holiness, a Church is in the ascendant of the pastor it venerates and loves. His standard is rarely *exceeded* by theirs."[83] For these reasons, the pastor should watch his life and doctrine closely.

The Pastor's Motives: Glory and Judgment

Holy actions should spring from holy motives. Winslow found motivation for pastoral ministry in two primary sources: the glory of God and the coming judgment. He believed God's glory should serve as the chief motive:

> What a persuasive motive to ministerial holiness!—The glory of God!... Let it be ours, my brethren, our one, sole, undeviating aim. Let us sacrifice every thing that would divert us from it—fame, applause, reputation, popularity, worldly comfort, the dearest interests of self, if these come in competition with the honour of divine truth and the glory of God, *let them go.*[84]

Additionally, the minister should always remember his accountability before God. Winslow believed such a view should thwart the temptation to trivialize any task. He proclaimed, "We are soon to stand before God in judgment. The record of our ministry will be unrolled, and every circumstance and every movement, and every sermon and every prayer, and every motive and every principle, will be set in the light of his countenance, and pass the searching

---

81. Winslow, *Personal Declension*, 99.
82. Winslow, *Eminent Holiness*, 69.
83. Winslow, *Eminent Holiness*, 73–74.
84. Winslow, *Eminent Holiness*, 77.

scrutiny of his piercing eye."[85] These core convictions concerning the pastor's holiness and the sanctification of his people served as the basis for Winslow's five pastorates and led him to pursue ministerial excellence.

Winslow's Pastorates

A minister's longevity often indicates the success of his ministry. Sadly, many ministers do not hold the shepherd's staff for long. At the same time, longevity alone does not confirm the success of a pastorate. A pastor should be judged first by the quality of his ministry. Over the course of forty-five years at five churches on two continents, Winslow had full opportunity to display the character and worth of his ministry.

Bowery/Central Baptist Church, New York, New York (1833–1835)
Winslow completed his service as moderator at Stanton Street in March of 1831 when the church invited Rev. G. Benedict to be their pastor.[86] He was then dismissed by letter on May 18, 1831, to become the founding pastor of the Bowery Baptist Church.[87] The congregation was formally organized in March of 1833 when Winslow began preaching in the Military Hall on the Bowery. A church of twenty members quickly formed in the southern part of Manhattan.[88] Winslow was a twenty-four-year-old church planter. Not surprisingly, God brought him a "youthful band" of congregants.[89] In light of his future transition to the Church of England, it should be noted that Winslow was decidedly a Baptist in his early days as a minister. Just before his first pastorate, he took advantage of a six-week voyage across the North Atlantic to convert an Anglican to his Baptistic views.[90]

After meeting for a year in the Military Hall, the new congregation relocated to Broadway Hall and renamed itself Central Baptist Church. During

---

85. Winslow, *Eminent Holiness*, 83.

86. Stanton, *Stanton Street*, 37. Not surprisingly, Octavius continued to have a fond "attachment to the church, and undiminished interest in her welfare" throughout his life and ministry (27).

87. Breed, *Calvinism and Communion*, 605n16.

88. Greenleaf, *History of the Churches*, 260.

89. Octavius Winslow, *The Minister's Final Charge: A Discourse, Delivered on Relinquishing the Pastoral Care, of the Central Baptist Church, New York, December 20, 1835* (New York: Leavitt, Lord, & Co., 1836), 30.

90. See Lucy Kendall Herrick, *Voyage to California Written at Sea, 1852*, ed. Amy Requa Russell, Marcia Russell Good, and Mary Good Lindgren (San Marino, Calif.: Huntington Library, 1998), 19–20.

this time, "a moderate degree of prosperity seemed to attend them."[91] Nevertheless, these early years were not devoid of struggle. Correspondence from his mother reveals Winslow battled depression early in his ministry. She wrote:

> I perceive by your letters that you are often depressed. This is natural, from the many trials and difficulties connected with your office. But you must remember that you are called to endure hardship as a good soldier of Jesus Christ; and must expect to be tried and buffeted if you would be an experimental minister of the cross. And do not forget He is infinite in wisdom, who selects and orders all your trials as those best suited to your case, and most qualified to prepare you for your work. Be assured no other would have done. May we be more sanctified by what we suffer![92]

Some if not most of these trials may have surfaced through interaction with his congregants. Winslow knew the remedy consisted in taking his case to Christ, and the Good Shepherd sustained him through this season of despondency.[93]

God not only carried him through these trials, but He also brought great personal blessing. On April 2, 1834, Winslow married Hannah Ann Ring. Hannah, too, was a follower of Christ, and their marriage brought new responsibilities for each of them.[94] Octavius had to set an example of godliness and lead in family worship.[95] Hannah Ann also had unique responsibilities as a minister's wife. Mary, the faithful mother-in-law, once wrote to Octavius, "Tender love to dear [Ann]. Tell her I have never been so firmly convinced as of late of the absolute necessity of the holy, wise walk of a minister's wife. It is my constant prayer that God will fully qualify her for her high

---

91. Greenleaf, *History of the Churches*, 260–61.

92. Winslow, *Life in Jesus*, 98.

93. On another occasion his mother wrote, "I was grieved to hear your spirits were depressed. My precious child, when you accepted the pastoral office, you commenced a life of trial both from saint and from sinner. Oh, do not be surprised at all you meet with. Look to Jesus. Do not let difficulties distress you. The cause is Christ's, and all you have to do is to take them to Him." Winslow, *Life in Jesus*, 91.

94. For an account of her radical conversion, see Octavius Winslow, *Instant Glory: A Reflection for the Year 1867 with a Short Biographical Notice of the Late Mrs. Winslow* (London: John F. Shaw, 1867), 72–75.

95. Concerning these responsibilities his mother wrote to Octavius and his brothers, "Your wives are professors of the same blessed hope. But, the husband is the head of the wife, even as Christ is the head of the church; and they will look to you for an example. Walk before them circumspectly; pray with them, and pray for them, and allow nothing to interrupt family worship." Winslow, *Life in Jesus*, 74–75.

and solemn position."[96] It can be assumed that Hannah Ann received much encouragement from her mother-in-law.[97] Their household grew quickly as God blessed them with ten children, three born during their New York years. On January 27, 1835, they welcomed their first-born son, John Whitmore.[98] Then they celebrated the birth of two daughters, Mary Forbes (1837) and Hannah (1838).[99]

Much of the character and focus of Winslow's first pastorate can be gleaned from reading his farewell sermon, delivered on December 20, 1835. He chose Philippians 4:1 as his text and exhorted his people to "stand fast." The overarching purpose of this message was to review the most important doctrines he had "set distinctly and prominently before" them throughout his ministry.[100] He unpacked the following six doctrines: the original fall and universal depravity of all mankind; the sinner's justification through the imputed righteousness of the Lord Jesus Christ; the expiatory nature of the sufferings and death of Christ; the distinct office of the Holy Spirit in the work of regeneration; the coming Savior; and the holiness of the gospel.[101]

Winslow stressed the importance of this final doctrine, claiming that all of the other doctrines should be worked out in holy living. He explained: "Every doctrine and precept which has been advanced in the ministry of this pulpit, when sealed upon the heart by the blessed Spirit's power, and interwoven in the soul's experience, will lay self in the dust, and exalt Christ in the heart; will make sin more exceeding sinful; holiness more beautiful; a throne of grace more endearing; God more loved, and Jesus more precious."[102] This statement reveals the priority Winslow placed on experimental Christianity early in his ministry. He preached strong doctrinal content with a view toward a practical experience of the truth.

The flock of Central Baptist also engaged in various ministries. Toward the close of his sermon, Winslow reflected, "It is my privilege to know that the holy cause of Domestic and Foreign Missions, of Sabbath School instruction,

---

96. Winslow, *Life in Jesus*, 98–99.

97. On another occasion Mary wrote of the minister's wife, "A minister's wife is, of all others, placed in the most responsible situation in the church of God. Much of his usefulness depends upon her. She must be a helpmate to the Lord's servant, and a servant of the Lord herself." Winslow, *Life in Jesus*, 143.

98. Winslow, *Hidden Life*, 4–5.

99. Jennifer Townsend, e-mail message to the author, November 17, 2009.

100. Winslow, *Minister's Final Charge*, 4.

101. Winslow, *Minister's Final Charge*, 5–29.

102. Winslow, *Minister's Final Charge*, 28.

of Ministerial Education, the Bible [Society], the Tract [Society], and kindred institutions, have found in your midst, and in proportion to your circumscribed enclosure, a healthy soil for their growth, and ready hands for their culture."[103] With his conclusion, he exhorted them to shine their light even though it may be smaller than that of larger churches. The general tone of the sermon was warm and affectionate. In his first pastorate Winslow led the church to be founded on doctrine and engaged in deeds.

One comment in his farewell sermon reveals Winslow experienced some trying moments during his days at Central Baptist. These comments may be relevant to his bouts with depression. He wrote, "My confidence in the sustaining faithfulness of God towards you as a Church, has never wavered. *True, there have been periods, when the difficulties of sustaining its interests have been such, as to tinge your pastor's days with anxiety, and render his nights sleepless.* Yet through it all, his faith in the kindness and love of God toward this youthful band, has never been permitted for a moment to falter" (emphasis added).[104] In spite of some difficulties, Winslow maintained his love for the flock. There is no official indication as to why he relinquished his pastoral duties.

Second Baptist Church, New York, New York (1836–1838)

After resigning from Central Baptist, Winslow became pastor of the Second Baptist Church in Brooklyn. The church gathered at the corner of Tillary and Lawrence Streets.[105] Winslow's high involvement in missions marked this season of ministry. This was not a new passion for Winslow nor would it soon fizzle. At the age of twenty-two, he was already noted for presenting "evangelical and spirit-stirring addresses" concerning global missions.[106] In 1838, he delivered an argument later to be published on the spread of home missions to the developing western frontier of the United States.[107] At the same time, Winslow did not see any competition between home and foreign missions. He pled for both: "We would not construct an argument for Domestic Missions, behind which, the lukewarm professor of the truth might

---

103. Winslow, *Minister's Final Charge,* 31.

104. Winslow, *Minister's Final Charge,* 30.

105. Nathaniel Prime, *History of Long Island: From Its First Settlement by Europeans to the Year 1845 with Special Reference to Its Ecclesiastical Concerns* (New York: Robert Carter, 1845), 400.

106. See American Tract Society, "Tract Meeting in New York," *The American Tract Magazine for the Year 1830* 5, no. 12 (December 1830): 157.

107. See Octavius Winslow, *Christ, The Theme of the Home Missionary: An Argument for Home Missions* (New York: John S. Taylor, 1838).

screen himself from the powerful claims which Foreign Missions urges upon him."[108] He desired for God's salvation to reach the ends of the earth through the preaching of Christ.

During his time at Second Baptist, Winslow also entered the controversy over a new version of the New Testament. Many Baptists wanted to produce their own translation representing their view of baptism. The controversy swirled around whether or not "the present authorized version of the New Testament be sufficiently explicit as to the mode and subject of baptism."[109] Some Baptists answered negatively, asserting that "immerse" and "immersion," or some equivalent, be substituted for the words "baptize" and "baptism."[110] Winslow presented his views in a book authored by William T. Brantly titled *Objections to a Baptist Version of the New Testament*. One of Winslow's primary contributions was a call for unity that was missiologically motivated. Because Baptists had just started disseminating the Word of God to millions in India, he argued:

> It requires then, no profound sagacity to perceive, that, to call off the attention of the whole denomination at the present moment from the consideration of a subject so momentous, to divide its interests and distract its counsels, by the agitation of a question comparatively so insignificant, is inconsiderate and impolitic; and did we not think the remark might be considered uncharitable, we would say, that it argued a painful lack of sensibility to the true interests of the kingdom of Christ.[111]

Winslow's writing as a young pastor displayed his theological and missiological concern.

Sadly, the church dissolved in the fall of 1838, and the building was sold to the Free Presbyterian congregation.[112] This event concluded Winslow's years in the United States. Once again, no records were located indicating why Second Baptist closed its doors. Winslow would soon move back to England and enjoy greater measures of fruitfulness in the years to come.

---

108. Winslow, *Christ, The Theme*, 104.

109. Octavius Winslow, "Additional Reasons for Preferring the English Bible As It Is," in William T. Brantly, *Objections to a Baptist Version of the New Testament* (New York: J. P. Callender, 1837), 2.

110. Brantly, *Objections to a Baptist Version*, 8.

111. Brantly, *Objections to a Baptist Version*, 65.

112. Prime, *History of Long*, 400. Contra Breed, who suggests that the church dissolved in 1840. *Calvinism and Communion*, 605–6n16.

Warwick Street Chapel, Leamington Spa, England (1839–1857)

After concluding his time in New York, Winslow moved his young family back to the land of his birth. They settled in Leamington Spa, Warwickshire, an area that experienced significant population growth during the mid-nineteenth century.[113] The Baptist cause in Leamington commenced a short time before Winslow became the pastor in June of 1839.[114] He followed the Rev. George Cole, who initiated the work, and the short pastorate of the Rev. D. J. East.[115] Alfred Phillips described Winslow's years at Warwick Street as a "brilliant pastorate." He also said Winslow's ministry "attracted a throng of the fashionable residents and frequenters of the 'Spa.'"[116] Though Warwick Street was a Baptist chapel, "his evening services were largely supported by Evangelical Churchmen."[117]

While in Leamington, God blessed Octavius and Hannah Ann with seven more children: James (1840), Thomas (1842), Ann Bruce (1846), Sarah Joanna (1848), Octavius Jr. (1850), Georgina (1853), and Lyndhurst (1855).[118] Winslow's mother, Mary, and sister, Emma, lived with them for many of these years. Winslow sought to lead his family in the ways of the Lord. The recollections of John Taylor, a lawyer from Lancashire who became friends with Winslow after reading several of his books, confirm their domestic pursuit and hospitality. He reflected in his diary:

---

113. From 1831 to 1861, the population nearly tripled, increasing from 6,269 to 18,768. See Adam Black and Charles Black, *Black's Guide to Leamington and Its Environs: Including Warwick, Stratford-on-Avon, & Kenilworth* (Edinburgh: Adam & Charles Black, 1883), 2.

114. Geoffrey Breed, *Particular Baptists in Victorian England and Their Strict Communion Organizations* (Didcot, U.K.: Baptist Historical Society, 2003), 347. For a history of Warwick Street Baptist Church, see James Begg, *The Baptist Church, Warwick Street, Leamington Spa: A Short History* ([Leamington?]: n.p., 1980), 3–11.

115. Alfred Phillips, "The Coventry District," in *Records of an Old Association: Being a Memorial Volume of the 250th Anniversary of the Midland, Now the West Midland, Baptist Association, Formed in Warwick, May 3rd, 1655*, ed. J. M. Gwynne Owen (Birmingham, U.K.: Press of Allday, 1905), 160–61.

116. Phillips, "Coventry District," 160–61.

117. John Taylor, *Autobiography of a Lancashire Lawyer, Being the Life and Recollections of John Taylor, Attorney-at-Law, and First Coroner of the Borough of Bolton, with Notice of Many Persons and Things Met During a Life of Seventy-Two Years Lived in and about Bolton*, ed. James Clegg (Bolton, U.K.: The Daily Chronicle Office, 1883), 194. Interestingly, one of England's most famous preachers of the nineteenth century, R. W. Dale, often attended Warwick Street as a sixteen-year-old young man. A. W. W. Dale, *The Life of R. W. Dale of Birmingham*, 6th ed. (London: Hodder & Stoughton, 1905), 27.

118. Jennifer Townsend, e-mail message to the author, November 17, 2009.

Arrived at Leamington at five, washed, and went to my appointment with Rev. Octavius Winslow. Was shown into the drawing-room, and shortly after met Miss Winslow, an only sister to Mr. Winslow, and his mother, Mrs. Winslow the elder. We sat down to tea without ceremony after a blessing asked, and our conversation soon became general and pious. We discussed freely and good-humouredly on many points of doctrine and experience, and a pleasing sight it was to see a mother, daughter, son, and his wife, all converted persons, talking of Christ, living after the example of Christ, and believing in Christ. Mr. Winslow read a chapter and prayed, mentioning myself as their visitor, and praying that I might be enabled to resist the temptations of an exciting and worldly profession (calling). I left them at ten, after an evening spent with the Lord.[119]

Taylor also supplied a rare description of Winslow: "He appeared to be about 40 years of age, genteel in appearance, and, though accomplished, yet without much display."[120]

If length of years indicates the effectiveness of his ministry, it could be argued that Warwick Street was Winslow's greatest pastoral assignment. He labored there for nineteen years. He called it a "pleasant pastorate" and possessed great love for his people.[121] One of the clearest demonstrations of his affection occurred when he was summoned to become the pastor of a large church in London. His son John Whitmore recorded this event: "To-day my dear father returned from London, where he has been invited to the pastoral charge of a large church, but not seeing his way clear, has decided to remain where he is, to the great joy of his flock, whose affection for him is very great."[122] Obviously, the congregants at Warwick Street loved their pastor just as he loved them.

One event during the summer of 1852 provides precious insight into Winslow's ministry at Warwick Street. During the midsummer school vacation, Octavius, Whitmore, and a few other family members visited the European continent. They planned to extend their tour to Switzerland but were forced to stop in Paris because of an illness suffered by Octavius. A letter from Whitmore to Hannah Ann sheds some light on the cause of his sickness: "I think he will be in much better health after this illness than

---

119. Taylor, *Autobiography of a Lancashire Lawyer*, 180.

120. Taylor, *Autobiography of a Lancashire Lawyer*, 173. In another place he was described as "a man of dignified and aristocratic bearing." Agnus, *Henry Dunckley*, 6.

121. Octavius Winslow, *The Inner Life: Its Nature, Relapse, and Recovery* (London: John F. Shaw, 1850), v.

122. Winslow, *Hidden Life*, 18.

before, for besides relieving him from the sad effects of past exertions of the brain (which have really brought on his illness), it will make him cautious for the future."[123] These comments indicate that Winslow's intense ministerial labors brought great stress and fatigue, even to the point of sickness.[124]

After settling in Dover, England, to complete his recovery, Winslow wrote a candid letter of encouragement to his congregation. He spoke directly about the health of their corporate worship. Although he was pleased with their improvement in public singing, he viewed the fact that some failed to bring their Bibles with them as "a serious defect."[125] He said, "A twofold object is gained by following the minister with the eye upon the book in the public reading of the word. The attention is kept from wandering, and the portions read are more vividly and indelibly impressed upon the mind."[126] Winslow also thought they needed to enhance their reverence in corporate prayer. Some stood and looked around rather than kneeling or bowing their heads. He also encouraged some to be more punctual and to treat visitors with greater courtesy.[127] These instructions display his concern for excellence in their corporate gatherings and a willingness to correct his flock.

Winslow also exhorted his congregation to persevere in his absence. In what may be the greatest unveiling of his heart as a minister, he wrote:

> It has been the distinctive aim, and the sincere desire of my ministry amongst you, to make known and to endear the Saviour to your hearts. A vision by faith of his glory, and a conviction by the Spirit of his worth, were coeval with my divine life. From the moment that that believing vision burst upon my view, and that spiritual conviction fastened itself upon my heart, "Redeeming love has been my theme, And shall be till I die." And may I, as from a languid couch, still press the Saviour's claims to your regard? Oh, how worthy is he of your most exalted conceptions,—of your most implicit confidence,—of your most self-denying

---

123. Winslow, *Hidden Life*, 76.

124. An indication of Winslow's tireless efforts as a minister is provided by R. W. Dale, who as a sixteen-year-old wished to start a "Leamington Royal Literary and Scientific Institution." In a letter to a friend, he lamented the fact that he had little influence or help: "I have, of course, but a small influence in either my own or the Baptist church…. Mr. Winslow is so much engaged that I cannot hope to make him more than an occasional auxiliary." Dale, *The Life of R. W.*, 34.

125. Octavius Winslow, *A Pastoral Letter, Addressed to the Church and Congregation Assembling in the Warwick-Street Chapel, Leamington* (London: Houlston & Stoneman, 1852), 12.

126. Winslow, *Pastoral Letter*, 12.

127. Winslow, *Pastoral Letter*, 13.

service,—of your most fervent love. When he could give you no more—and the fathomless depths of his love, and the boundless resources of his grace, would not be satisfied by giving you less—he gave you *himself.* Robed in your nature, laden with your curse, oppressed with your sorrows, wounded for your transgressions, and slain for your sins, he gave his entire self for you. And let it be remembered that it is a continuous presentation of the hoarded and exhaustless treasures of his love. His redeeming work now finished, he is perpetually engaged in meting out to his church the blessings of that "offering made once for all." He constantly asks your faith,—woos your affection,—invites your grief,—and you repair with your daily trials to his sympathy, and with your hourly guilt to his blood. You cannot in your drafts upon Christ's fullness be too coveteous, nor in your expectations of supply be too extravagant. You may fail, as, alas! the most of us do, in making too little of Christ,—you cannot fail, in making too much of him.[128]

The profound goal of Winslow's ministry was to proclaim Christ in all of His glory and see His people love Him supremely.

One of his greatest moments at Warwick Street was the conversion of his son Whitmore. Although he had apparently experienced conversion at an earlier age, Whitmore had not publicly confessed his commitment to Christ for fear that his conduct would not accurately display his faith. After hearing his father preach from 1 Kings 18:21, he decided to publicly declare his faith. That night, when Octavius went to bed, he found a note from Whitmore and read it "with awe-struck emotions."[129] Whitmore wrote,

Your sermon to-night was irresistible. Long, long, have I been halting between two opinions; not whether I should embrace Christ or not, for He has long been my Saviour and the staff of my youth; but whether it was right for me to confess it, feeling, as I have done, that my conduct has often been so contrary, that to make such a profession would seem but hypocrisy.... I tell this first to you, dear Papa, for it is under your ministry my soul has been led to Christ.[130]

Octavius described his joy in the following words: "Such was the announcement which met my eye. The effect was stunning—overpowering—indescribable. The first sensation was that of a pleasant dream that seemed too blissful to

---

128. Winslow, *Pastoral Letter*, 6–7.
129. Winslow, *Hidden Life*, 59.
130. Winslow, *Hidden Life*, 59.

realize.... The prayers which preceded his birth—which cradled his infancy—which girded his youth—were answered—my son was Christ's!"[131]

Whitmore professed his faith by baptism on January 4, 1852.[132] Octavius had the great privilege of baptizing him and serving him the Lord's Supper for the first time that evening. Whitmore wrote in his journal, "In the evening I received the Lord's Supper—another precious privilege—which, indeed, I felt sweet and solemn. Much was I affected when dear papa, in giving me the right hand of fellowship, said, that 'When he was laid in the grave, he trusted that I would be a faithful minister of the Gospel which it was his privilege to preach.'"[133] Octavius enjoyed an affectionate relationship with his son, unquestionably adding to the joy of these years.

Winslow's years at Leamington were also checkered with suffering. Aside from his own health problems, he experienced the most severe time of loss in his life. His infant daughter Sarah Joanna died on July 3, 1848, at the residence of his brother George.[134] That same year he lost his two-year-old daughter, Ann Bruce. Both of these precious children passed away from inflammation of the bowels.[135] On the occasion of one daughter's death, his mother wrote him a letter of encouragement: "The Lord has mercifully housed our dear little sufferer.... She is not lost; she is in the tender bosom of Jesus; and this was designed from eternity. May your hearts be comforted, and you be enabled to say, 'The Lord gave, and the Lord hath taken away; blessed be the name of the Lord.'"[136]

Then, on Tuesday evening, October 3, 1854, his precious mother, Mary, entered the presence of God.[137] To console her before her death, one of her

---

131. Winslow, *Hidden Life*, 59–60.

132. It was reported that "the crowd was so great that the doors had to be bolted." Begg, *Baptist Church*, 7.

133. Winslow, *Hidden Life*, 61.

134. Joseph Foulkes Winks, ed., "Deaths," *The Baptist Reporter and Missionary Intelligencer* 22, no. 264 (August 1848): 328.

135. Jennifer Townsend, e-mail message to the author, November 17, 2009.

136. Winslow, *Life in Jesus*, 199. Winslow's sister Emma also experienced an "alarming illness" during this period. Her sickness occasioned one of Winslow's books, *Midnight Harmonies*, which he dedicated to her. In the preface, Winslow wrote, "The Author had completed his arrangements for a sea-voyage, when the sudden and alarming illness of a beloved relative interposed to prevent its accomplishment. A period of much anxiety ensued, during which the idea and the themes of this little volume suggested themselves to his mind." *Midnight Harmonies, or, Thoughts for the Season of Solitude and Sorrow* (New York: Robert Carter & Brothers, 1853), v.

137. For the affecting account of her death, see Winslow, *Life in Jesus*, 331–33.

sons, probably Octavius, repeated Scripture passages from memory for three hours "as the Holy Spirit aided his memory."[138] In those moments, she gave her final charge to the family: "Meet me in heaven!" Her dying words were uttered softly, "I see Thee!—I see Thee!—I see Thee!—I see Thee!"[139] She died in the home of her beloved son Octavius at the age of eighty.[140] Reflecting on his mother's death, he wrote:

> The sepulcher has closed in silence over her; but her inspiration, vital and balmy as the breath of spring, still floats over life's dreary way, gladdening, moulding, and guiding.... The authority to which as children we bowed so submissively, in later life, when the snow-flakes of time have frosted our brow, still lives to sway; and the maternal influence which shaped our youthful step, yet holds us in its deathless enchantment.[141]

While the death of his mother was expected, Winslow was completely unprepared for the horrific news of his next loved one who would meet the grave.

During the summer of 1856, Whitmore Winslow returned from Trinity College in Dublin, Ireland, for summer break. After spending a few weeks with his family in Leamington, he went to London to visit his sick Uncle Isaac. He then met his mother and sisters in Dover for a time of vacation. Two days after his arrival on Wednesday morning, August 6, Whitmore joined the family for morning worship in perfect health. Afterward he went down to the beach to bathe at the bathing machine.[142] Upon entering the water, it is believed his body went into shock, and he immediately went unconscious, drowning at the age of twenty-one.[143] Winslow experienced a "sudden shock and convulsed agony" at the loss of his son.[144] In the middle of this thriving pastorate, Winslow was intimately acquainted with suffering.

Winslow's theology buoyed his soul during these trials. He knew the Christ of the cross was both willing and able to bear his burdens. This is evident from a chapter he penned on suffering:

---

138. Winslow, *Life in Jesus*, 332.

139. Winslow, *Life in Jesus*, 332.

140. *Annual Register, or, a View of the History and Politics of the Year 1854* (London: F. & J. Rivington, 1855), 342.

141. Winslow, *Life in Jesus*, 127–28.

142. Bathing machines were roofed and walled wooden carts that rolled into the sea and allowed people to change out of their clothes and enter the ocean to bathe in a discreet manner.

143. Winslow, *Hidden Life*, 185–96.

144. Winslow, *Hidden Life*, vi. Winslow expressed gratitude for "the affectionate sympathy of his own beloved congregation, and of the feeling and attached community among whom he dwells." Winslow, *Hidden Life*, vii.

Jesus stands at your side and lovingly says—"Cast your burden upon Me and I will sustain you. I am God Almighty. I bore the load of your sin and condemnation up the steep of Calvary, and the same power of omnipotence, and the same strength of love that bore it all for you then, is prepared to bear your need, and sorrow now. Roll it all upon Me. Child of My Love! Lean hard! Let Me feel the pressure of your care. I know your burden, child! I shaped it—I poised it in My own hand and made no proportion of its weight to your unaided strength. For even as I laid it on, I said I shall be near, and while she leans on Me, this burden shall be Mine, not hers. So shall I keep My child within the circling arms of My own love. Here lay it down! Do not fear to impose it on a shoulder which upholds the government of worlds! Yet closer come! You are not near enough! I would embrace your burden, so I might feel My child reposing on My breast. You love Me! I know it. Doubt not, then. But, loving me, lean hard!"[145]

By God's grace he continued to exercise unwavering faith in God's sovereign goodness.[146]

Though the Leamington years brought great personal trial, they also delivered great ministerial blessing. The building of galleries to hold the growing congregation provides an indication of Winslow's popularity.[147] The church was also blessed financially under his ministry.[148] T. B. Dudley summarized Winslow's ministry by noting that "he conferred special lustre on the Church and the Spa for the space of eighteen years by his erudition, eloquence and zeal.... When he resigned a void was created in the pulpit and on the platform difficult to fill."[149] In 1857, Winslow completed his ministry at Warwick Street. The family then moved to Bath, hoping the area would benefit his health.[150]

---

145. Octavius Winslow, *The Ministry of Home, or, Brief Expository Lectures on Divine Truth Designed Especially for Family and Private Reading* (London: William Hunt & Co., 1867), 355.

146. Due to the many trials experienced throughout his life, Winslow's theology of suffering would provide a fascinating topic for further study.

147. Lyndon F. Cave, *Royal Leamington Spa: Its History and Development* (Chichester, U.K.: Phillimore & Co., 1988), 167.

148. The church minutes in March of 1848 reveal they paid off £1,200 ($128,851.46 in today's currency) in building debts and raised Winslow's salary to £250 ($26,844.06). Begg, *Baptist Church*, 7.

149. Dudley, *From Chaos to the Charter*, 246–47.

150. Jennifer Townsend, e-mail message to the author, November 17, 2009. Begg also noted, "During the latter part of his ministry Dr. Winslow was plagued with illness and eventually, in 1857, left Leamington to settle in Bath." *Baptist Church*, 7.

Kensington Chapel, Bath, England (1857–1867)

Upon arriving in Bath, Winslow leased a proprietary chapel belonging to the Church of England and started a Baptist church. As his friend John Taylor described, "It was used by him as a Baptist place of worship, though fitted up in every respect as belonging to the Church of England."[151] Thus, he became the founder of Kensington Chapel in 1858.[152] Taylor also described the make-up of his congregants: "As at Leamington, his popularity extended to members of the English Church, and many of that body took pews and settled under his pastorship."[153] This last statement is worthy of deeper investigation.

Why would Anglicans "settle" at a Baptist church? On the one hand, it is not surprising Winslow would draw members from outside the Baptist ranks. He was a prolific author and well respected in the religious community. He also had been heavily involved in the Evangelical Alliance since its inception in 1846, working with those outside of "party lines."[154] J. H. Y. Briggs notes that Kensington Chapel consisted of both credobaptists and paedobaptists.[155] Winslow was optimistic the two groups would stay united and led the church to join the Baptist Union as an open membership church in 1865.[156] Apparently, things did not go as planned and the church ultimately split because of conflict between the two groups.[157]

During his days in Bath, Winslow engaged in one of England's greatest theological controversies. On June 5, 1864, Charles Haddon Spurgeon preached a sermon titled "Baptismal Regeneration." It set off shock waves that reverberated throughout England. Spurgeon's sermon decried the Anglican position on baptismal regeneration. This is not surprising. What was

---

151. Taylor, *Autobiography of a Lancashire Lawyer*, 197.

152. J. H. Y. Briggs, "Winslow, Octavius" in *The Blackwell Dictionary of Evangelical Biography*, ed. Donald M. Lewis (Oxford: Blackwell Publishers, 1995), 1213.

153. Taylor, *Autobiography of a Lancashire Lawyer*, 197.

154. Evangelical Alliance, *Evangelical Alliance: Report of the Proceedings of the Conference, Held at Freemasons' Hall, London, From August 19th to September 2nd Inclusive, 1846* (London: Partridge & Oakey, 1847), 146. Winslow also served as one of three Honorable Secretaries for the Bath Committee in 1866. Evangelical Alliance, "Evangelical Alliance," *Evangelical Christendom; A Monthly Chronicle of the Churches. Conducted by Members of the Evangelical Alliance* 7 (October 1866): 519.

155. Briggs, "Winslow, Octavius," 1213.

156. Here Winslow aligned himself with one of his Puritan predecessors, John Bunyan, who had argued for open membership two centuries earlier. See John Bunyan, *Differences in Judgment about Water Baptism, No Bar to Communion*, in *The Works of Bunyan*, ed. George Offor (Glasgow, U.K.: W. G. Blackie & Son; repr., Edinburgh: Banner of Truth, 1991), 2:616–47.

157. Jennifer Townsend, e-mail message to the author, November 17, 2009.

surprising about Spurgeon's sermon was how he lambasted the evangelical clergymen in the church as hypocrites, saying they had signed off on doctrinal statements with which they knowingly disagreed.[158] This compelled many to respond, including Winslow.

Winslow undoubtedly agreed with Spurgeon's theology. He abhorred the doctrine of baptismal regeneration, believing it helped send people to hell. Winslow called it a "soul-destroying heresy"[159] and delineated his views with fierce boldness, writing, "We hesitate not to pronounce the Romish dogma of sacramental grace—the Papistical doctrine of baptismal regeneration—to be the pre-eminent lie of Satan—the most subtle and fatal weapon which this arch-foe of our race ever forged for the destruction of men's souls in perdition."[160] Moreover, he abhorred the doctrine because it undercuts and disregards the Spirit's work. He wrote, "It is just as fatal an error to believe in the dogma of Baptismal Regeneration—the antagonistic error to the work of the Spirit—as to believe in the dogma of the Mass—the antagonistic error of Christ's sacrifice."[161] Although Winslow agreed with Spurgeon theologically, he strongly opposed Spurgeon's verbal assault on his evangelical Anglican friends.[162]

Winslow chided Spurgeon's attack on the evangelical clergy in a sermon preached from Ephesians 6:24.[163] He announced:

> To denounce the Evangelical clergy of the church of England because they do not preach the doctrine of Baptismal Regeneration; to stigmatise their conduct on this ground as "equivocal and shuffling," their course as "inconsistent and dishonest," as "one of the gravest pieces of

---

158. For a summary of Spurgeon's sermon and the ensuing controversy, see Lewis Drummond, *Spurgeon: Prince of Preachers* (Grand Rapids: Kregel, 1992), 483–500.

159. Octavius Winslow, *Born Again, or, From Grace to Glory* (London: John F. Shaw, 1864), 89.

160. Winslow, *Born Again*, 30.

161. Octavius Winslow, *The Precious Things of God* (London: James Nisbet, 1860; repr., Ligonier, Pa.: Soli Deo Gloria, 1993), 231.

162. Another magazine cited Winslow as declaring, "I will give place to no man living in my abhorrence of the doctrine of Baptismal Regeneration. I believe it to be one of the most insidious, ensnaring, and fatal heresies which the genius of error ever invented.... But repugnance to this doctrine, and a solemn protest against its dissemination, do not necessarily involve a violation of Christian charity, an impeachment of the piety, integrity, and honesty of any order of Christian men, or the excommunication of any one branch of the Christian Church." "Monthly Retrospect: Rev. Mr. Spurgeon and Baptismal Regeneration," *The United Presbyterian Magazine* 8 (October 1864): 477.

163. Ephesians 6:24 reads, "Grace be with all them that love our Lord Jesus Christ in sincerity."

immorality perpetrated in England," as ministers "whose friendship honest men neither ask nor accept," is to come under the censure, in its greatest breadth, which our Divine Master once pronounced upon those who breathed a like spirit of condemnation, "Ye know not what manner of spirit ye are of." I have no right to stand between God and a man's conscience. Who made me a judge of my brother? To his own Master he stands or falls. It were an impertinence and a presumption in me to foist my interpretation of any article of faith subscribed to by godly men, either upon their conscience or their ministry.[164]

Winslow believed Christian charity demanded a different response than Spurgeon's "spirit of condemnation." Furthermore, he did not think the evangelical clergy really believed that the Book of Common Prayer taught the doctrine. He also highly esteemed many servants in the Anglican ranks. Winslow "shudder[ed] at the thought" of withdrawing affection and fellowship from men such as Charles Simeon and Henry Martyn of yesteryear and other godly men of the present.[165]

Another angle in the controversy was the presence of the Evangelical Alliance. Winslow spoke as someone firmly rooted in the Alliance and would have agreed with his friend the Honorable Reverend Baptist Noel that Spurgeon's words broke the spirit of the Alliance's fourth resolution.[166] This surely caused friction in his friendship with Spurgeon. Just three years earlier Spurgeon had invited Winslow to preach at the opening of the Metropolitan Tabernacle.

The years in Bath brought another agonizing hardship. On October 9, 1866, Hannah Ann died suddenly in their home.[167] After her death, Winslow provided a short biographical sketch of her life in a reflection titled *Instant Glory*. He honored her by writing, "Her life in all its relations, duties, and trials, was the Lord's, regulated and hallowed by the holy principles of the

---

164. Evangelical Alliance, "Home Intelligence: Mr. Spurgeon and Charity," *Evangelical Christendom: A Monthly Chronicle of the Churches* 5 (October 1864): 513.

165. Evangelical Alliance, "Home Intelligence," 513.

166. The fourth resolution read: "Then when required by conscience to assert or defend any views or principles wherein they differ from Christian brethren who agree with them in vital truths, the members of the Alliance will aim earnestly, by the help of the Holy Spirit, to avoid all rash and groundless insinuations, personal imputations, or irritating allusions; and to maintain the meekness and gentleness of Christ by speaking the truth in love." Spurgeon withdrew from the Alliance shortly thereafter. See Drummond, *Spurgeon: Prince of Preachers*, 497–98.

167. For a stirring account of Mrs. Winslow's final two days of life, see Winslow, *Instant Glory*, 59–71. For her obituary, see Sylvanus Urban, ed., "Deaths," *The Gentleman's Magazine July–December 1866* 221 (1866), 704.

divine religion she professed. As a mother, she was devoted, affectionate and self-denying; as a minister's wife, sympathizing and helpful, often supplying a wanting link in pastoral service; as a friend, loving, gentle and true."[168] For thirty-two years of marriage, she had displayed "a life of unswerving fidelity to duty and love."[169] From all indications, Hannah Ann and Octavius enjoyed a great partnership in the gospel. Their final moments together supply ample evidence.

The morning before her death, Octavius had to catch a train for a pulpit engagement in town. At the time, he was battling an unusual "depression of spirits."[170] She reminded him of the precious truths of God's Word and left him with these parting and final words: "We must look *up*, and not *down*; the Lord is all-sufficient, and will do all things well, good-bye."[171] A delegation from the Evangelical Alliance attended the funeral, bestowing "numerous and sincere" expressions of sympathy.[172] Shortly after this sorrowful event Winslow moved to Brighton, where he would spend his final years of life and ministry.

Emmanuel Church, Brighton/Hove, England (1868–1878)
When Winslow's lease expired at Bath, he sought another place of ministry. Through the assistance of many readers of his works and other friends, he raised the funds to build Emmanuel Church.[173] His final pastorate originated in the same manner as his first, as a church plant.

The enigmatic distinction of the Emmanuel pastorate resided in Winslow's ecclesiological shift. This new church, situated on the boundary line of Hove and Brighton,[174] was not a place of Baptist worship.[175] The *Brighton Gazette* explained, "When Dr. Winslow first came to Brighton, and gathered round him the numerous and influential congregation that worshipped at Emmanuel's, he and his followers were of the sect known as 'Free

---

168. Winslow, *Instant Glory*, 75.
169. Winslow, *Instant Glory*, 61.
170. Winslow, *Instant Glory*, 60.
171. Winslow, *Instant Glory*, 62.
172. Evangelical Alliance, "Evangelical Alliance: The Bath Conference," *Evangelical Christendom A Monthly Chronicle of the Churches* 7 (November 1866): 551. Incidentally, Winslow was supposed to present a paper on some practical resolutions of the principles of the Alliance on October 17. His paper was read by another member (554).
173. Taylor, *Autobiography of a Lancashire Lawyer*, 198.
174. Middleton, *Encyclopaedia of Hove and Portslade*, 4:74.
175. One source called Winslow a "Baptist minister" during this time. Evangelical Alliance, "Monthly Retrospect: Home," *Evangelical Christendom: A Monthly Chronicle of the Churches* 9 (October 1868): 400.

Church'—Episcopal, not Presbyterian, and not Methodist."[176] This concluded thirty-four years as a Baptist pastor. His transition did not spring from any discernible theological revision. John Campbell recorded, "A new church has opened at Brighton, of which the Rev. Dr. Octavius Winslow—only a few months ago a Baptist preacher in Bath—is minister. The church is 'for the accommodation of those who love the Church of England Liturgy, but yet desire to sever themselves from the Establishment.' Dr. Winslow does not, in the position he has taken, abjure his old Nonconformist principles."[177] Thus, Winslow was still identified as a Nonconformist. This is evident from the controversial opening of Emmanuel Church. Winslow invited Rev. I. Knapp, an Evangelical Anglican, to preach one of the inaugural sermons. The staunch Ashurst Turner Gilbert, bishop of Chichester, reprimanded Rev. Knapp for "fraternizing" with Winslow and inhibited him from officiating until he purged himself of his "grievous and audacious" offense.[178] Obviously, the bishop did not want other Anglicans to be friendly with Nonconformists.[179] One of the first tasks Winslow accomplished involved the publication of a hymnbook for Emmanuel Chapel.[180] Someone, presumably from the established church, said nearly all of the hymns were "dissenting effusions."[181]

Winslow completed his ecclesiological transition in 1870. On July 12, Winslow was ordained as a deacon in the Church of England by Bishop Richard Durnford of Chichester in the Cathedral Church.[182] Five months

---

176. "Death of the Rev. Dr. Winslow," *Brighton Gazette*, March 7, 1878.

177. John Campbell, ed., "Church News of the Month," *The Christian's Penny Magazine and Friend of the People* 4 (1868): 306.

178. Campbell, "Church News," 306. For a short biographical sketch on Gilbert, see "Gilbert, Ashurst Turner (1786–1870)," *The Dictionary of National Biography*, ed. Leslie Stephen and Sidney Lee (London: Oxford University Press, 1922), 7:1200.

179. Interestingly, the bishop was forced to inhibit another rector for his "Ritualistic extravagances" because the people of Brighton were indignant that Rev. Knapp was inhibited for association with Winslow while the "highest Ritualistic practices" of another were ignored. Campbell, "Church News," 327.

180. See Octavius Winslow, *Hymns: Selected and Arranged for the Use of Emmanuel Church, Brighton* (London: W. Hunt, 1868). It is evident that Winslow loved hymns as he often quoted them in his books and sermons. It seems that one of his favorite hymns was "There Is a Fountain." In a letter to Octavius his mother wrote, "I have just been trying to sing your tune my dear child, that sweet hymn we have often sung together,—There is a fountain fill'd with blood...." Winslow, *Life in Jesus*, 151. He also referenced that hymn when testifying of his conversion. Winslow, *Pastoral Letter*, 6.

181. Middleton, "Emmanuel Church," 74.

182. "Ordinations," *The Ecclesiastical Gazette, or, Monthly Register of the Affairs of the Church of England and of its Religious Societies and Institutions* 33 (July 12, 1870): 21. It would not be surprising to discover that the appointment of Bishop Durnford played a part in the

later, on December 18, Winslow was ordained as a priest.[183] Although Winslow was welcomed to address gatherings of Anglican ministers, it seems that his relationship with the Church of England was delicate. Bishop Durnford later wrote to Winslow's successor concerning Emmanuel Church: "It is not a 'church' nor, strictly speaking, even a 'chapel' but simply a building licensed for divine service. And let me remind you that without the Bishop's license you could not as a clergyman of the Church officiate in it, and that such license is by the terms of it revocable."[184]

Winslow's transition to the Church of England has been clouded in mystery. Even his contemporaries were perplexed as to why he seceded. *The United Presbyterian Magazine* wrote, "The Rev. Dr. Octavius Winslow... [has] been received into the Church of England. Dr. Winslow has been long and favourably known as the author of a number of popular and pious publications.... Of his conversion to the Episcopal Establishment we have not had any explanation."[185] The *Brighton Gazette* also stated, "Somehow or other Dr. Winslow and his congregation came to see the falsity of their position in the Christian world [apparently referring to Emmanuel's "Free Church" position]. Thus it came about that Brighton witnessed the rare example of a pastor and his whole congregation leaving Dissent to enter the folds of Mother Church."[186] So, why *did* Winslow transition to the Church of England? Any definitive answer without historical evidence would be sheer conjecture. Conceding that, several possible factors exist concerning his decision.

First, a position on church government did not rank high on the list of Winslow's theological priorities. He said "that it was a cause for thankfulness that Christ did not leave any particular order of government in His Church. He had left it open for each individual to form his own judgment, as far as he could, guided by the unerring light of the revealed Word."[187] This seems to be a major reason. Second, there is a clear progression of ecclesiological elasticity

---

timing of Winslow's ordination, especially in light of the insulting greeting Bishop Turner had bestowed just two years earlier.

183. Joseph Irving, *The Annals of Our Time: A Diurnal of Events, Social and Political, Home and Foreign, from the Accession of Queen Victoria, June 20, 1837* (London: MacMillan & Co., 1871), 967.

184. William Richard Wood Stephens, *A Memoir of Richard Durnford, D.D., Sometime Bishop of Chichester: With Selections from His Correspondence* (London: John Murray, 1899), 241.

185. "Monthly Retrospect: Home Affairs," *The United Presbyterian Magazine* 15 (1871): 95.

186. "Death of the Rev. Dr. Winslow."

187. Evangelical Alliance, "Public Meeting," *Evangelical Christendom* 3 (November 1862): 567.

as evidenced by Kensington Chapel becoming an open membership Baptist church. This move completed his progression from a Baptist pastor, to the pastor of a Baptist church with both credo and paedobaptist members, to serving in the Church of England.[188] Third, as mentioned above, Winslow apparently loved the liturgy in the Church of England. Fourth, he began attracting people from the Anglican Church as early as his Warwick Street pastorate. There was a growing affinity for Winslow among Anglicans, probably due to the popularity of his preaching and writings.[189] Fifth, he shared a great affection for the evangelical clergy in the Church of England. This is observed in numerous instances, including the controversy with Spurgeon, his inviting Anglican ministers to preach in his church, and the memorial tributes he presented for ministers in the established church.[190] Sixth, Winslow clearly exhibited an ecumenical spirit, which he articulated and displayed through the Evangelical Alliance. During an address delivered at an annual gathering of the Evangelical Alliance, Winslow called for a "greater breadth, and more visible manifestation, of brotherly love and Christian union."[191] Seventh, the influence of his family may have also played a role in his secession. Mary was influenced by ministers from various churches, as evidenced in her love for John Newton. Moreover, Winslow's brothers, George and Isaac, were both Anglican ministers, and Forbes Winslow was also a member of the Anglican Church.[192] Finally, one could speculate on whether Winslow desired to be a positive influence in the reform of the church. He clearly sided with the Low Church Evangelicals and did not fear exposing the heresies of the Tractarians (High Church) or Broad Church Movement. Perhaps some or all of these

---

188. Remember that Winslow began his ministry seeking to persuade those in the Anglican church to accept his Baptistic views.

189. It is also interesting that Columbia College, the school that honored Winslow with a doctor of divinity, was an Episcopal school.

190. See Octavius Winslow, *Jesus and John, or, The Loving and the Loved: A Tribute to the Memory of the Late Rev. William Marsh, D.D.* (London: James Nisbet & Co., 1859); and Octavius Winslow, introduction to *A Short Memoir of the Rev. John Finley, Late Ministerial Trustee of the Countess of Huntington's Connexion…with a Brief Account of His Two Sons,* by Harriet Finley (London: James Nisbet, 1856). In the preface to his tribute to William Marsh, Winslow wrote, "Alas! The race of godly ministers, of whom William Marsh and John Angell James were distinguished types, is fast diminishing. Who among us will wear their mantles? Let us perpetuate their Christian excellencies, and seek grace from God to imitate their holy example, as they imitated Christ." Winslow, *Jesus and John,* 5.

191. Octavius Winslow, *Practical Suggestions Appropriate to the Present Religious Crisis* (London: William Hunt & Co., 1868), 15.

192. Whittington-Egan, *Doctor Forbes,* 30.

factors converged later in life, making the transition somewhat inconsequential for him.

Although he compromised in areas of polity, Winslow held firm to his orthodox convictions and confronted others in the established church who wavered from pure doctrine and practice. In fact, Winslow observed many detestable flaws within the Church of England and did not hesitate in exposing the dangers of the rationalistic and ritualistic wings of the church. At a meeting of the Church Congress held in Nottingham on October 13, 1871, Winslow was asked to present a paper on how the church must regain her spiritual vitality. His closing remarks were bold and pointed. Note the editorial comment in brackets revealing the impact of his piercing statement:

> Let the Church of England cease to be a Christ-witnessing Church, a "burning and shining light" of God's truth—let her abjure her ancient Protestantism, sacrifice her evangelical faith, and prostrate herself before the golden image which rationalistic philosophy and an idolatrous worship have set up within her pale—[The President hoped the speaker would kindly withdraw an expression which must necessarily exasperate many persons present.] Then the days of her existence are numbered, the splendour of her glory is departed, and her sun, draped in funereal gloom, will have gone down while it was yet day![193]

With these words he denounced both the "rationalistic philosophy" of the Broad Church Movement and the Tractarians' "idolatrous worship."

Winslow's final years of ministry in Brighton were very fruitful. He continued to publish books at a rapid pace, and Emmanuel Church grew to 1,300 regular worshipers.[194] Ironically, the church was demolished in 1965, and a Baptist church now stands in its place.[195] In all, Winslow planted three churches, and the other two churches he pastored were very young churches.[196]

---

193. Church Congress, *Authorized Report of the Church Congress Held at Nottingham October 10, 11, 12, & 13* (London: Wells Gardner, 1871), 441. The number Winslow offended was potentially great as the Congress was very well attended with 3,205 present over the four days of meetings (vi).

194. "Death of the Rev. Dr. Winslow."

195. Middleton, "Emmanuel Church," 74.

196. Second Baptist was founded in 1830, six years before Winslow became the pastor. Prime, *History of Long*, 400. Warwick Street was also founded in 1830, eight years before Winslow's pastorate. Begg, *Baptist Church*, 3.

The Writings of Octavius Winslow

One of the distinct features of Winslow's ministry throughout all of his pastorates was his industrious pen. By the end of his life, his literary output culminated in the publication of more than forty books, numerous tracts and pamphlet sermons, and various addresses and articles published in a variety of magazines.[197] His series of annual addresses enjoyed "extensive circulation."[198] Upon the publication of two new works, *Our God for Ever and Ever* and *Consider Jesus*, one reviewer wrote, "Dr. Winslow's pen is never at rest, and its products are much prized by many good and devout people."[199] Apparently, he often burned the midnight oil in order to publish at such a rapid pace. He wrote in the preface of *The Sympathy of Christ with Man*: "Composed under the pressure of important ministerial, extended pastoral, and continuous public labour, it necessarily partakes of the imperfections of a work thus written, and often at a season when the jaded powers, both of mind and body, demanded the restorative of sleep."[200] Winslow made significant sacrifices to maintain his writing ministry.

One could make the argument that Winslow was more widely known for his writing ministry than for his preaching or pastoral ministry. One reviewer wrote, "Dr. Winslow is certainly a very prolific author, and exercises his ministry as effectively from the press as he does from the pulpit. But through the press he addresses a far more numerous audience. To how many Christians he has been the means of imparting comfort and strength, it would be impossible to calculate."[201] In many instances his writing and sermons were almost indistinguishable. The following review of *Personal Declension and Revival in the Soul of Man* provides evidence:

> The statements of doctrine are clear and discriminating, and the practical operation of truth in the heart and life of a believer, is accurately unfolded. But the great charm of the book is the spirit of elevated piety which pervades it from the beginning to the end, and this it appears

---

197. See appendix 3 for an annotated bibliography of Winslow's works.

198. Evangelical Alliance, "Home Intelligence: The Late Dr. Winslow," *Evangelical Christendom, Christian Work, and the News of the Churches: Also a Monthly Record of the Transactions of the Evangelical Alliance* 19 (April 1878): 120. Several of Winslow's annual addresses were compiled and published. See Octavius Winslow, *Divine Realities, or, Spiritual Reflections for the Saint and Sinner* (London: John F. Shaw & Co., 1860).

199. John Campbell, ed., "Notices of New Books," *The Christian Witness and Congregation Magazine* 6 (1870): 478.

200. Winslow, *Sympathy of Christ with Man*, v.

201. Baptist Missionary Society, "Brief Notices," *The Baptist Magazine* 55 (1863): 517.

to us, must commend it to all who love the faith and holiness of the Gospel. The reader will feel the inspiration of a fervour very different from that which distinguishes many of the religious publications of the day.[202]

Like his preaching, Winslow's writing sought to transform the mind and the heart. On the one hand, his works were theological and full of Scripture. On the other hand, they were grounded in truth so that people might experience and practice those truths in life. His style was devotional, vivid, and passionate. The vast majority of his books went to press numerous times.

Death and Legacy

On March 5, 1878, at the age of sixty-nine, Octavius Winslow died suddenly at his residence in Brighton. One source said the cause of death was heart disease.[203] His obituary in the *Brighton Gazette* read:

> We regret to have to announce the death of the reverend Dr. Winslow, the incumbent of Emmanuel Church. This melancholy event took place at the residence of Dr. Winslow early on Tuesday morning. Dr. Winslow had preached at his own church on Sunday and his death was unexpected. Dr. Winslow was a man who well adorned his sacred office. His unaffected piety, burning eloquence, uprightness, and genial, courteous, benign character caused him to be respected in life by all who came into contact with him, and loved by those who had closer opportunity of observing his sterling worth. His death will be mourned particularly by the large congregation who Sunday after Sunday were attracted to hear the masterly expositions and the earnest exhortations which were delivered from his pulpit. Generally his loss will also be felt by the Evangelical party in the Church, to whom his name was a tower of strength.[204]

John Taylor, a man who had known Winslow for more than thirty years, described him in the following words: "He was a gentleman of a high-toned

---

202. "Critical Notices," *Southern Presbyterian Review: Conducted by an Association of Ministers in Columbia, S.C.* 1 (December 1847), 156.

203. "Our Memorial Record: The Rev. Octavius Winslow," *The Sunday Magazine for Family Reading* 1 (1878), 504.

204. "Death of the Rev. Dr. Winslow." One month later his possessions were auctioned off. They included much "excellent furniture" and "450 volumes of books." See "This Day. Lyndhurst Lodge, Wilbury Road, Hove. Messrs Wilkinson and Son," *Sussex Advertiser*, April 9, 1978. This was uncovered by Jennifer Townsend and made public by Matthew Blair, who established "The Octavius Winslow Archive" at http://octaviuswinslow.org/.

character—a laborious worker in his Master's service—of piety the most elevated, and, as his writings testify, deeply taught in the work of the Holy Spirit."[205]

Throughout his life Winslow sought to avoid the disgrace of making a shipwreck of his faith. He knew the danger of not finishing well. He said, "The bleak shores of eternity are strewed with the fragments of many a beautiful wreck—men who once stood high in the church,—too high for their own safety,—but who made shipwreck of their profession and their faith, and now serve as beacons of warning to those who follow."[206] Thankfully, God enabled him to finish his race with integrity and grace, and those who followed Winslow found in him a beacon of encouragement and example.

Concerning the reality of death, Winslow wrote: "Remember, my reader, you must depart this world, but your influence will survive you.... The dead never die! Their memory speaks! Their character speaks! Their works speak, and speak forever!"[207] Through his numerous books, experimental preaching, and the lives he touched for God's glory, Octavius Winslow continues to speak.

---

205. Taylor, *Autobiography of a Lancashire Lawyer*, 194.

206. Winslow, *Eminent Holiness*, 84.

207. Octavius Winslow, *Grace and Truth* (London: John F. Shaw, 1849), 35e. In a few cases, I was unable to obtain copies of some of Winslow's rare original works. Thus, all books with page numbers ending in "e" can be downloaded in an electronic PDF format at: http://grace-ebooks.com/library/ index.php?dir=Octavius%20Winslow/. The page numbers correspond to the electronic versions.

2

THEOLOGY AND METHOD
OF PREACHING

Richard Lints insightfully warned, "[People] who are not driven by a theological vision will be driven by a vision of expediency."[1] This applies to the
ministry of proclamation. Without a theological vision, preaching is destined
to fall short of God's great design of changing lives and claiming worship from
all people. In order to regain their homiletical compass and chart the course
toward faithful and effective proclamation, preachers must think theologically. When this happens, methodology will fall into place. When it fails to
happen, sermons will devolve into something less than biblical preaching.
J. I. Packer alluded to this when he wrote, "Not every discourse that fills the
appointed 20- or 30-minute slot in public worship is actual preaching, however much it is called by that name."[2] In contrast, Winslow grounded his
sermons in a healthy theology of preaching.

This chapter provides the foundation for understanding Winslow's
experimental preaching by examining his theology of preaching. The first
two sections cover his thoughts on the nature of preaching and the Holy
Spirit's role in the task. An assessment of Winslow's experimental methodology follows. It will be concluded that he combined a robust theology of
preaching with faithful pulpit practice.

The Nature of Preaching
D. Martyn Lloyd-Jones was one of England's greatest preachers in the twentieth century. Although a century divided his ministry from Winslow's, his
theology of preaching could hardly be more congruent. Lloyd-Jones said:

> So often when people are asked to lecture or to speak on preaching they
> rush immediately to consider methods and ways and means and the

---

1. Richard Lints, *The Fabric of Theology: A Prolegomenon to Evangelical Theology* (Grand
Rapids: Eerdmans, 1993), 4.

2. J. I. Packer, "Why Preaching?," in *The Preacher and Preaching: Reviving the Art in the
Twentieth Century,* ed. Samuel T. Logan Jr. (Phillipsburg, N.J.: P&R, 1986), 3.

mechanics. I believe that is quite wrong. We must start with the pre-suppositions and with the background, and with general principles; for unless I am very greatly mistaken, the main trouble arises from the fact that people are not clear in their minds as to what preaching really is.[3]

Winslow was clear "as to what preaching really is." He had strong convictions concerning the nature of preaching, the gravity of the task, the pleasure of preaching, and the source of his sufficiency as a herald of God's truth.

Speaking God's Words

Winslow loved to preach and possessed an extremely high view of the task. Speaking of the minister he said, "The great design of [Christian ministry]... is the preaching of the gospel to a dying world. From this, as his chief and most honourable work, no other and inferior should dissuade or beguile him."[4] Though a formal definition of preaching is difficult to find in his writings, Winslow clearly had convictions about what constituted biblical preaching. If someone would have asked him the question, "What is preaching?" he likely would have directed them to the example of the prophet Micaiah in 2 Chronicles and stated that the primary task of preaching is speaking God's words. Reflecting on what it means to revere God's Word, Winslow held up Micaiah as an example of supreme fidelity.[5] When urged to predict a favorable outcome for King Ahab and King Jehoshaphat concerning an upcoming military endeavor, unlike the false prophets who surrounded him, Micaiah refused to speak anything contrary to what God had spoken. Second Chronicles 18:13 records his response: "As the LORD liveth, even what my God saith, that will I speak." These words crystallize Winslow's view of preaching. He wrote, "Am I a minister of Christ? Then, as the Lord lives, what my God says, that must I speak, nothing more and nothing less."[6] Winslow held that faithful preachers simply proclaim what they receive from God's Word.

For Winslow, preaching was a response to seeing the glory of Christ. He believed one must *see* before he *speaks*. Another prophet, Isaiah, provided him with this insight: "Isaiah not only beheld the glory of Christ, but he also

---

3. D. Martyn Lloyd-Jones, *Preaching and Preachers* (Grand Rapids: Zondervan, 1971), 10.

4. Octavius Winslow, *Eminent Holiness: Essential to an Efficient Ministry* (London: Houlston & Stoneman, 1843), 17.

5. Octavius Winslow, *Thus Saith the Lord, or, Words of Divine Love* (London: John F. Shaw, 1872), 1st Day. This work is organized as a month of devotionals. Thus, reading days rather than page numbers are designated.

6. Winslow, *Thus Saith*, 1st Day.

'spake of it.' While he mused upon the wondrous sight, 'the fire burned, then spake he with his tongue.' He could not but speak of that which he saw and felt. And who can behold the glory of the Redeemer, and not speak of it? Who can see His beauty and not extol it—who can taste His love and not laud it?"[7] Such a view of preaching carries a significant sense of duty. Winslow went on to say, "How tremendous the responsibility of my ministerial office! I am under the most solemn obligation to preach the Gospel, the whole Gospel, and nothing but the Gospel, as God has spoken it in His Word."[8] A deep reverence for God's Word dominated Winslow's preaching.

The task for preachers is exposition.[9] Speaking to preachers, Winslow declared, "We are but the expositors of what God has seen most consistent with his glory to make known.... O for grace to preach as God has commanded; neither taking from, nor adding to, his revealed word!"[10] His sermons were always drawn from a text of Scripture and supported by numerous cross-references throughout.[11] It is evident Winslow affirmed the Reformation dictum: Scripture interprets Scripture. This type of preaching requires frequent meditation by the preacher. Winslow announced, "O to have the word of God dwelling in us so richly, and our hearts so intensely glowing with the love of Christ, as to be ever ready to open our lips for God—a well always full, and running over."[12] Expositors of Scripture must love and meditate on God's Word in order to proclaim it faithfully.

At the same time, faithful exposition involves applying the text in its gospel context. In a sermon meditating on Psalm 58:4–5, Winslow refers to preachers as "gospel charmers" and defines preaching in this way: "To charm

---

7. Octavius Winslow, *The Glory of the Redeemer*, 8th ed. (London: John F. Shaw, 1865; repr., Pittsburgh: Soli Deo Gloria, 1997), 117.

8. Winslow, *Thus Saith*, 1st Day.

9. Exposition involves the communication of God's truth. Contemporary homiletician Ramesh Richard says, "Biblical exposition expounds, expresses, and exposes the Bible to an audience and the audience to the Bible." *Preparing Expository Sermons: A Seven-Step Method for Biblical Preaching* (Grand Rapids: Baker, 2001), 21.

10. Octavius Winslow, *Glimpses of the Truth As It Is in Jesus* (Philadelphia: Lindsay & Blakiston, 1856), 83.

11. For example, in a sermon titled "A Full Christ for Empty Sinners," Winslow utilized nearly forty direct quotations of related biblical texts. See *Patriarchal Shadows of Christ and His Church: As Exhibited in Passages Drawn from the History of Joseph and His Brethren* (London: John F. Shaw, 1863; repr., Grand Rapids: Sovereign Grace Treasures, 2005), 47–65. See appendixes 1 and 2 for more examples.

12. Octavius Winslow, *The Inner Life: Its Nature, Relapse, and Recovery* (London: John F. Shaw, 1850), 94.

wisely, then, is so rightly to divide God's word, as not to confound truth with error—so discriminatingly to preach it, as to separate the precious from the vile—and so distinctly and prominently to hold up the cross of Christ, as to save immortal souls."[13] According to this statement, the primary aims of preaching involve faithfully dividing God's Word, applying it to the hearers, and holding up the cross of Christ that souls might be saved. These categories shaped Winslow's methodology.

Winslow said true preachers are "men of God who preach not themselves, but with beautiful simplicity, holy fervor, and fresh anointing, preach Jesus in all His personal glories, and in all the fulness and perfection of His atoning work—men who do not shun to declare the whole counsel of God."[14] Winslow practiced this by consistently preaching Christ from the Old and New Testament.[15]

The Weight of Preaching

The task of preaching carries a tremendous weight of responsibility. When preachers speak for God, eternal souls hang in the balance. This understanding accompanied Winslow to the pulpit each time he preached God's Word. Regarding the magnitude of the minister's work, Winslow said, "A greater work than theirs was never entrusted to mortal hands. No angel employed in the celestial embassy bears a commission of higher authority, or wings his way to discharge a duty of such extraordinary greatness and responsibility."[16] There was no levity in his approach to the pulpit.

The reason for such an understanding was twofold. First, it stemmed from the significance of the One he served and the task set before him. Speaking of gospel ministers, he explained, "He is a minister of the Lord Jesus Christ—an ambassador from the court of heaven—a preacher of the glorious gospel of the blessed God—a steward of the mysteries of the kingdom."[17] The minister serves Jesus Christ, the Creator and Redeemer of fallen man. He also possesses and proclaims the inestimable treasure of the gospel.

Secondly, the task is infinitely important because it possesses an outcome of infinite consequence. Winslow's theology of language is important here. He

---

13. Winslow, *Glimpses of the Truth*, 28–29.
14. Winslow, *Inner Life*, 206.
15. For more on Winslow's Christ-centered preaching, see chapter 4, "Preaching Centered in Christ."
16. Winslow, *Glimpses of the Truth*, 89.
17. Winslow, *Glimpses of the Truth*, 89.

believed language is bestowed on humanity as a divine gift, and the tongue is employed as "a mighty instrument for good or for evil."[18] As Proverbs 18:21 says, "Death and life are in the power of the tongue." Winslow believed this truth held "awful" ramifications for ministers because God holds them accountable for every word they preach. That is why he exhorted his fellow gospel laborers, "Oh, see that your speech is seasoned with grace, administering instruction and edification to the hearer. Let no corrupt thing, no false doctrine, no untruthful statement, no harsh, unkind, unsympathizing, heart-wounding word flow from your lips. Speak for God, for Christ, for souls."[19] Winslow approached the pulpit with sobriety because he believed people will spend an eternity in heaven or hell based on their response to the gospel.

Understanding God has chosen preachers as His instruments of proclaiming salvation, Winslow viewed preachers as "those who stand between the living and the dead."[20] He said a preacher "comes with a message from the court of heaven of the most absorbing interest, to a world in arms against its sovereign Majesty. He throws himself in the midst of a race of rebels against the blessed and only Potentate, the King of kings, and Lord of lords: and with weeping eye, and outstretched hands, and persuasive voice, he beseeches them to ground their weapons before the cross, and submit to the laws and government of God."[21] Thus, as one who stands between God and man, preachers serve as imperfect but bold instruments of grace who call people to believe in Christ.

In his pursuit of souls, Winslow was careful to focus his praying and preaching on individuals. He wrote, "The thought of *one* soul saved, the spectacle of *one* soul lost, were sufficient to inspire the highest joy, the deepest woe. Think only of the latter—*a soul lost*—lost to all eternity!"[22] Winslow preached with the conviction that no one was beyond the reach of God's grace. He believed God could convert the vilest sinner:

> It is the theological creed of some that to those who are spiritually dead, we ought neither to write, nor to preach. But with all meekness would we say, we have not so read God's word, nor have we "so learned Christ."

---

18. Octavius Winslow, *The Sympathy of Christ with Man: Its Teaching and Its Consolation* (New York: Robert Carter & Brothers, 1863; repr., Harrisonburg, Va.: Sprinkle, 1994), 27.

19. Winslow, *Sympathy of Christ*, 28.

20. Octavius Winslow, *Personal Declension and Revival of Religion in the Soul* (London: John F. Shaw, 1841; repr., Edinburgh: Banner of Truth, 2000), 147–48.

21. Winslow, *Eminent Holiness*, 12.

22. Octavius Winslow, *Pisgah Views, or, The Negative Aspects of Heaven* (London: John F. Shaw, 1873), 137.

The prophet Ezekiel was commanded to prophesy over the "dry bones"; and Jesus himself not only warned the impenitent, but wept over them! Who can tell while we are writing and preaching, warning and inviting, the "breath of the Lord" may come forth and breathe over them, and they live![23]

The gravity of this responsibility, as well as his accountability before God, caused him to exclaim, "Woe is unto me, if I preach not the pure, simple, unadulterated Gospel of Christ! The blood of souls will God require at my hands!"[24] In light of these truths, Winslow believed that one additional element should be present in the ministry of sincere preachers: tears. He said:

> Oh, let us who deal with souls, who preach Christ and in view of eternity, not fail to steep the precious seed we sow in tears of the deepest sensibility. Where is there an office more worthy, a work more befitting, an end more in harmony with the tears of the deepest sympathy, than that of the Christian minister addressing himself to deathless and endangered souls speeding to the judgment-seat?[25]

This perspective gave Winslow's preaching a sense of urgency and earnest conviction.[26] However, according to Winslow, preachers should not only focus on the burden of their responsibility. They should also recognize the great privilege and pleasure of proclaiming the gospel.

The Pleasure of Preaching

Winslow also believed preachers should both find pleasure in their task and preach for the pleasure of God. The weight of the office should in no way lessen the immense joy of preaching. While Winslow was acquainted with the vast responsibility of preaching, he also knew the great delight of the pulpit. He explained:

> To proclaim that gospel which has often charmed his own soul—to preach that Jesus, at times so precious to his own heart—to comfort others with the comforts with which he himself has been comforted by God—to wipe a solitary tear from the eye—to chase a single grief from

---

23. Octavius Winslow, *Grace and Truth* (London: John F. Shaw, 1849), 97e.

24. Winslow, *Thus Saith*, 1st Day.

25. Winslow, *Pisgah Views*, 137.

26. Speaking of the preacher to the students at Stepney College, Winslow declared, "It is no marvel that night and day with tears, in season and out of season, he should warn every man, and teach every man, becoming all things to all men, if by *any means* he might save some. My brethren, in view of such a picture, the astonishment is, not that we feel so much, but that we feel no more!" *Eminent Holiness*, 12.

the heart—to smooth a dying pillow—to save a soul from death—to guide a saint to glory—O to him it were worth a million lives, were they even lives of tenfold toil and trial![27]

Winslow believed all true preaching should have a doxological dimension. He saw preaching as an existentially satisfying endeavor that brings God glory and holds great personal reward.[28]

When preachers preach for the pleasure of God, they are free to serve God and their people to the fullest. The apostle Paul exemplified such preaching. Winslow wrote, "Human opinion weighed lightly with him. What men thought of him as a preacher was a matter of very little moment; the grand point, the all-absorbing thought and one aim of his life was, so to preach as to please God."[29] Winslow's godly mother prayed this truth for her son. In a letter to Octavius, Mary Winslow wrote, "You are now in the midst of your sermons. May the Lord's sensible presence be with you. May you preach as if the Lord's eye, not the eyes of the people, were full upon you."[30] Two important results flow from preaching centered on the pleasure and glory of God.

First, it frees the preacher from the fear of man. In reflecting on the gospel, Winslow declared: "I must not dilute, nor pervert, nor withhold it. I must not preach it with reservation, either to exalt myself or to please man."[31] Second, it enables boldness. If Satan, sin, error, and the kingdom of darkness are so bold in their attack upon Christ's church, Winslow argued that ministers of the gospel should possess greater boldness. He wrote, "How can they be faithful and efficient preachers of the truth, if awed by a corrupt public sentiment, or fettered by a pusillanimous fear of man? How much is the glory of the truth shaded, and its power impaired, and the dignity of their office compromised, by the man-pleasing, man-fearing spirit which, alas, so much prevails!"[32] Winslow observed many preachers in his day who were captured by a spirit of man-pleasing and

---

27. Winslow, *Glimpses of the Truth*, 26.
28. Winslow set forth a proverb related to this: "Only honor the God of grace in all the means of grace, and God will honor you by imparting to you all grace through the means." *Inner Life*, 106.
29. Octavius Winslow, *No Condemnation in Christ Jesus: As Unfolded in the Eighth Chapter of the Epistle to the Romans* (London: John F. Shaw, 1853; repr., Edinburgh: Banner of Truth, 1991), 109.
30. Octavius Winslow, *Life in Jesus: A Memoir of Mrs. Mary Winslow Arranged from Her Correspondence, Diary, and Thoughts* (London: John F. Shaw, 1890; repr., Grand Rapids: Reformation Heritage Books, 2013), 349.
31. Winslow, *Thus Saith*, 1st Day.
32. Winslow, *Glimpses of the Truth*, 86–87.

lamented that "few preach a whole gospel and a full Christ."[33] That is why he called for "holy intrepidity and uncompromising fearlessness."[34]

Preaching in the Sufficiency of God

Winslow was astounded that the triune God would choose weak vessels to declare His glorious gospel. He said the gospel preacher should be "often alarmed by the thought, that truth so divine and so pure should flow through a channel so earthly and so defiled; and that to an office so spiritual, and to a work so great, he should bring grace so shallow, and attainments so limited."[35] Winslow pointed to Jeremiah as an example of a prophet who entered the Lord's work in much weakness. Like Jeremiah, preachers must draw confidence and sufficiency not in their natural abilities but in the presence of God, which Winslow said was "enough to quell every fear, to meet every objection, and to inspire the timid servant of the Lord with a giant's strength, and a martyr's fortitude."[36] He understood ministers are in perpetual need of God's presence and grace.

Winslow believed our most sanctified acts, including preaching, are tainted with sin. His view of man's depravity surfaced in a sermon on Psalm 130:3 titled "Contrition and Confession." He proclaimed, "All that we do for God, and for Christ, and for our fellows, is deformed and tainted by human infirmity and sin. A close scrutiny and analysis of our most saintly act would discover the leprosy of iniquity deeply hidden beneath its apparent loveliness and sanctity."[37] Therefore, ministers must go to Christ's atoning work. Winslow explained, "When our most fervent prayer has been breathed, and our most self-denying act has been performed, and our most liberal offering has been presented, and our most powerful sermon has been preached, and our sweetest anthem has poured forth its music, we have need to repair to the 'blood that cleanses from all sin,' even the sins of our most holy things!"[38] Because Winslow was acutely aware of his need for the gospel, Christ's finished work served as the empowering principle of his ministry.[39]

---

33. Winslow, *Glimpses of the Truth*, 88.

34. Winslow, *Glimpses of the Truth*, 88. "Intrepidity" is another word for courage.

35. Winslow, *Glimpses of the Truth*, 25.

36. Winslow, *Thus Saith*, 5th Day.

37. Octavius Winslow, *Soul-Depths & Soul-Heights: Sermons on Psalm 130* (London: John F. Shaw, 1874; repr., Edinburgh: Banner of Truth, 2006), 44.

38. Winslow, *Soul-Depths*, 44.

39. Chapter 4, "Preaching Centered in Christ," explains his doctrine of the cross in greater detail.

Winslow also believed preachers who sense their insufficiency are most useable to God. He asserted, "He who sees his own poverty sees something of Christ's wealth; who feels his own emptiness realizes in some measure Christ's fulness. Thus the Lord impoverishes, that He might enrich us; weakens, that He might strengthen us; casts us down, that faith may look for uplifting."[40] He also offered words of encouragement to those who recognized their infirmities and lacked confidence in their ministrations:

> Let them remember that however humble their gifts, narrow their acquirements, and limited the range of their influence, it is impossible that they can exhibit the Lord Jesus without some fragrance breathing from His name, and some blessing distilling from His grace, for which some sin-distressed soul, or some tried and tempted believer shall thank them in heaven.[41]

God uses the simple preaching of Christ to glorify Himself and bless His people.

Finally, Winslow knew preachers must trust in the Spirit's power, not their own resources. This requires great faith. Winslow grew frustrated over unbelief in his day. He explained, "If the Spirit of the Lord is able to convert one soul, He is able to convert a hundred? and if a hundred, why not a whole congregation? Oh! are not our stinted faith, our low expectations, our languid desires, the causes of the few, the *very* few, conversions to God which result from the preaching of the Gospel in the present?"[42] Winslow desperately desired conversion through the ministry of the Holy Spirit.

An examination of Winslow's homiletic reveals the priority he placed on speaking God's words and on understanding the gravity and pleasure of preaching, as well as the source of the preacher's sufficiency. All of these factors were essential elements in Winslow's approach. However, this list is

---

40. Octavius Winslow, *The Tree of Life: Its Shade, Fruit, and Repose* (London: John F. Shaw, 1868), 124e.

41. Winslow, *Tree of Life*, 124e. "Ministrations" is an archaic term for duties a pastor would perform, including preaching.

42. Octavius Winslow, *"Is the Spirit of the Lord Straitened?" A Plea for a National Baptism of the Holy Ghost with Incidents of American Revival* (London: John F. Shaw, 1858), 14. Winslow addressed those who might dismiss their lack of faith with theological excuses: "Jesus '*did not many mighty works because of their unbelief.*' In the face of this declaration, will you assert that it was His secret decree, His Divine sovereignty, that restrained Him? It was the wicked *unbelief* of the people. By a parity of argument we are justified in maintaining that, but for the unbelief, the restrained prayer, the low expectations of the Church, we should hear multitudes, moved by one common, irresistible influence of the Spirit, exclaim, 'Men and brethren, what shall we do to be saved?'" (14).

not exhaustive. His understanding of the work of the Holy Spirit supplied another key facet in his theology of preaching.

Winslow's Theology of the Spirit and Preaching

Winslow viewed the work of the Holy Spirit as indispensable for preaching. He acknowledged that only the Spirit effectually reaches and transforms the heart. In arguing for home missions, he emphasized the necessity of the Spirit's work in gospel proclamation: "Infinite and complete as was the sacrifice offered by Christ upon the cross; glorious and free as is the Gospel that proclaims it, yet, had not provision been made in the covenant of redemption for the life giving influences of the Holy Spirit, not an individual of our race would ever have availed himself of the blessings spread before him in the great charter of redemption."[43] Only the influence and blessing of the Spirit can prevent a stagnant and powerless ministry.[44] Conversely, he knew the Spirit was the driving force that ignited the apostles' preaching. He proclaimed, "To what divine agency, then, did the apostles themselves trace the extraordinary result of their preaching? To what, but the demonstration of the Spirit? O for tongues of fire to proclaim the glad tidings of the gospel!"[45] This is why he earnestly sought the Spirit's work and empowerment for the homiletical task.

Winslow also saw an inseparable relationship between the Word and the Spirit. Speaking of the Bible, he wrote:

> Divine as is the record, and precious as is the revelation it affords of Jesus, it yet is but an instrument, and nothing more. Unaccompanied with the power of the Holy Spirit, it is inactive, inoperative, a mere dead letter. It quickens not, it sanctifies not, it comforts not. It may be read constantly, and searched deeply, and known accurately, and understood partially, and quoted appropriately; yet, left to its own unassisted power, 'it comes but in word only,' producing no hallowing, no abiding, no saving results.[46]

Divine truth works effectually in those who hear when accompanied by the empowering presence of the Spirit. That, however, does not diminish the power of the Word as an instrument in "the hands of the Spirit" by which

---

43. Octavius Winslow, *Christ, The Theme of the Home Missionary: An Argument for Home Missions* (New York: John S. Taylor, 1838), 57–58. He went on to say, "Friends of this holy cause! your Missionaries preach and labour but in vain, unassisted by the influences of the Spirit of God" (58).

44. Winslow, *Personal Declension*, 126.

45. Winslow, *Glimpses of the Truth*, 28.

46. Winslow, *Glory of the Redeemer*, 346.

God accomplishes His intended purposes.[47] Winslow said, "As God never works apart from instrumentality, when instruments are made ready for His use, so the Holy Spirit never accomplishes this great and marvelous change in the soul apart from the truth of God."[48] This inextricable relationship between Word and Spirit is paramount for preaching.

Winslow's reflection on Peter's sermon at Pentecost in Acts 2 draws some helpful distinctions between the Word and the Spirit. Speaking of the crowd's response he said:

> The Eternal Spirit was the efficient cause, and the preached truth but the instrument employed, to produce the effect; but for his accompanying and effectual power, they would, as multitudes do now, have turned their backs upon the sermon of Peter, though it was full of Christ crucified, deriding the truth, and rejecting the Savior of whom it spoke. But it pleased God, in the sovereignty of his will, to call them by his grace, and this he did by the effectual, omnipotent power of the Holy Spirit, through the instrumentality of a preached gospel.[49]

Winslow exercised his preaching ministry convinced the Spirit must bless his efforts in order to bear fruit for God. He actively depended on the Spirit's indispensable work in four key areas: regeneration, illumination, anointing and sanctification.[50]

Regeneration: A Work of the Spirit

One of the primary reasons Winslow sought the blessing of the Holy Spirit was his deep belief that regeneration is exclusively a work of the Spirit. If his hearers were going to experience new life in Christ, they must be born again by the Spirit. That is why he called regeneration "the sole and special work of the Holy Spirit."[51]

---

47. Winslow referred to the Word being wielded as an instrument in the hands of the Spirit on multiple occasions. See Octavius Winslow, *Born Again, or, From Grace to Glory* (London: John F. Shaw, 1864), 61–65.

48. Winslow, *Born Again*, 61.

49. Winslow, *Personal Declension*, 114.

50. One should not conclude that Winslow lacked a comprehensive understanding of the Spirit's work beyond these four key areas. He also believed that the Spirit was active in bringing conviction, calling, and other areas of the Christian life. See Octavius Winslow, *The Inquirer Directed to an Experimental and Practical View of the Holy Spirit* (London: John F. Shaw, 1840; repr., *The Work of the Holy Spirit: An Experimental and Practical View* [Edinburgh: Banner of Truth], 2003).

51. Winslow, *Holy Spirit*, 57.

Winslow grounded his doctrine of regeneration in his understanding of man's total depravity.[52] Aligning his theology with the apostles and Reformers, he believed anything less than affirming the utter helplessness of man and the necessity of the Spirit's work should be considered "subversive of the Scripture doctrine of regeneration, and destructive of the best interests of the soul."[53] Contrary to some, he argued that regeneration is not bestowed through a mere outward profession, an external reformation of habit, or the ordinance of baptism.[54] The latter was particularly egregious to Winslow. Concerning baptismal regeneration, he wrote, "Oh, did every professed minister of Christ but study the third chapter of John's Gospel, with earnest prayer for the teaching of the Spirit, before he attempted to expound to others the way of salvation, how soon would the heresy of baptismal regeneration be expelled from our pulpits, and banished from the land!"[55] This heresy was serious but correctable through careful exegesis.

Winslow understood God uses various means in bringing people truth. These may include the hearing of a sermon, the loss of a friend, a severe illness, or any other exposure to God's Word.[56] However, the essential means by which God works is always His Word. God's Word is effectual as the Spirit impresses it on the heart. Although God uses diverse means to bring people the gospel, the ultimate work of salvation belongs to Him alone. He explained, "The work of regeneration is supremely the work of the Spirit. The means may be employed, and are to be employed, in accordance with the Divine purpose, yet are they not to be deified. They are but means, 'profiting nothing' without the power of God the Holy Spirit. Regeneration is His work, and not man's."[57] In sum, Winslow believed salvation is the monergistic work of God.

Illumination: A Work of the Spirit

The doctrine of illumination comprises another key aspect of Winslow's theology of Word and Spirit. In a sermon titled "Christ's Knowledge of His People—Their Ignorance of Him," he declared, "The words of Christ are enigmas, the language of Christ is a foreign tongue, the revelations and mysteries of Christ unintelligible and inexplicable, and Christ himself unknown,

---

52. Winslow, *Holy Spirit*, 32.
53. Winslow, *Holy Spirit*, 32.
54. Winslow, *Holy Spirit*, 33–37.
55. Winslow, *Holy Spirit*, 33.
56. Winslow, *Holy Spirit*, 61.
57. Winslow, *Holy Spirit*, 62.

unseen, until the Holy Spirit becomes our Teacher. The Interpreter of the Bible is He who wrote the Bible."[58] If people are going to understand the words of Scripture, the Holy Spirit must illumine their minds.

As with regeneration, Winslow grounded his view of illumination in the doctrine of depravity. He explained, "We cannot place this fact too prominently before the reader, that the human intellect is fallen and benighted; and that without the life of Christ and the illumination of the Spirit, it cannot find its way to God, or up to heaven."[59] He viewed 1 Corinthians 2:14 as a pivotal verse pointing to our need for illumination.[60] In light of man's depravity apart from the grace of God, it is easy to understand why Winslow put such a high priority on praying for the illumination of the Spirit.[61] That's why he encouraged others to "study the Scriptures of truth with a heart in prayerful uplifting for the accompanying power, light, and anointing of the Holy Ghost."[62] Not surprisingly, Winslow often began his sermons by asking the Spirit to illumine the hearts of his hearers.[63]

Winslow also believed the Spirit's illumination is essential during sermon preparation. The pastor should consistently seek the gracious aid of the Holy Spirit. He exhorted:

> Ever remember that the Divine Author of the Bible is at your side—invisible and noiseless—when you sit down to read it. Graciously and kindheartedly He is bending over you, prepared to explain what is difficult, to harmonize what is contradictory, and to shed a flood of light upon each page, causing Heaven's glory to dart into your soul from the diamond spark of a single passage![64]

Preachers are ever tempted to rely on human resources, the latest books and commentaries, and the teaching of man more than they depend on the Spirit. That is why Winslow exclaimed, "Oh, there is more real value in one ray

---

58. Winslow, *Patriarchal Shadows*, 34.

59. Octavius Winslow, *Lights and Shadows of Spiritual Life* (London: John F. Shaw, 1876; repr., *The Spiritual Life* [Stoke-on-Trent, U.K.: Tentmaker, 1998]), 19.

60. "But the natural man receiveth not the things of the Spirit of God: for they are foolishness unto him: neither can he know them, because they are spiritually discerned" (1 Cor. 2:14).

61. Winslow, *Our God* (London: John F. Shaw, 1870; repr., Grand Rapids: Reformation Heritage Books, 2007), 143.

62. Octavius Winslow, *The Precious Things of God* (London: James Nisbet, 1860; repr., Ligonier, Pa.: Soli Deo Gloria, 1993), 275.

63. For example, in his introduction to a sermon titled "The Aged Christian," Winslow said, "There are three or four suggestive features in the portrait; may the Spirit of truth make our meditation of them instructive and sanctifying!" See Winslow, *Patriarchal Shadows*, 250.

64. Winslow, *Precious Things*, 275–76.

of the Spirit's light, beaming in upon a man's soul, than in all the teaching which books can ever impart!"[65]

Anointing: A Work of the Spirit

A third key aspect of the Holy Spirit's work in the homiletical task involves his anointing the preacher for fruitful ministry. Winslow referred to anointing, or unction, as the empowering presence of the Spirit by which preachers effectively carry out their work. This anointing flows from the Spirit's divine blessing. Winslow said, "The unbounded power, love, and grace of the Holy Spirit spring from His essential Deity. His power is what it is—illimitable; His love is what it is—fathomless; His grace is what it is—boundless; His energy is what it is—invincible; because He is what He is—divine."[66] The following exhortation sheds light on his view of anointing: "Beloved, live not, as a priest of God, without the sensible inbeing of the Holy Spirit. Live in conscious union and communion with Him—seek to be filled with His influences."[67] According to Winslow, anointing involves a (1) conscious awareness of the indwelling Spirit, (2) walking in close communion with Him, and (3) being filled with His influential working.

Winslow believed preachers are in perpetual need of the fresh oil of God's Spirit. It is not enough to rely on past blessings for present service. Ministers need the Spirit's anointing to keep them from a fruitless ministry. He explained:

> Why is it that we sow so much, and reap so little? Why, after our studious preparation, and exhausting toil, there is so little real power in our preaching, and from that preaching so little immediate result? Why is it that our words, instead of burning upon our lips, and thrown like glowing embers into the bosoms of our hearers, enkindling holy fires, alas! do but drop like icicles, congealing before they reach a solitary heart? Is it not, verily, because we lack the fresh oil? Necessary as is education—valuable as is learning—useful auxiliaries as are all the treasures we can draw from science—enriching as is intellect—and entrancing as is eloquence, these alone constitute not the able minister of the New Testament. Other and far more important requisites are needed to

---

65. Winslow, *Inner Life*, 187.

66. Winslow, *"Is the Spirit,"* 9. He went on to say, "Beware, my reader, how you limit and fetter the Holy Spirit in the blessings He would bestow upon you, by any secret doubt in your mind, touching His personal dignity" (9–10).

67. Winslow, *Precious Things*, 197–98. By "inbeing," Winslow meant the sensible indwelling of the Spirit.

compose and perfect this high and holy character. Without the anointing of the Holy Spirit, what spiritually enlightening, sanctifying, saving power has the most erudite, and eloquent, and convincing ministry? None whatever![68]

If preachers do not seek the Spirit's active influence, they do so to the detriment of the truth they preach, the souls they instruct, and the Master they serve.[69] Winslow believed they are responsible to seek this anointing. He wrote, "If prayer languishes—if grace decays—if affection chills—if there is any discovered relapse of your soul in the divine life, seek at once and earnestly the fresh communication of this divine anointing."[70] Without such anointing, power for ministry will be missing.

Winslow followed Paul in striving to depend solely upon the Spirit's power. In a sermon addressing Paul's request for prayer in Ephesians 6, Winslow reflected on Paul's approach to ministry: "He knew that He who made man's mouth could only open his lips to proclaim the unsearchable riches of Christ. Great as were his natural endowments, and rich and varied as were his intellectual acquirements, he felt their inadequacy when working alone. We should never fail to distinguish between the natural eloquence of man, and the holy utterance which the Spirit gives."[71] Thus, he went on to exhort, "Be very jealous for the honor of the Spirit in the ministry of the word.... It is mournful to observe to what extent the idolatry of human talent and eloquence is carried, and how little glory is given to the Holy Spirit in the gospel ministry."[72] He believed ministry success depended completely upon the sovereign work of the Holy Spirit. While man may sow and water the seed, only God gives the growth.[73] Therefore, preachers should pursue this anointing every time they study, serve, and preach the gospel. He wrote:

> Be exhorted to seek large communications of this holy anointing. The growth of your spiritual life—the holiness of your Christian walk—the glory of Him whose you are and whom you serve, demand that your head should be anointed—daily and abundantly—with holy oil. "Be filled with the Spirit." The anointing of Christ, our true Aaron, flows down to the fringe of His robe; and those who sit lowest and the closest at His feet in the spirit of penitence, love, and docility will

---

68. Winslow, *Inner Life*, 204.
69. Winslow, *Inner Life*, 203.
70. Winslow, *Precious Things*, 198.
71. Winslow, *Glimpses of the Truth*, 84.
72. Winslow, *Glimpses of the Truth*, 84.
73. See Winslow, *Precious Things*, 276–78.

partake the most richly of this holy unction. Oh with what power you will then testify for Jesus! If a minister of Christ, you will preach as with "a tongue of fire," with such unction, wisdom, and demonstration of the Spirit as no enemy of the truth shall be able to gainsay; sinners shall be converted to God, and the flock confided to your care will exhibit all the marks of a manly, vigorous Christianity, built up in sound doctrine and holiness of life. Oh! never cross the threshold of your pulpit but with the prayer—"Anoint me, O Christ, for this service with fresh oil."[74]

Anointing provides all of the spiritual resources preachers need for their task. Winslow knew this and sought it earnestly.

Sanctification: A Work of the Spirit

The doctrine of sanctification was central to Winslow's preaching theology and methodology. This also happens through the Word and Spirit. Winslow valued the Word because "as the instrument of…sanctification, the Bible is beyond all price."[75] Faithful, text-driven preaching is so important because it allows the Word to perform its transformative work. Through the preached Word God teaches, corrects, rebukes, equips, and comforts His people.[76] At the same time, sanctification happens primarily through the Spirit: "The work of holiness in the soul is preeminently the product of the Holy Spirit. He is the author of all true holiness in the regenerate heart."[77] Winslow depended on the Spirit's transforming power through the work of the Word.

Winslow also viewed the work of the Word and Spirit in sanctification as inseparable from Christology. In fact, one could argue that his sermons were so Christ-centered precisely because of his theology of Word and Spirit. He believed Jesus is the center of the Bible and the One whom the Spirit glorifies. He explained:

> And not only thus, but by employing the truth which especially testifies of Jesus, as the grand instrument of producing that holiness in the soul of which He is the Divine Author, He confers unspeakable honor on Christ

---

74. Octavius Winslow, *The Nightingale Song of David: A Spiritual and Practical Exposition of the Twenty-Third Psalm* (London: John F. Shaw, 1876), 122–23.

75. Winslow, *Precious Things*, 274.

76. Of the latter Winslow wrote, "God comforts us by the ministry of His Word. For this purpose, He furnishes His servants with gifts and grace, and while some are like John the Baptist, 'crying in the wilderness,' others like Barnabas, 'sons of consolation,' able to speak a word in season to those who are weary." *Our God*, 64.

77. Winslow, "Is the Spirit," 19.

in the word. The Spirit of God undertakes the achievement of a stupendous work. He enters the soul, and proposes to restore the empire of grace, the reign of holiness, and the throne of God. He engages to form all things anew—to create a revolution in favor of Christ and of heaven. He undertakes to change the heart, turning its enmity into love; to collect all the elements of darkness and confusion, educing from them perfect light and perfect order; to subdue the will, bringing it into harmony with God's will; to explore all the recesses of sin, turning its very impurity into holiness— in a word, to regenerate the soul, restoring the Divine image, and fitting it for the full and eternal enjoyment of God in glory. Now, in accomplishing this great work, what instrumentality does He employ? Passing by all human philosophy, and pouring contempt upon the profoundest wisdom and the mightiest power of man, He employs, in the product of a work, in comparison with which the rise and the fall of empires were as infants' play, simply and alone, the "truth as it is in Jesus."[78]

This doctrine was vital to Winslow because he felt the church's lack of power, spiritual knowledge, and spiritual progress could be traced to stinted views of the Spirit's work in sanctification. He wrote, "Why is our spiritual knowledge so shallow, and why are our spiritual attainments so dwarfish? Even because we limit the Holy Spirit in the great work of personal sanctification."[79] Wise preachers will place great emphasis on the Spirit's work of sanctification in the lives of their people.

Since God accomplishes His saving purposes through the instrumentality of the preached gospel and a preacher in need of divine anointing, Winslow believed a healthy and experimental view of the Holy Spirit's work must accompany faithful pulpit ministry. Overall, his theological convictions provided the basis for his pulpit practice.

Winslow's Methodology

Every preacher has an approach by which he executes his task. Winslow was no different. Before examining Winslow's experimental methodology in detail, a few other general observations are in order. First, Winslow often utilized the "sermon series" in planning and organizing his sermons. Sometimes he employed the *lectio continua* method and preached through Scripture passages.[80] At other times he preached thematic series.[81] It seems that most of his

---

78. Winslow, *Glory of the Redeemer*, 343.
79. Winslow, *"Is the Spirit,"* 20.
80. For examples, see Winslow, *Patriarchal Shadows*; *Soul-Depths*; and *No Condemnation*.
81. For an example, see Winslow, *Inner Life*.

sermons were delivered extemporaneously.[82] Winslow preached in a popular style, "always animated" and often "florid."[83] He believed preaching should be "a Christ-exalting, soul-awakening, soul-winning, soul-searching, soul-loving ministry."[84] To understand his methodology, it is helpful to examine those who influenced him and the elements contained in his sermons. Finally, I will provide a closer look at his experimental preaching.

The Preaching of Jesus: The Minister's Preeminent Example
Jesus was a prophet, and He preached with authority. Winslow recognized the uniqueness of Christ's prophetic office when he said: "The only authoritative Teacher in the Church of God, the only true Prophet, is the Lord Jesus Christ."[85] Revering Christ's role as the highest authority in the church was important because many people were looking elsewhere for their source of authority. Winslow explained, "We need to hold firmly, and to contend earnestly for the prophetical office of Christ in the present day. There are those whose cry is, 'Hear the *Church!*' The voice from the excellent glory is, 'This is my beloved Son, hear ye Him!'"[86] Winslow believed Jesus provided an example in experimental preaching. Aside from pressing His hearers to apply the truths He taught, Jesus displayed marks of an experimental preacher in other ways.[87]

Jesus exemplified the experimental qualities of discriminating and interrogating preaching. Discriminating preaching occurs when the preacher addresses different groups of hearers based on their spiritual condition. Interrogating preaching involves the skill of helping hearers to deal with their consciences through penetrating questions. This often helps bring conviction by causing them to evaluate their lives. Winslow said:

> How important, may we not pause to remark, that the ministers of the Gospel—those who stand between the living and the dead—should

82. Winslow, *No Condemnation*, v.

83. "Literary Notices," *The Boston Review: Devoted to Theology and Literature* 3 (May 1863): 333. This American reviewer noted that Winslow's sermons had "more of poetical recitation in them than our severer pulpit taste would approve; we understand that British preaching is much more florid, in this direction, than among ourselves is customary."

84. Winslow, *Inner Life*, 64.

85. Octavius Winslow, *The Man of God, or, Spiritual Religion Explained and Enforced* (London: John F. Shaw, 1865), 71.

86. Octavius Winslow, *Jesus and John, or, The Loving and the Loved: A Tribute to the Memory of the Late Rev. William Marsh, D.D.* (London: James Nisbet and Co., 1859), 18.

87. This does not mean Winslow would not have added other features of Jesus' preaching, but these were the only ones he explicitly mentioned as uncovered in the present research.

model their ministry, as closely as they can, after their blessed Lord's; that they should be careful how they preach—that their preaching should be discriminating without being harsh, pointed without being personal, searching without being caustic; that no hearer should go away from beneath their ministrations, without a faithful delineation of his own character, the voice sounding in his conscience, and following him amid all his windings and his wanderings, "You are the man."[88]

One other feature of Jesus' experimental preaching included the way He practiced what He preached. In other words, Jesus preached *from* the heart *to* the heart. He loved His hearers to the point of weeping over their lostness.[89] Winslow was inspired by how Jesus embodied love and preached sermons with words of love.[90] As is apparent in Winslow's words as well as actions, he tried to emulate what he observed in the preaching of Jesus.

The Puritan Influence

As explained earlier, the Puritans deeply influenced Winslow's ministry. Predictably, there are many similarities between Winslow's preaching and the Puritans. The Puritans were also known for their experimental preaching.

William Perkins was arguably the most influential writer on preaching among the English Puritans in the seventeenth century and beyond.[91] Perkins advocated a "plain style" of preaching.[92] He said, "Preaching the Word is prophesying in the name and on behalf of Christ. Through preaching those who hear are called into a state of grace, and preserved in it."[93] Perkins summarized his approach by saying preaching involves reading the text,

---

88. Winslow, *Personal Declension*, 147–48.

89. Winslow, *Grace and Truth*, 97e.

90. See Winslow, *Patriarchal Shadows*, 173.

91. Joel Beeke highlights the wide influence Perkins exercised when he writes, "By the time of his death from kidney stones at the age of forty-four, Perkins had produced writings which, in England, were outselling those of Calvin, Beza, and Bullinger combined." *The Quest for Full Assurance: The Legacy of Calvin and His Successors* (Edinburgh: Banner of Truth, 2000), 83–84.

92. Sinclair Ferguson, foreword to *The Art of Prophesying with The Calling of Ministry*, by William Perkins (n.p.: n.p., 1606; rev. ed., Edinburgh: Banner of Truth, 2002), ix. For a deeper study on Perkins's influence on Puritan preaching and those who followed him, see Joseph Pipa Jr., "William Perkins and the Development of Puritan Preaching" (PhD diss., Westminster Theological Seminary, 1985).

93. William Perkins, *The Art of Prophesying with the Calling of Ministry* (n.p.: n.p., 1606; rev. ed., Edinburgh: Banner of Truth, 2002), 7.

explaining the meaning, expounding a few points of doctrine, and applying the doctrines to the congregation.[94]

All of these efforts were for one great purpose: the sanctification of the hearers. The Puritans were intensely concerned with hearers applying the text.[95] Sinclair Ferguson says Perkins's and subsequent Puritan preaching "was more than just a formula for biblical exposition; it was marked by a further apostolic credential: power. At its centre lay a searching examination of and appeal to the consciences of those who heard the exposition of the meaning of Scripture." He continues, "Perkins believed that preaching should 'rip up the hearts' of those who heard it; but by the same token he saw the preacher as a spiritual apothecary whose knowledge of biblical remedies enabled him to bathe the wounds and heal the spiritual sicknesses of God's people with the grace of Christ."[96] In order to do this well, preachers must know their hearers and address their needs accordingly. This describes discriminating preaching.

In summary, the main goal of Perkins and the Puritans was "to preach Christ and to reach the heart. Everything was subservient to this."[97] When we take into consideration the primary elements of Perkins's methodology (i.e., explaining the text, preaching Christ, expounding doctrine, and faithful application), we see Winslow following in lockstep.

Sermonic Elements

Winslow's sermons followed a typical structure whereby he introduced his text and topic, divided the argument into main points (usually three), and provided a conclusion. His sermon structure was similar to the Puritan form of Doctrine, Reason, Use, but he often wove these elements together within a single point or throughout the sermon as a whole.[98] Winslow typically spent minimal time expositing the text in its grammatical, historical, and literary contexts. He devoted most of his energy to unpacking the doctrine of the text before applying it in various ways. This can be illustrated by Winslow's

---

94. Perkins, *Art of Prophesying*, 79.

95. David Larsen notes, "The practicality and profitability of the Scriptures have been an emphasis from the beginning of biblical preaching (cf. 2 Timothy 3:16–17), but few eras have been as plush and prolific in application as the Puritans." *The Company of the Preachers* (Grand Rapids: Kregel, 1998), 258.

96. Ferguson, foreword to *Art of Prophesying*, x.

97. Ferguson, foreword to *Art of Prophesying*, x.

98. See Horton Davies, *The Worship of the English Puritans* (Westminster, U.K.: Dacre Press, 1948), 191–92.

sermon titled "Hoping in the Lord" from Psalm 130:7.[99] The following analysis of that sermon will serve as a case study demonstrating the characteristic elements found in his preaching.

In the introduction to this sermon, Winslow accomplished three things: he introduced his text and theme, provided his outline, and prayed for the Spirit's illumination. Then, moving into his first point, he discriminated between unbelievers, who have no hope, and believers, who possess every reason to hope in God. He also employed what contemporary homiletician Bryan Chapell calls the "Fallen Condition Focus," which reveals the fallen condition of the human heart that requires the grace of the passage.[100] Winslow declared, "But what is all human hope, as to its nature and object, but a phantom and a dream as the foam on the crest of the billow, the shadow on the mountain's brow—unsubstantial and fleeting? Yet, how does the soul cling to it! How do men, looking only to the things that are seen and temporal, cling to human hopes, pursuing a bubble, building upon a shadow, grasping the wind!"[101]

In his second point, Winslow displayed how easily he took his doctrinal explanation to the cross. He declared, "There is everything in God to inspire and encourage hope.... The atonement of Christ touches the soul, and meets its case at every point. There could be no hope of the sinner's pardon and justification consistently with divine justice, holiness, and truth apart from the obedience, death, and resurrection of the Lord Jesus."[102] Winslow's knowledge of Scripture and use of cross-referencing is also seen in his encouragement to those outside of God's grace. He exhorted and encouraged:

> Behold your true and only hope of heaven! You are, perhaps, bowed to the earth under the sight and conviction of your sinfulness; you have come to the end of all your own doings, perfection, and merit; you are on the brink of despair! Look up! there is hope now! "Christ died for the ungodly." "This Man receives sinners." "He who comes to me I will in no wise cast out." "Christ is the end of the Law for righteousness to every one that believes." "And when they had nothing to pay He frankly forgave them both." "The blood of Jesus Christ His Son cleanses us from all sin." "By grace are you saved."[103]

---

99. See Winslow, *Soul-Depths*, 92–108. Psalm 130:7: "Let Israel hope in the LORD: for with the LORD there is mercy, and with him is plenteous redemption."

100. See Bryan Chapell, *Christ-Centered Preaching: Redeeming the Expository Sermon* (Grand Rapids: Baker, 1994), 42.

101. Winslow, *Soul-Depths*, 94.

102. Winslow, *Soul-Depths*, 95.

103. Winslow, *Soul-Depths*, 97.

With seven consecutive passages, Winslow encouraged his hearers to embrace the Christ of the cross. Even from these brief extracts, Winslow's experimental methodology surfaces.

A couple of other noteworthy elements are discovered in the sermon's conclusion. Rather than using illustrations like many contemporary preachers, Winslow typically illustrated his points by painting word pictures. Moreover, he often closed his sermons with a flurry of exhortations and by pointing to eschatological truth. For example:

> Oh, cling only and firmly to Christ! Look not so much to your hope as to him who is your hope!... Fight on, toil on, hope on, you soldier of Christ, you laborer for Jesus, you tried and suffering one! Soon you shall put off your travel-stained garments, unclasp your dust-covered sandals, lay down your pilgrim-staff; and, attired in glory-robes, enter the palace, and feast your eyes upon the beauty of the King forever.[104]

Throughout his sermons he sought to equip and encourage his hearers to practice the truth. While these elements are not exhaustive, they are representative of many qualities found in Winslow's experimental homiletic.

His Experimental Preaching

Experimental preaching was the touchstone of Winslow's ministry. He came by this methodology honestly. The influence of the Puritans on his ministry is obvious, but this tradition was also a part of his Baptist heritage. Francis Wayland said that the early English Baptists "were remarkable for what was called experimental preaching."[105] In addition to the influences of tradition and Scripture, Winslow also believed experimental preaching was practical and powerful. Henry Ward Beecher, one of his American contemporaries, said, "I often hear myself out-preached by some new convert who can hardly put words together. Some say experimental preaching is shallow. Shallow! It is deep as the soul of God."[106] For all of these reasons, Winslow practiced this method.[107]

---

104. Winslow, *Soul-Depths*, 107–8.

105. Francis Wayland, *Notes on the Principles and Practices of Baptist Churches* (New York: Sheldon, Blakeman, & Co., 1857), 41.

106. Henry Ward Beecher, *Life Thoughts Gathered from the Extemporaneous Discourses of Henry Ward Beecher*, ed. Edna Dean Proctor (Boston: Phillips, Sampson, & Co., 1858), 63.

107. While some might contend Winslow's preaching should be labeled "doctrinal" or even "doctrinal-experimental," a proper understanding of experimental preaching should defuse such claims. This is because true experimental preaching is grounded in doctrine. Sadly, one could be a doctrinal preacher without applying truth to life, but a true experimental

The key to Winslow's experimental homiletic is the relationship between doctrine and life. He believed truth must be embraced, felt, and lived. For example, note how Winslow connects christological truth with its application to life:

> To taste or to drink of a thing is to have an *experimental* knowledge of it. There are many religious professors who read of Christ's blood, and hear of Christ's blood, and outwardly commemorate Christ's blood, but who never *spiritually* and *experimentally* drink of Christ's blood. Oh, let us not be mere professing, theoretic Christians; but real, vital, experimental Christians—living *by* Christ, living *on* Christ, and, having Christ in us the hope of glory, looking forward to that blessed hope of being *with* Christ forever.[108]

Winslow was convinced doctrine and experience should always go together. Andrew Fuller agreed and argued, "Doctrinal and experimental preaching are not so remote from each other as some persons have imagined; and that to extol the latter, at the expense of the former, is to act like him who wishes the fountain to be destroyed, because he prefers the stream."[109] For Winslow and Fuller, there was no competition between sound doctrinal preaching and pressing for application in one's experience.

Winslow's methodology reflects what some have highlighted as "indicative-imperative" preaching.[110] This kind of preaching balances strong doctrinal content with its application to life. This is important because some preachers fill their sermons with doctrine to the neglect of application.[111] Still others fill their preaching with a flurry of practical instruction to the neglect of sound biblical and theological principles.[112] Winslow would agree with the

---

preacher must unpack the truths of God's Word in order to reach the heart and encourage life transformation.

108. Octavius Winslow, *The Lord My Portion* (London, 1870), 42e.

109. Andrew Fuller, *The Complete Works of Andrew Fuller* (Philadelphia: American Baptist Publication Society, 1845), 1:170. Charles Bridges also wrote, "Scriptural preaching will expound doctrines practically, and practice doctrinally; omitting neither, but stating neither independent of the other, or unconnected with experimental religion." *The Christian Ministry with an Inquiry into the Causes of Its Inefficiency* (London: R. B. Seely and W. Burnside, 1830; repr., Edinburgh: Banner of Truth, 2006), 266–67.

110. See John Carrick, *The Imperative of Preaching: A Theology of Sacred Rhetoric* (Edinburgh: Banner of Truth, 2002), 5.

111. Daniel Kidder said in Winslow's day, "No sane man will contend for mere dogmatic abstractions in the pulpit." *A Treatise on Homiletics: Designed to Illustrate the True Theory and Practice of Preaching the Gospel* (New York: Carlton & Porter, 1864), 275.

112. Lloyd-Jones decried this in his day: "There are those who need to be warned against mere exhortation. So often men seem to think that preaching is just an extended exhortation. They start exhorting the people at the beginning of their sermon; it is all application. They do

conclusions of contemporary homiletician John Carrick when he speaks of the *irreversibility* and *inseparability* of the indicative-imperative relationship. First, there is a particular, even irreversible, structure to good preaching. Carrick states, "'Christianity begins with a triumphant indicative'; Christianity does not begin with an urgent imperative. The initial emphasis is upon that which God has done in Christ, not upon that which man must do. There is, then, a primacy about the indicative mood."[113] Second, good preaching never separates the indicative from the imperative. Carrick states simply, "The indicative always moves on to the imperative."[114] Winslow understood this and utilized the preaching of sound doctrine as the foundation for application.

Very few descriptions of Winslow's experimental preaching are available. Interestingly, the longest is found in his son Whitmore's journal. The following entry says much about his father's experimental homiletic:

> Just returned from hearing a delightful sermon—delightful, because it found its way to the intellect and the heart. His sermons are such as few can appreciate—those only whose minds are rich and tender, like mellowed soil, opening to receive the seed. As such, they must be, to a great degree, intellectual. But I should say their character is less that of intellectual truth than of heart-experience, with a torrent of sanctified feeling, savouring all of Jesus, which sweeps away every minor consideration, and produces permanent benefit upon the soul. Persons going to hear him, expecting merely deep erudition, soft persuasive eloquence, and graceful delivery, may often come away disappointed; but they will find, instead, deep pathos, energy almost to excess, and truth full, free and spiritual. You need not ask his theme—you may anticipate it. His theme, in fact, his *one* theme, is—Jesus and His cross, and all the rest, like graceful festoons, but surround this glorious centre-piece. This is the reason why his preaching would not, perhaps, be denominated "popular," simply because his feeling, not his language, is unintelligible to the general mass. But the "poor in spirit," the downcast, and the afflicted, thrive beneath it. Those who are living much in the world in thought and action, who love not what he terms "the cross," cannot

---

not present the Truth first and then make the inevitable application. They spend the whole time 'getting at' their people, and slashing them and exhorting them, calling them to do this and that and forcing them." *Preaching and Preachers*, 258.

113. Carrick, *Imperative of Preaching*, 27–28. Speaking of the primacy of indicatives does not necessarily mean that a preacher should not have the freedom to give an exhortation and then follow with biblical and theological justification. Carrick is quoting J. Gresham Machen when he says, "Christianity begins with a triumphant indicative." See J. Gresham Machen, *Christianity and Liberalism* (Grand Rapids: Eerdmans, 1977), 47.

114. Carrick, *Imperative of Preaching*, 28.

comprehend him. This term, like many employed by Latin and Greek poets, expresses in a concrete form a vast range of general and abstract truth, and it is the burden of his whole discourse. What it means is— Jesus, His life and death, His grand Atonement, and His undying interest in His Church. The reason that so few preachers make this their great and chief theme, and that so many hearers dislike it as their habitual food, is evident to any one in the least degree acquainted with the human heart. Alas! how often have I had to class myself amongst these rebellious and unprofitable hearers. So true is it that spiritual preaching can never find its way to any but a spiritual understanding.[115]

Whitmore's description provides valuable insight into his father's experimental approach. Winslow's preaching engaged "the intellect and the heart." His aim was to effect "permanent benefit upon the soul." Additionally, Christ and His cross formed the center of his messages. Indeed, Jesus was "the burden of his whole discourse." Experimental preaching, for Winslow, also meant employing a vigorous style, full of passion, "deep pathos," and "energy almost to excess." In this regard, he embodied his methodology in the sense that he preached as though captured and invigorated by the truth he had experienced.[116] In sum, the nature of his delivery, "a torrent of sanctified feeling," and the substance of his content, "savouring all of Jesus," worked together to produce "spiritual preaching." This entry provides valuable insight into Winslow's experimental methodology.

Finally, Winslow practiced experimental preaching because it requires preachers to exercise their office with authenticity and sincerity. In true experimental preaching, there exists an inextricable link between the method and the man. The heart must be gripped by God's truth before aiming at the hearts of others. In an address to those preparing for ministry, he declared, "God will have his true ministers experimentally acquainted with the truth they preach. They shall not lift up a Christ whose glory they have not seen, whose grace they have not experienced, whose voice they have not heard, whose love they have not felt, whose fullness, tenderness, sympathy,

---

115. Octavius Winslow, *Hidden Life: Memorials of John Whitmore Winslow* (London: John F. Shaw, 1872), 18–19.

116. G. Campbell Morgan said, "I cannot see how any one can really handle these things until he is handled by them.... When his text handles him, when it grips and masters and possesses him, and in experience he is responsive to the thing he is declaring, having conviction of the supremacy of truth and experience of power of truth, I think that must create passion." *Preaching* (New York: Fleming H. Revell, 1937), 36–37. Morgan continued, "I don't think any preacher can lift his hearers above the level of his own experience" (37).

and compassion they have not tasted."[117] Preachers should live the sermons they preach.

He also stressed the importance of authentic living because of the effect on one's congregation. He announced:

> We must, in all the circles where we move, and in all the engagements in which we are occupied, exhibit and illustrate the hallowed spirit and commanding influence of our office. Not only must our pulpit ministrations, in the matter and manner of their performance, carry conviction to the minds of our hearers, that the solemn truths we preach, we firmly believe; but, when descending from the pulpit, and mingling among our people, the deepest caution is needed, lest our spirit, our conversation, or our demeanour; should weaken the conviction, and lessen the impression, which the pulpit has produced. Such should be the sobriety, solemnity, meekness, heavenly-mindedness, lowliness, and sincerity, marking and pervading our entire conduct and conversation,—so fragrant upon us should be the anointing oil, and such a "savour of Christ" should we be in every place,—that, wherever we moved, we should be centres of holy light, thought, feeling, and action; everywhere witnessing for God, exalting Jesus, and saving souls.[118]

This primary goal should always be kept in view. In his preaching, praying, and living, Winslow desired to see people transformed by the power of the gospel. This motivated his experimental preaching.

Conclusion

Winslow's theology of preaching set the foundation for his preaching practice. His understanding of the nature of preaching, including how the preacher speaks for God, the weight and pleasure of preaching, as well as the source of the preacher's sufficiency, bolstered his pulpit ministry. His theology of the Holy Spirit also greatly influenced his homiletic practices. These convictions, in turn, shaped his experimental methodology. The next two chapters cover the two foundational pillars of Winslow's methodology: his doctrinal and Christ-centered preaching.

---

117. Winslow, *Eminent Holiness*, 42–43.
118. Winslow, *Eminent Holiness*, 51.

3

PREACHING GROUNDED
IN DOCTRINE

Much like his Puritan predecessors, Winslow was a doctrinal preacher.[1] In a day when many "played" with the key doctrines of the faith, he made them a staple of his experimental homiletic.[2] Without sound doctrinal preaching, believers have no basis for what to believe or how they should glorify God in their daily lives. In short, they have no foundation for what their experience should look like in practice. Because of this understanding, Winslow consistently unpacked doctrine after doctrine in his sermons. Many of his contemporaries did not employ the same approach. He wrote, "This is a day of much criminal reserve, of holding back bold, uncompromising statements of these great and essential verities of our faith. Men styled evangelical seem afraid to place in the front rank of their preaching these great doctrines of the Gospel."[3] Winslow detested such weak preaching. He did not gather his sermon themes from the latest cultural happenings, nor did he preach what he thought people wanted to hear. On the contrary, he preached the great doctrines of the gospel. This chapter will explore Winslow's view of the Bible, the gospel and doctrinal precision, and his practice of doctrinal preaching as demonstrated in his heralding of the doctrines of grace.

---

1. Contemporary homiletician Stephen Rummage provides an understanding of doctrinal preaching that reflects Winslow's handling of the text when he writes: "In a sense, all biblical preaching is doctrinal preaching because every teaching of Scripture is doctrine.... But when I speak of doctrinal preaching...I am talking about sermons specifically concerned with the central theological truths of the Bible." *Planning Your Preaching: A Step-by-Step Guide for Developing a One-Year Preaching Calendar* (Grand Rapids: Kregel, 2002), 138. For an introduction to the Puritan view of the pulpit, see Bruce Bickel, *Light and Heat: The Puritan View of the Pulpit* (Morgan, Pa.: Soli Deo Gloria, 1999).

2. In an address to the Evangelical Alliance, Winslow declared, "Never were the doctrines of our holy Faith, and the principles of our glorious Reformation, more ignobly the football of the sceptic and the sport of the Papist than now." *Practical Suggestions Appropriate to the Present Religious Crisis* (London: William Hunt & Co., 1868), 6.

3. Octavius Winslow, *The Tree of Life: Its Shade, Fruit, and Repose* (London: John F. Shaw, 1868), 122–23e.

Winslow's View of the Bible

When it came to man's knowledge of God, Winslow did not deny that general revelation pointed to the existence of God and left unbelievers without excuse. Nevertheless, he knew the witness of nature, along with the gifts of reason and conscience, were not enough to bring a saving knowledge of God's person and work. He wrote, "Beloved reader, the kingdom of nature, replete as it is with the wisdom, power, and benevolence of Jehovah, every spire of grass, every lowly flower, every towering mountain, every glimmering star, rebuking the 'fool's' denial of a God, can never disclose how you may be pardoned, justified, and saved."[4] God must reveal Himself and His plan of redemption.[5] He does this by His Word.

Winslow declared that the Bible should serve as the "supreme authority" for believers rather than the "human and fallible standards of the Church."[6] Emphasizing the divine nature of the Bible, he wrote, "And when the believer opens the Bible, it is with the profound and solemn conviction that he is about to listen to the voice of God!"[7] In light of these convictions, it is little wonder Winslow displayed so much zeal for truth in his writing and preaching ministry. For example, observe his passion as he reflected on the prospect of seeing Christ:

> Our glimpses of Him are dim, imperfect, transient; though sometimes, blessed be His name! ravishing, sanctifying, and heaven-attracting. But the full, the perfect, the unclouded vision, yet awaits us. Oh the magnitude of the spectacle! Oh the magnificence of the scene! Oh the exceeding and eternal weight of glory! To drop the glass, and be in a moment ushered in to the presence of the glorified Son of God! To see Him as He is! To be with, to be near, to be like Him![8]

This passion was often evident in Winslow's sermons.

Furthermore, Winslow encouraged every believer to spend significant amounts of time reading God's Word. He wrote, "Be exhorted to an intimate acquaintance with God's holy word, as supplying a powerful help to the progress of the soul in deep spirituality. And if your time for reading is

4. Octavius Winslow, *The Precious Things of God* (London: James Nisbet, 1860; repr., Ligonier, Pa.: Soli Deo Gloria, 1993), 246.

5. Winslow, *Precious Things*, 250.

6. Winslow, *Practical Suggestions*, 19.

7. Winslow, *Precious Things*, 250.

8. Octavius Winslow, *The Glory of the Redeemer in His Person and Work*, 8th ed. (London: John F. Shaw, 1865; repr., Pittsburgh: Soli Deo Gloria, 1997), viii–ix.

limited, limit it to *one* book, and let that one book be—the Bible."[9] Progress in experimental Christianity depends largely on one's devotion to Scripture. To understand his experimental methodology, it is imperative to examine Winslow's view of the inspiration, truthfulness, and power of God's Word.

The Bible Is Inspired by God

Winslow ministered in a day of acute biblical criticism, especially during his latter years. He courageously engaged in the battle, taking every opportunity to defend his evangelical convictions. He wrote, "The giant evil of the day is infidelity unblushingly assailing the truth, and impeaching the integrity of the Sacred Scriptures. Be vigilant and prayerful here. Lose your Bible, and you lose your all."[10] He witnessed increasing hostility to the doctrine of inspiration. Various factors stemming from the Enlightenment, such as the exaltation of human reason and the historical-critical method of biblical scholarship, challenged the historic beliefs of the church and fueled widespread skepticism.

Winslow believed the error of his opponents resided primarily in their theological method. Namely, they did not begin with the reality of Christ and His culminating work on the cross. He explained:

> Here is the grand mistake men make, in not *commencing* their study of God's Word, their inquiries after the truths of revelation, at *the cross of Jesus*. Do you think that the skeptics of the day would be found, in this advanced age of Biblical research, questioning the truth of the Bible, ignoring the Divine inspiration of the Scriptures, and, with effete weapons borrowed from the dusty arsenals of error, whose edge had long since been turned, attacking the integrity of the Pentateuch, involving in its fall the destruction of the entire fabric of truth, had they made *the cross of Christ* the starting point of their investigations, the foundation of their inquiries? Alas! men, for the most part, commence at the farthest circumference of truth, and endeavor to work their way to the center; thus reversing God's order, which is to commence at the center and so reach the circumference.[11]

Moreover, because Christ was the controlling reality for Winslow, he also consulted Jesus' view of the Scriptures. He wrote:

---

9. Winslow, *Precious Things*, 229.

10. Octavius Winslow, *Our God* (London: John F. Shaw, 1870; repr., Grand Rapids: Reformation Heritage Books, 2007), 150.

11. Octavius Winslow, *The Foot of the Cross and the Blessings Found There* (New York: Robert Carter, 1868; repr., *Atonement and The Cross* [Stoke-on-Trent, U.K.: Tentmaker, 2008]), 89.

Beware, my reader, of indulging in doubts concerning the divine veracity or the correct rendering of any part of God's word. The most profound human judgment is after all, fallible, and human learning often contradictory. The safest path is to accept the Bible as it is, and not to allow your confidence in its Divine integrity to be disturbed by this rendering or by that, by one manuscript or by another. Hold fast the memorable and precious declaration of the Savior—a declaration which may be fearlessly asserted in the face of every doubt cast upon the divine inspiration of the Scriptures—"Thy Word is truth."[12]

Though some claimed only parts of the Bible are reliable and inspired, Winslow affirmed plenary inspiration.[13] He wrote, "Beware of that false reasoning that teaches that God's Word is in the Bible, but that the Bible is not God's Word."[14] The Bible does not simply contain God's Word; it *is* the Word of God. Winslow knew the slippery slope that accompanies the partial view of inspiration. He wrote:

It is no light thing in the present day to maintain the integrity of God's word. On every hand, and from every quarter it is malignantly and fiercely assailed. Men deeply erudite, religious in profession, and eminent in their relation to the Church, are devoting all the power and influence their learning and position can command, to the destruction of the Bible. I speak advisedly—*the destruction of the Bible!* The Word of God is wholly divine; and as a volume thus wholly divine, it must, in faith, humility, and love, be received. Impugn the integrity of any one part, and you have impugned the integrity of every other. Loosen one stone of the sacred fabric, and you have loosened all. Tamper with the integrity of this book, or question the veracity of that narrative; reject the inspiration of this gospel, or doubt the canonical integrity of that epistle, and you have taken away my Bible, and what have I left? The God dishonoring theories, therefore, which several modern writers have advanced, the refined and subtle shades of inspiration which many have drawn, all converge to one point—the virtual denial of inspiration

12. Winslow, *Our God*, 105–6.

13. It is not surprising Winslow also defended the inspiration of Scripture when preaching to his flock. His pastoral sensitivity is evident in a sermon titled "Go and Tell Jesus." He declared, "Let your faith in, and your reverence for, the Divine inspiration of the Scriptures of truth become firmer and deeper; for, be assured, 'holy men of God spoke as they were moved by the Holy Spirit,' and all that they have said, both of mercy and judgment, shall literally and surely come to pass!" Octavius Winslow, *Patriarchal Shadows of Christ and His Church: As Exhibited in Passages Drawn from the History of Joseph and His Brethren* (London: John F. Shaw, 1863; repr., Grand Rapids: Sovereign Grace Treasures, 2005), 6.

14. Winslow, *Our God*, 150.

entirely; and all tend to one solemn and inevitable result—the over-throw of God's Word.[15]

Clearly, Winslow revered God's Word and defended it with great vigor. The honor he gave the Old and New Testament Scriptures in his preaching stemmed from his view of divine inspiration.

The Bible Is True and Trustworthy

Because of its divine inspiration, Winslow believed God's people could trust the Bible. He announced, "The Bible is our only rule of faith, whose teaching is infallible, and whose decision is ultimate."[16] He also believed the truthfulness of Scripture is rooted in the character of God Himself. Because the Bible originates from the God of truth, it must be true since it partakes of the same nature.[17] Winslow also pointed to fulfilled prophecy as evidence for the veracity of Scripture. He explained, "Accept, then, with gratitude every fulfilled prophecy as evidencing the truth of the Bible.... Hold fast to the integrity of these two witnesses—the Old and the New Testament. They confirm and establish each other. The Old Testament predicts the New, and the New Testament fulfils the Old; and thus both unitedly testify, 'Your Word Is Truth.'"[18] According to Winslow, the harmony of the Bible confirms its truthfulness though it was written across the span of hundreds of years.

Winslow drew practical importance from this teaching. He said, "As divine truth, then, it is most precious to the believer who has staked his all of future and eternal happiness upon its veracity. Let your faith, beloved reader, have more close dealing with the truth of God's Word."[19] When Winslow set biblical truth before his hearers, he believed they could take God at His Word because the Scriptures are infallible and completely trustworthy.[20]

---

15. Octavius Winslow, *Emmanuel, or, Titles of Christ: Their Teaching and Consolations* (London: John F. Shaw, 1869), 3e.

16. Winslow, *Practical Suggestions*, 19.

17. Winslow, *Precious Things*, 259.

18. Winslow, *Emmanuel, or Titles of Christ*, 3e.

19. Winslow, *Precious Things*, 260.

20. In writing on how the believer can cast his care upon God, Winslow again affirmed the infallibility of the Bible. He stated, "In the directions which we suggest we would give prominence to the exercise of unquestioning faith. Here there must be a taking God at his word. Our warrant for an act apparently so impossible and presumptuous as the transferring of every thought of anxiety, and feeling of sadness, and pressure of want, to the great Jehovah must be as divine and unquestionable as the act itself. That warrant is God's revealed, infallible, unalterable word." *Help Heavenward: Guidance and Strength for the Christian's Life-Journey* (London: James Nisbet, 1869; repr., Edinburgh: Banner of Truth, 2000), 107.

The Bible Is Powerful and Effective

Winslow also believed that the Bible, in the hands of the Spirit, possessed power to transform lives. This is why he saturated his preaching with Scripture from beginning to end. The implications for his experimental homiletic are obvious. He knew one simple word of the gospel, breaking into the heart, had the power to kill a man's sins, grant faith, and convert the soul. He wrote, "This, and this only, is the preaching which will beget souls again, people the world with new creations, and erect, from the ruins of the fall, living temples of the Holy Spirit.... To supplement it with human teaching is to blunt the edge of the sword, and to veil the luster of the diamond, and to render the Word of God of no effect."[21] In other words, Winslow did not mix the proclamation of the Bible with his own ingenuity and teaching agenda. He simply sought to preach the great doctrines of the Bible.

When the Bible is preached, God's power is unleashed to work on the soul. In order to preach to the heart, the preacher must wield the only instrument that cuts to the heart. This is why Winslow loved the metaphor of the Bible as the sword of the Spirit. He wrote, "The Word of God is a 'sword,' but the sword is effectual only as it is wielded, by the power of the Spirit.... Expect, then, this Word to be powerful in your own souls, as in the souls of those upon whom you bring it to bear, only as it is clothed with the divine and irresistible might and energy of the Holy Spirit."[22] The efficacy of the Word works in a variety of ways. Winslow explained:

> As the word of life, it *quickens*. As a divine word, it *converts* the soul. As the truth which is after godliness, it *sanctifies*. As a nourishing word, it promotes *growth in grace*. As a word of consolation, it *comforts*. As a storehouse of supply, it thoroughly *furnishes us unto all good works*. As the divine light, it is our *guide*. As a spiritual sword, it is *a mighty weapon in the hands of the Spirit*. And when the books are opened, *it will judge us at the last day*. Such is the word of God, which lives and abides forever.[23]

Winslow believed a thriving preaching ministry will witness the power of the Word in the hearts of the preacher and congregation.

---

21. Octavius Winslow, *Born Again, or, From Grace to Glory* (London: John F. Shaw, 1864), 65.

22. Winslow, *Precious Things*, 275–76.

23. Octavius Winslow, *Grace and Truth* (London: John F. Shaw, 1849), 28e.

The Gospel and Doctrinal Precision

Winslow believed the duty of preachers is to "exposit" doctrine.[24] All doctrine must be rooted in Scripture. As preachers expound the text, they must also expound the doctrines embedded in those texts, which communicate the life-changing gospel to their hearers. Because the content and essential importance of the gospel is unchanging, Winslow argued, "We are not to adapt our preaching to the education, the philosophy, or the politics of the times. We are to preach the same old glorious Gospel which the apostle Paul preached when he uplifted the cross of Christ as the only hope of a lost and a ruined world."[25] Additionally, preachers should not be selective in what doctrines they preach, no matter how challenging they are to understand or communicate. Winslow exhorted, "Let no minister of the gospel withhold any part, or doctrine, or truth of God's word, because it is 'hard to be understood.'"[26] In order to understand Winslow's practice of doctrinal preaching, one must grasp his convictions about the importance of preaching the gospel and doctrinal precision.

The Importance of the Gospel

Winslow argued that "the Gospel is the most valuable treasure the believer possesses. Everything else is shadowy, chimerical, transitory, passing away."[27] It is safe to conclude that few things possessed greater importance to Winslow than the gospel. The gospel supplied both the content and motivation for his preaching. In a sermon on Romans 8:2 titled "Freedom from the Law of Sin and Death," he offered a description of the gospel:

> The Gospel is the law which *reveals the way of salvation by Christ*. It is the development of God's great expedient of saving man. It speaks of pardon and adoption, of acceptance and sanctification, as all flowing to the soul through faith in his dear Son. It represents God as extending his hand of mercy to the vilest sinner; welcoming the penitent wanderer back to his home, and once more taking the contrite rebel to his heart.[28]

While many in the church reduced the gospel to nothing more than a ticket to heaven, Winslow painted a more robust picture. He knew the gospel reveals

---

24. Winslow, *Glory of the Redeemer*, 370.

25. Winslow, *Tree of Life*, 123e.

26. Octavius Winslow, *Glimpses of the Truth As It Is in Jesus* (Philadelphia: Lindsay & Blakiston, 1856), 83.

27. Winslow, *Precious Things*, 255.

28. Octavius Winslow, *No Condemnation in Christ Jesus: As Unfolded in the Eighth Chapter of the Epistle to the Romans* (London: John F. Shaw, 1853; repr., Edinburgh: Banner of Truth, 1991), 26.

God's heart in both His saving and sanctifying work. In short, the gospel is the good news of the truth as it is in Jesus. Consequently, it is emphatically doctrinal in content. When addressing those who neglected the great gospel doctrines, Winslow would have likely asked, "How can people come to a saving knowledge of Christ without understanding the doctrines of the incarnation, the deity of Christ, the atonement, regeneration, justification by faith, and the resurrection?"

The preacher's assignment, therefore, is to preach the whole counsel of God. He must not withhold any of the great doctrines of Scripture. Just as Jesus revealed all that the Father made known to Him, so preachers must unfold all God has revealed in His Word.[29] Winslow argued, "There must be no adulteration of the Word, nothing doubtful in our statement of the Deity and Atonement of Christ, no mental reservation in preaching the doctrines of grace, no denying or neutralizing the Person and work of the Spirit.... Woe unto us if we preach not the great truths of the gospel as Christ taught them!"[30] Every sermon should expound the Bible's grand redemptive narrative, which culminates in the person and work of Jesus.[31]

In addition, Winslow affirmed that the gospel is not only the *content* of preaching but also the *impetus*. He wrote, "Oh, if I did not believe that Jesus Christ came to save the worst of sinners, will never cast out the very chief who comes in penitence at His feet, and takes hold of His blessed cross, resting on his finished work, I would never more preach."[32] The truthfulness and transformative power of the gospel were pillars of Winslow's preaching ministry. That is why he sought doctrinal precision in order to unfold the truth and guard the church from heresy.

The Importance of Doctrinal Precision

One of the greatest responsibilities of preachers is to communicate truth without error. In order for the church to thrive, she must guard and proclaim truth. Winslow noted that "God has appointed the Church the sacred depository of His truth, and His truth the conservative principle of the Church. No chapter of ecclesiastical history is more richly replete with

---

29. Octavius Winslow, *Consider Jesus: Thoughts for Daily Duty, Service, and Suffering* (London: John F. Shaw, 1870), 18e.

30. Winslow, *Consider Jesus*, 18e.

31. For Winslow, every biblical doctrine and every Bible passage should be tied to the gospel because of the centrality of Christ. For more on Winslow's Christ-centered preaching, see chapter 4, "Preaching Centered in Christ."

32. Winslow, *Tree of Life*, 124e.

instruction than that which illustrates the influence of fundamental error as an element of spiritual decay."[33] The monumental consequences of preaching sound doctrine can hardly be overstated. Preachers expound the path of death or the path of life. Winslow had strong words for false teachers who led hearers toward destruction and warned people to flee from their instruction. He wrote:

> There is also death in the tongue of him who preaches false doctrine. The minister of soul-destroying error is the minister of death! All teaching which is opposed to the Gospel of Christ, which misleads men on their way to eternity by failing to show to them the way of life—all preaching which denies the work of the Spirit in regeneration; which substitutes human merit for the atoning work and sacrifice of Christ; which builds up men in their *own doings and works* as a meritorious preparation for heaven. All pulpit instruction which tends to lower the holiness of the truth, to relax the bond of moral obligation, to suppress, in the professor of the Gospel, an ardent desire after godliness—we say all such teaching is fatal to souls, and that, therefore, there is death in the power of the preacher's tongue. As you value your eternal well-being go not in the way of such false teachers—*these murderers of souls!* Recoil from them as you would from the wily serpent; reject their ministries as you would the poisoned cup; cease to hear the instruction that causes to err from the words of knowledge and from the way of life.[34]

In contrast to the false teachers, Winslow asserted, "There is life in the power of the tongue of him who preaches the Lord Jesus Christ. When we preach Jesus we preach the only true life. Jesus is emphatically the Way of Life—Yes, He is Life itself."[35] Clearly, Winslow drew a sharp distinction between true and false teachers.

One primary reason false teaching was and continues to be so prevalent is because men abandon God's Word. Winslow said, "Men would rather learn of their fellow men than of the God-man; they prefer human writings to the Divine—the school of man, to the school of God. And this is one reason why there is so much false doctrine, the teaching that causes to err, both

---

33. Octavius Winslow, "The Deepening of the Spiritual Life: Its Hindrances and Helps among Clergy and People," in Church Congress, *Authorized Report of the Church Congress Held at Nottingham October 10, 11, 12, & 13* (London: Wells Gardner, 1871), 439.

34. Octavius Winslow, *The Ministry of Home, or, Brief Expository Lectures on Divine Truth: Designed Especially for Family and Private Reading* (London: William Hunt and Co., 1868), 127.

35. Winslow, *Ministry of Home*, 128.

from the pulpit and from the press."[36] He believed the great dangers of liberal rationalism and ritualistic Romanism resulted from such a departure and could only be avoided by adhering to biblical authority. He explained:

> The two shoals through which the Church of God has need to steer are—*Rationalism* and *Romanism*. The slightest divergence to the one or to the other imperils her safety, and is treason against her Lord. The true and safe passage is only to be found in a strict adherence to the revealed and written Word of the living God. The moment she removes her eye from this Divine compass, and ceases to consult this heaven-constructed chart, her danger commences. Holding firmly the Divine inspiration of the Scriptures, recognising no other authority, and guided by no other teaching than the Bible, she may brave every danger, and smile defiantly at every storm.[37]

Preaching the gospel is the only means by which the church will be built and preserved.[38] Therefore, ministers must fearlessly refuse to compromise the bedrock doctrines of the faith.[39]

Winslow's Doctrinal Preaching in Practice: The Doctrines of Grace

An examination of Winslow's sermons reveals the soteriological foundation for his preaching was grounded in the doctrines of grace. He affirmed the utter freeness of the gospel and God's sovereignty in salvation through the work of Christ. Winslow loved the doctrines of grace:

> The doctrine of God's eternal, sovereign, and unconditional election of a people, his redemption of them by the sacrifice of his Son Jesus Christ, his particular and effectual calling of them by the Eternal Spirit, their complete pardon and justification, and their preservation to eternal

---

36. Octavius Winslow, *The Man of God, or, Spiritual Religion Explained and Enforced* (London: John F. Shaw, 1865), 71.

37. Octavius Winslow, *Jesus and John, or, The Loving and the Loved: A Tribute to the Memory of the Late Rev. William Marsh, D.D.* (London: James Nisbet & Co., 1859), 34–35.

38. At a conference for evangelical ministers, Winslow declared, "But the question still returns: 'What is the healing branch you propose to fling into these bitter waters of the Church?' We most conscientiously and unhesitatingly reply,—*the Gospel of Christ can alone meet the case.* The Bible, the old-fashioned Bible, as inspired men wrote it, as vigilant sentinels guarded it, as Reformers battled and as martyrs died for it—God's pure Word undiluted and undefiled—is the only branch that can sweeten the Marah waters of the Church, the one and only instrument that can effectually say to the proud waves of Rationalistic belief and Romish ritual, 'Thus far shalt thou come, and no further.'" *Practical Suggestions*, 12.

39. Octavius Winslow, *Personal Declension and Revival of Religion in the Soul* (London: John F. Shaw, 1841; repr., Edinburgh: Banner of Truth, 2000), 126.

glory,—these are God's truths, and not to be rejected. They come *from* God, and, when received in the heart, they lead *to* God; they have their origin in him, and to him they draw the soul. Precious truths! How they abase the sinner, how they exalt the dear Redeemer; how they glorify God, how they empty, humble, and sanctify the soul! We would not be the individual to speak [anything] against them, or think slightingly of them, no, not for our right hand, or for our right eye.[40]

He also loved to proclaim the gospel truth found in Isaiah 55:1: "Ho, every one that thirsteth, come ye to the waters, and he that hath no money; come ye, buy, and eat; yea, come, buy wine and milk without money and without price." In commenting on this verse, he wrote, "The most unworthy, the most vile, the most penniless, may come and drink water freely out of the wells of salvation. This is the language of God, by the mouth of his prophets. What a gospel, then, is here revealed! how full the supply! how free the gift!"[41]

Though Winslow was not alone in preaching the doctrines of grace, many did not follow suit. He lamented over how many failed to preach the truth he saw so clearly:

Is there not in the present day a criminal keeping back by some, and a painful undervaluing by others, of the scriptural and holy doctrines of grace?—The doctrines which unfold the eternity of God's love to his people—the sovereignty of his grace in their election—the effec- tual power of the Spirit in their calling—the free justification of their persons through the imputed righteousness of Christ, and the entire putting away of their sins by his atoning blood—the solemn obliga- tion to "live soberly, righteously, and godly in this present evil world," and the certainty of their final glorification in the world to come,—are not these Divinely-revealed truths, at the present moment, and by the great mass of Christian professors and preachers, excluded from our pulpits and exiled from our land? are they not considered mean and unfashionable? and, having lost their savor with the many, are they not cast out and trodden under foot of men? We verily and solemnly believe that it is so. By some they are professedly received, but criminally held back; by others they are professedly preached, but with such timidity and obscurity, as to render them of none effect: and by the many they are disbelieved altogether, and therefore openly and boldly denied! And yet, these are the doctrines which shine so luminously in every page of

---

40. Octavius Winslow, *The Inquirer Directed to an Experimental and Practical View of the Atonement* (London: John F. Shaw, 1839; repr., *Atonement and the Cross* [Stoke-on-Trent, U.K.: Tentmaker, 2008]), 69.

41. Winslow, *View of the Atonement*, 84.

the apostle's writings,—these are the doctrines which formed the grand themes of Christ's ministration.[42]

Several points emerge from this statement. First, Winslow demonstrates how the doctrines go beyond the five points of Calvinism. In fact, Winslow never seemed to place himself in the Calvinist camp, although his theology was thoroughly Reformed.[43] Second, he believed the doctrines of grace are grounded in apostolic teaching and, more importantly, the teaching of Jesus. Third, the doctrines of grace are essential to the believer's sanctification. They are practical doctrines with great significance for daily living. Fourth, the doctrines of grace are not always well received. For that reason, many retreat from preaching them.

In order to take a closer look at Winslow's understanding of the doctrines of grace, an examination of some of them will be offered. Each of the following sections will include sermon extracts in order to demonstrate how Winslow practiced doctrinal preaching. A look at the results of preaching the doctrines of grace will follow.

Preaching the Doctrines of Grace: The Content

The doctrines of grace answer the question of how God saves. They speak to one's view of God, man, the world, and Christian ministry. Several key doctrines that demonstrate how Winslow preached the doctrines of grace include total depravity, the love of God, unconditional election, effectual calling, particular redemption, and perseverance and assurance.

Total Depravity. Winslow believed man is wicked in his natural state, and, apart from God's grace, a man's heart is his own worst enemy.[44] This nature has been passed down from the fall of Adam. He explained, "Adam fell, and in his fall transmitted to his posterity a nature totally corrupt in every part."[45] Winslow believed this corruption touched every aspect of man's soul. Concerning man's depraved state he said, "The understanding, the will, the affections were all dark, perverted and alienated from God, with enmity and

---

42. Winslow, *Personal Declension*, 121–22.

43. Winslow was clearly numbered among the Particular Baptists of his day. See Geoffrey R. Breed, *Particular Baptists in Victorian England and Their Strict Communion Organizations* (Didcot, U.K.: Baptist Historical Society, 2003), 347.

44. Octavius Winslow, *The Inquirer Directed to an Experimental and Practical View of the Holy Spirit* (London: John F. Shaw, 1840; repr., *The Work of the Holy Spirit: An Experimental and Practical View* [Edinburgh: Banner of Truth, 2003]), 36.

45. Winslow, *Personal Declension*, 170.

death marking every unconverted man."[46] This understanding provides the backdrop for his convictions on the work of God's love and grace in salvation.

In a sermon titled "Christ Our Brother," Winslow articulated the importance of understanding man's total depravity. He declared:

> Oh, how utterly fallen, low totally depraved, how entirely void of spiritual holiness, strength, and love are we! Talk of our nature being in a salvable state—preposterous idea! "When we were without strength, in due time Christ died for the ungodly." "There dwells in our flesh no good thing." "There is none righteous, no, not one." If there is any, the least, moral power, or inclination, or light innate in the soul, by which we can assist the work of our recovery, then Christ becomes a "helper" only, and not a Savior, and the Holy Spirit is simply a secondary and subordinate Agent, aiding a mind already spiritually enlightened, a will already rightly disposed, a heart already pulsating with love, and yearning with desire toward God! See to what a "reduction to absurdity" the theory of innate moral ability in the natural and unrenewed man conducts the reasoner.[47]

Winslow's argument highlights how his preaching of this doctrine exposes other crucial doctrines related to God's salvific work. He taught that man's sinfulness offends God's holiness, leaving him exposed to His just condemnation. Moreover, if man is less than totally depraved, then Christ is less than a Savior.

The Love of God. As stated earlier, the doctrines of grace encompass more theological truth than the classic five points of Calvinism. For example, the doctrines of imputation, regeneration, and adoption (and many more) are all doctrines of grace. Chief among these is the doctrine of the love of God. Winslow's understanding of God's love is central because he viewed it as the "concentric truth" around which God's redeeming work revolves.[48] He declared:

> If one perfection of God shines out in redemption with greater effulgence than any other, it is this. Love is the focus of all the rest, the golden thread which draws and binds them all together in holy and beautiful cohesion. Love was the moving, controlling attribute in God's great expedient of saving sinners. *Justice* may have demanded it, *holiness* may have required it, *wisdom* may have planned it, and *power* may have executed it, but love originated the whole, and was the moving

---

46. Winslow, *Personal Declension*, 56.
47. Winslow, *Patriarchal Shadows*, 117.
48. Winslow, *Our God*, 2.

cause in the heart of God; so that the salvation of the sinner is not so much a manifestation of the justice, or holiness, or wisdom, or power of God, as it is a display of His love.[49]

It is the great love of the triune God that secured man's salvation. The Father demonstrated His love in sending His Son. The Son expressed His love in His sacrificial death, and the Spirit reveals His love in applying the work of Christ to sinners.[50] Winslow viewed the cross as the greatest spectacle of God's infinite and indiscriminate love. He wrote, "Behold Christ upon the cross! Every pain that He endures, every stroke that He receives, every groan that He utters, every drop of blood that He sheds, proclaims that God is love, and that He stands pledged and is ready to pardon the vilest of the vile. Justice, sheathing its sword, and retiring satisfied from the scene, leaves mercy gloriously triumphant."[51] The love of God serves as the cornerstone for the great work of salvation.

In a sermon titled "No Separation from Christ Jesus," Winslow expounded on the doctrine of God's great love:

> The love of Christ! such is our precious theme! Of it can we ever weary? Its greatness can we ever know? Its plenitude can we fully contain? Never! Its depths cannot be fathomed, its dimensions cannot be measured. It passes knowledge. All that Jesus did for his Church was but the unfolding and expression of his love. Traveling to Bethlehem—I see love incarnate. Tracking his steps as he went about doing good—I see love laboring. Visiting the house of Bethany—I see love sympathizing. Standing by the grave of Lazarus—I see love weeping. Entering the gloomy precincts of Gethsemane—I see love sorrowing. Passing on to Calvary—I see love suffering, and bleeding, and expiring. The whole scene of his life is but an unfolding of the deep, and awesome, and precious mystery of redeeming love.
>
> The love of the Father! Such, too, is our theme;… The love of the Father is seen in giving us Christ, in choosing us in Christ, and in blessing us in him with all spiritual blessings. Indeed, the love of the Father is the fountain of all covenant and redemption mercy to the church. It is that river the streams whereof make glad the city of God. How anxious was Jesus to vindicate the love of the Father from all the suspicions and

---

49. Winslow, *Our God*, 1.

50. Octavius Winslow, *Morning Thoughts, or, Daily Walking with God: A Portion for Each Day in the Year* (London: John F. Shaw, 1858; repr., Grand Rapids: Reformation Heritage Books, 2003), 5–6.

51. Winslow, *Glory of the Redeemer*, 65.

fears of his disciples! "I say not unto you, that I will ask the Father for you, for the Father Himself loves you." "God so loved the world that he gave his only-begotten Son." To this love we must trace all the blessings which flow to us through the channel of the cross. It is the love of God, exhibited, manifested, and seen in Christ Jesus. Christ being, not the originator, but the gift of his love; not the cause, but the exponent of it. Oh, to see a perfect equality in the Father's love with the Son's love! Then shall we be led to trace all his sweet mercies, and all his providential dealings, however trying, painful, and mysterious, to the heart of God; thus resolving all into that from where all alike flow—everlasting and unchangeable love.

Now it is from this love there is no separation.[52]

Such preaching is typical of Winslow, heavy on theological content with the purpose of encouraging his hearers to see God more clearly and be comforted by that knowledge.

Unconditional Election. The doctrine of election is grounded in man's depravity and God's love. In spite of man's rebellion and helplessness to save himself, God, in His sovereign lovingkindness, predestines some for salvation who would never have chosen Him. Winslow defined election as "God's choice, of a beloved people."[53] Winslow recognized the mysterious nature of God's electing purpose.[54] He also understood that some do not accept this doctrine and "extract bitterness from one of the sweetest and clearest truths of God's word."[55]

He believed many struggle with election because they initiate their theological quest in the wrong place. When preaching on the doctrine of election, he likened our understanding of God's salvific work to links in a chain. He explained to his people:

The first and lowest link in the chain of your salvation is your *calling* by the Spirit. Called by sovereign grace to see your sinfulness, to accept Christ; and evidencing the reality of your calling by a pure and holy life, you have made sure of the last and the highest link of the chain, and may calmly leave the fact of your eternal election to everlasting life with God, in whose hands it is alone and safely lodged. *With the*

52. Winslow, *No Condemnation*, 388–90.
53. Winslow, *No Condemnation*, 365.
54. Winslow, *Help Heavenward*, 53.
55. Octavius Winslow, *Soul-Depths & Soul-Heights: Sermons on Psalm 130* (London: John F. Shaw, 1874; repr., Edinburgh: Banner of Truth, 2006), 14.

divine decrees, happily, you have nothing to do. You are not called to
believe that you are one of the elect; but you are called to believe in
Jesus Christ—that you are a poor, lost sinner, feeling your need of the
Savior, looking only to His blood and righteousness as the ground of
your pardon, justification, and final glory. Thus called by grace to be a
saint of God, election will become to you one of the most *encouraging,*
comforting, and *sanctifying* doctrines of the Bible.[56]

Thus, Winslow believed that through evidence of the Spirit's effectual calling, people can be confident of God's electing grace. He urged people not to
become consumed with searching out the secret things of God, but simply to
believe in Christ and walk in holiness.[57] This extract provides an example of
Winslow's theological acumen and his concern to carefully explain doctrines
many find difficult and even mysterious.

Effectual Calling. Winslow considered the calling of men to salvation to be
a work of the Holy Spirit. He distinguished between the external, or general, call and the internal, or effectual, call of the Spirit. The external call of
the gospel goes forth to every person.[58] This call of the Spirit places a great
responsibility and accountability on man. In addition to the general call,
"there is the special, direct and effectual call of the Spirit, in the elect of God,
without which all other calling is in vain."[59] This supernatural work of the
Spirit enables individuals to see their sinfulness and believe in Christ's salvific work on the cross.

Concerning the resistibility of the Spirit's work, Winslow knew that
fallen man opposes the work of the Spirit but cannot ultimately resist Him.
He explained, "We do not say that the Spirit is not resisted—He is resisted,
strongly and perseveringly. But He is not overpowered. All the enmity and
carnality of the heart rises in direct opposition to Him; but when bent upon
a mission of love, when in accordance with the eternal purpose He comes
to save, not all the powers on earth or in hell can effectually resist Him."[60]
The Holy Spirit overcomes all resistance and effectually calls men to Christ.
This truth evoked a doxological tone in the following sermon excerpt:
"O memorable moment, when Jesus, by the resistless but gentle power of his

56. Winslow, *Soul-Depths,* 14–15.
57. Winslow, *Soul-Depths,* 15.
58. Winslow, *No Condemnation,* 304–6.
59. Winslow, *Holy Spirit,* 69–70.
60. Winslow, *Holy Spirit,* 65.

grace, broke down every barrier, entered your heart, and planted there the germ of a life as Divine, as holy, and as immortal as his own!"[61]

Winslow's heralding of God's effectual call demonstrates another consistent feature of his doctrinal preaching, namely, supporting his claims with Scripture. He often quoted verse after verse, many times consecutively, as evidence for his assertions. For instance, after explaining the general call of the gospel, Winslow brought his hearers back to the internal call of the Spirit as found in Romans 8:30. He preached:

> But the call here referred to is the especial call of the Gospel—the secret, effectual call which has found its way to the heart by the power of the Holy Spirit. The connection of these two truths—an especial people, and an especial call—is thus conclusively shown—"And that he might make known the riches of his glory in the vessels of mercy, which he had afore prepared unto glory, even us, whom he has called." "Who has saved us, and called us with an holy calling, not according to our works, but according to his own purpose and grace, which was given us in Christ Jesus, before the world began." "Those who are sanctified by God the Father, and preserved in Christ Jesus, and called." Honored Church! Happy people! Called to be saints. Oh, to have the Divine testimony that we are among them![62]

This example reveals Winslow's use of the analogy of faith as well as how he exposed the relevance and devotional aspects of doctrine.

Particular Redemption. The prominence of the atonement in Winslow's theology is observed in the following words: "Were we to relinquish every other revealed truth, and concentrate upon this one our supreme and lasting study, resolving all our knowledge of the Bible into an 'experimental and personal acquaintance' with atoning blood—as, like a purple thread, it runs from Genesis to Revelation, it would not be a too exaggerated view of this vital and momentous subject."[63] Winslow emphasized striving for an "experimental and personal acquaintance" of the atonement. His first book, *The Inquirer Directed to an Experimental and Practical View of the Atonement*, was devoted to the topic.[64] His primary concern throughout his writings

---

61. Octavius Winslow, *The Inner Life: Its Nature, Relapse, and Recovery* (London: John F. Shaw, 1850), 36.

62. Winslow, *No Condemnation*, 305.

63. Winslow, *Consider Jesus*, 47e.

64. It should be noted that Winslow did not address the extent of the atonement in his first book, *An Experimental View of the Atonement*. This omission, though probably

was the practical implications of Christ's sacrifice rather than the extent of the atonement. The atonement was so central to Winslow that he wrote, "No single day should pass in the experience of a child of God without washing in the blood. The blood should be upon all his religious duties, engagements, and services."[65] Winslow believed everything should be filtered through Christ's atoning work.

In the sermon he delivered during the opening of the Metropolitan Tabernacle in London, Winslow preached on "Christ's Finished Work."[66] In that sermon he highlighted the expiatory and substitutionary purpose of the atonement. Christ's primary purpose in going to the cross was to bear the punishment and penalty of man's sin. He also emphasized Christ's victory on the cross over sin, Satan, and hell.

Just because Winslow focused on the practical features of the atonement does not mean he was undecided regarding the extent of the atonement. Winslow held that the finished work of Christ on the cross was limited in its application to the elect. He wrote, "In the eternal purpose of the Triune God the sins of the elect were laid upon Jesus, and He undertook to bear and die for them."[67] Even still, he argued that the atonement still holds implications for unbelievers.[68]

---

intentional, was noted by an early reviewer of this work. See Methodist Episcopal Church, "Critical Notices," *The Methodist Quarterly Review* 28 (October 1846), 632.

65. Winslow, *Our God*, 47.

66. Charles H. Spurgeon, *The Metropolitan Tabernacle Pulpit* (Pasadena, Tex.: Pilgrim Publications, 1986), 7:241–46.

67. Winslow, *Foot of the Cross*, 106.

68. In reflecting on the patience of God, Winslow explained his views:

If, then, the patience of our God was so manifest and glorious amid the dim shadows of the legal dispensation, how much more real and glorious does it appear in the full blaze of the gospel and the sublime and impressive scenes of Calvary! If God would patiently bear with men's rebellion because of the sacrifice of a lamb, a goat, or a heifer, how much more honorable and fitting on His part to extend to sinners His patience on the ground of Christ's only and complete sacrifice!

This explains the worldwide indirect influence of Christ's Atonement. That atonement has a particular reference to the elect church of God; but since it was necessary that the world should be kept in existence—a wicked, ungodly, mutinous world though it is—in order that God might take His chosen people out of it, the indirect effect of the sacrifice of Christ is to enable God to endure "with much patience the vessels of wrath fitted to destruction" (Rom. 9:22)!

Oh, the marvelous blessings that flow from the death of Christ! What variety of precious fruit grows on the cross of Calvary! So marvelous, so unheard of was it that, the incarnate God, the Maker of all worlds, the Creator of all beings, should die, it would seem impossible that there should be a spot in the

In his preaching, Winslow did not always spend a whole sermon expounding a specific doctrine. There were times when he would briefly set forth a particular doctrine when focusing on another truth. They could be called "doctrinal sidebars" or "doctrinal touchpoints." For example, he exposed his view of the atonement when preaching about the Father's role in the resurrection of the Son: "By this act of raising up his Son from the grave, the Father manifested his infinite delight in, and his full acceptance of, the sacrifice of Christ, as a finished and satisfactory expiation for the sins of people."[69] At other times, he was more explicit regarding the extent of the atonement. Preaching on the life of Joseph, Winslow tried to find a typological link in Joseph's care for his family by comparing it to Christ's saving work for His elect:

> But, for the Church of God alone, the chosen of God, the gift to Christ of the Father, His especial treasure, everlastingly loved and eternally elected, did the Son of God die upon the cross. On their behalf obedience was given to the law, satisfaction was offered to justice, the righteousness of God's government was upheld—its honor and dignity vindicated and maintained—"the Church of God which He has purchased with His own blood." Is God unrighteous in this? Who are you that replies against Him?—a worm—a moth—a vapor—sinful dust and ashes daring to impugn the holiness, the equity, the wisdom, the goodness of Jehovah! Believer in Christ! for you our true Joseph was raised up—for you the food in Egypt was provided to keep your soul alive in famine, and to save it everlastingly—by a great and glorious deliverance.[70]

Winslow not only proclaimed God's atoning grace for His special people but he also declared His persevering grace.

Perseverance and Assurance. As with all his theological convictions, Winslow believed the doctrine of the final perseverance of the saints was thoroughly biblical. He built his case for perseverance and assurance from Scripture, writing, "It is declared—written as with a sunbeam.... 'Being confident of this very thing, that he who has begun a good work in you will perform it until the day of Jesus Christ.' 'Kept by the power of God through faith unto salvation.' 'They shall never perish, neither shall any man pluck them out of

---

universe or a being on the globe to whom the influence of Christ's death should not reach, directly or indirectly, either of saving mercy, or of restraining and sparing power. *Our God*, 42–43.

69. Winslow, *Inner Life*, 259.
70. Winslow, *Patriarchal Shadows*, 133.

my hand.'"[71] Such passages highlight God's grace in bringing His saints to glory. Additionally, he said John 10:27–30 reveals "the double security of the believer in [Christ's] and his Father's hands."[72] These scriptural proofs Winslow pointed to demonstrate how God keeps believers from falling away and sustains them to persevere in the faith.

At one point, Winslow encouraged his people by telling them to look outside of themselves, namely, to Christ, for their assurance:

> Let it be your aim to know your present standing as in the sight of God. Upon so vital a question not the shadow of a doubt should rest. "We believe, and are sure." Faith brings assurance, and assurance is faith. The measure of our assured interest in Christ, will be the measure of our faith in Christ. This is the true definition of assurance, the nature of which is a question of much perplexity to sincere Christians. Assurance is not something audible, tangible, or visionary—a revelation to the mind, or a voice in the air. Assurance is believing. Faith is the cause, assurance is the effect. Assurance of personal salvation springs from *looking to, and dealing only with Jesus.* It comes not from believing that I am saved, but from believing that Christ is my Savior. The *object* of my salvation is not my faith, but Christ. Faith is but the instrument by which I receive Christ as a sinner. As the eaglet acquires strength of vision by gazing upon the sun, until at length, when fledged, it expands its wings and soars to the orb of day,—so *the eye of faith*, by "looking unto Jesus" *only*, gradually becomes stronger; and in proportion to its clear and still clearer view of Christ, brings increased, sweet, and holy assurance to the soul.[73]

This excerpt demonstrates how Winslow applied theological truth to his hearers' hearts.

These key soteriological convictions are in many cases mysterious, but together they form the foundation on which Winslow's doctrinal preaching rested. He consistently declared man's total depravity, God's everlasting love and unconditional election, the Spirit's effectual calling, Christ's atoning work, and the believer's final perseverance.

---

71. Winslow, *Grace and Truth*, 47–48e.

72. Winslow, *Personal Declension*, 196. John 10:27–30 says: "My sheep hear my voice, and I know them, and they follow me: and I give unto them eternal life; and they shall never perish, neither shall any man pluck them out of my hand. My Father, which gave them me, is greater than all; and no man is able to pluck them out of my Father's hand. I and my Father are one."

73. Winslow, *Soul-Depths*, 3–4. Winslow also affirmed that believers can look for assurance within because of the inner witness of the Holy Spirit.

Preaching the Doctrines of Grace: The Results

Winslow understood that preaching the doctrines of grace carried both positive and negative ramifications. Negatively, preaching the doctrines of grace often means many will turn away because of the hard sayings of the gospel. He observed this in the ministry of Christ: "Doctrine divides us from some. If we speak of God's eternal love, and free choice, and discriminating mercy, we offend. When our Lord preached the doctrine of sovereign grace, we read that 'from that time many of his disciples went back, and walked no more with him.'"[74] Moreover, when certain doctrines are resisted or difficult to explain, preachers are tempted to neglect proclaiming them. That is why Winslow exhorted his readers, "Let no minister of the gospel withhold any part, or doctrine, or truth of God's word, because it is 'hard to be understood.'… All revealed truth is unqualifiedly to be declared. The doctrines of grace, towering though they do above the comprehension of carnal reason, and humbling though they are to human pride, are yet fully and broadly to be stated."[75] Although some did not expound the doctrines of grace because they were unpopular, Winslow saw great benefit in preaching these truths.

Winslow believed that preaching the doctrines of grace delivered two great objectives in God's salvific work: conversion and sanctification. He pointed to Peter's sermon at Pentecost as evidence of God's saving work through the proclamation of sovereign grace. Referring to the crowd's favorable response to Peter's sermon, he wrote:

> This was the result of a simple preaching of the truth,—a faithful exhibition of the doctrines of grace. The stout-hearted Jews listened with awe: the men who had witnessed the awful scene of Calvary without emotion, now quailed, trembled, turned pale, and smote on their breasts, in all the anguish of a deep, pungent conviction of sin. How soon did their proud natures bend, their hard hearts melt; the strong fortress of their prejudices yield before the simplicity and the majesty of the truth![76]

Additionally, the doctrines of grace promote a great sanctifying influence. Regarding this, Winslow again pointed to the preaching of Jesus as evidence. He highlighted how Jesus' preaching of the doctrines of grace helped deliver the virtue of humility. He wrote, "They were all exhibited as doctrines that laid man's pride in the dust, and exalted the grace and mercy of God. There is

---

74. Octavius Winslow, *Midnight Harmonies, or, Thoughts for the Season of Solitude and Sorrow* (New York: Robert Carter & Brothers, 1853), 61–62.

75. Winslow, *Glimpses of the Truth*, 83.

76. Winslow, *Personal Declension*, 124.

not a doctrine in Christ's ministry that does not tend to abase the creature."[77] According to Winslow, preachers who desire to see their hearers grow in grace should emulate the preaching of Jesus and herald the Father's everlasting love, His gracious election, and His sovereign mercy.

Doctrinal preaching was the foundation of Winslow's preaching, but he always preached doctrine so that his hearers might become experimentally acquainted with truth. For him, doctrine was intensely practical and devotional. He believed anything less than applying the truth was a diluted form of preaching and Christianity.

Conclusion

Winslow possessed strong convictions concerning the homiletical task. His practice of doctrinal preaching was a natural result of his theology. His view of the Bible's divine inspiration, truthfulness, and power provided the necessary foundation for his preaching. Moreover, his understanding of the gospel and doctrinal precision, as well as his proclamation of the doctrines of grace, were the means by which he performed his ministerial work. The next chapter will address another essential aspect of his experimental homiletic, his Christ-centered preaching.

---

77. Winslow, *Man of God*, 52–53.

4

~

PREACHING CENTERED
IN CHRIST

Winslow's experimental preaching was centered in Christ. Like the apostle Paul, he "determined not to know anything among [those to whom he ministered], save Jesus Christ, and him crucified" (1 Cor. 2:2). Winslow consistently preached Christ as the doctrinal and practical fulfillment of each passage. For example, when addressing the doctrine of truth, he said: "The cross…is the central fact of God's moral universe. All Divine truth meets in Christ's cross. All glory beams from Christ's cross. All spiritual blessings distil from Christ's cross. It is at its feet that the studious, earnest mind receives the most luminous, comprehensive, and glorious revelations and views of the Divine Being; and from thence he draws the sweetest and richest blessings to his soul."[1] He also viewed Christ as the practical solution for applying the truth in one's life. For example, in a sermon on true versus false Christianity he explained:

> What course am I to adopt when…I find a spiritual drought and deadness in my soul, and cannot feel, nor weep, nor sigh, nor desire?—when to read and meditate, to hear and pray, seem an irksome task?—when I cannot see the Savior's beauty, nor feel him precious, nor labor as zealously, nor suffer as patiently for him as I would desire? The answer is at hand—Look again to Jesus. This is the only remedy that can meet your case. Search the Bible through, inquire of all the ministers who have ever lived, and still the answer would be—look again to Jesus. Go direct to Christ—he is the Fountainhead, he is the living Well. True, the well is deep—for its fulness is infinite—but faith, be it of the smallest capacity, can with joy draw sufficient to quench your thirst.[2]

Winslow believed such preaching should emanate from a Christ-centered hermeneutic. Moreover, his Christ-centered messages avoided the potential

---

1. Octavius Winslow, *The Foot of the Cross and the Blessings Found There* (New York: Robert Carter, 1868; repr., *Atonement and the Cross* [Stoke-on-Trent, U.K.: Tentmaker, 2008]), 84.
2. Octavius Winslow, *The Inner Life: Its Nature, Relapse, and Recovery* (London: John F. Shaw, 1850), 99–100.

danger of marginalizing the doctrine of the Trinity. His Trinitarian theology actually provided the motivation for his Christ-centered messages.

This chapter will examine Winslow's Christ-centered approach by analyzing his Christ-centered hermeneutic and fundamental convictions about Christ-centered preaching before providing different examples from his sermons. Finally, it will demonstrate how he found motivation for the practice through his Trinitarian theology.

An Examination of Winslow's Christ-Centered Preaching

A cursory glance at Winslow's ministry will reveal his focus on the person and work of Christ. In many respects, Christ was the theme of his ministry. Winslow's love for the glory of Christ is evident in his writings and preaching.[3] The starting point for grasping his Christ-centered preaching involves analyzing his hermeneutic.

Winslow's Christ-Centered Hermeneutic

Winslow repeatedly argued that the Bible must be interpreted christocentrically. He was convinced that "the Bible is, from its commencement to its close, a record of the Lord Jesus."[4] Fundamental to his Christ-centered hermeneutic were his convictions on Scripture's progressive revelation, the unity of the testaments, and the hermeneutic of Jesus.

---

3. The titles of Winslow's books uncover the christocentric emphasis of his ministry. These include *Christ and the Christian in Temptation: Counsel and Consolation for the Tempted* (London, 1878); *Christ, The Theme of the Home Missionary* (New York: John S. Taylor, 1838); *Consider Jesus: Thoughts for Daily Duty, Service, and Suffering* (London: John F. Shaw, 1870); *Emmanuel, or, Titles of Christ: Their Teaching and Consolations* (London: John F. Shaw, 1869); *Foot of the Cross; Glimpses of the Truth As It Is in Jesus* (Philadelphia: Lindsay & Blakiston, 1856); *The Glory of the Redeemer in His Person and Work*, 8th ed. (London: John F. Shaw, 1865; repr., Pittsburgh: Soli Deo Gloria, 1997); *The Inquirer Directed to an Experimental and Practical View of the Atonement* (New York: M. W. Dodd, 1838); *Life in Jesus: A Memoir of Mrs. Mary Winslow Arranged from Her Correspondence, Diary, and Thoughts* (London: John F. Shaw, 1890; repr., Grand Rapids: Reformation Heritage Books, 2013); *No Condemnation in Christ Jesus: As Unfolded in the Eighth Chapter of the Epistle to the Romans* (London: John F. Shaw, 1853; repr., Edinburgh: Banner of Truth, 1991); *None Like Christ* (New York: A. D. F. Randolph, 1863); *Patriarchal Shadows of Christ and His Church: As Exhibited in Passages Drawn from the History of Joseph and His Brethren* (London: John F. Shaw, 1863; repr., Grand Rapids: Sovereign Grace Treasures, 2005); and *The Sympathy of Christ with Man* (New York: Robert Carter & Brothers; repr., Harrisonburg, Va.: Sprinkle, 1994). Winslow's Christology stands out as one of the more prominent possibilities for future research and writing.

4. Octavius Winslow, *The Precious Things of God* (London: James Nisbet, 1860; repr., Ligonier, Pa.: Soli Deo Gloria, 1993), 263.

Progressive Revelation and "The Sun of Righteousness." While Winslow believed all Scripture centers in Christ, he also held that the types and shadows that point to Jesus unfold throughout the Old Testament in a particular way. He wrote, "It was thus the wisdom and the will of God that the revelation of Jesus to the Church should assume a consecutive and progressive form."[5] The progressive nature of God's revelation was gradual and increasing until Christ appeared. Winslow called Jesus "the great Antitype of all the types, the glowing substance of all the shadows, the full signification of all the symbols."[6] He made use of metaphor to explain the necessity of interpreting Scripture through a Christ-centered lens. He explained:

> The personal glory of the Lord Jesus is to the Bible what the sun is to our planet. In the deep and dark recesses of nature, as well as scattered upon its broad surface, there are many objects of great intrinsic value, whose beauty and fitness remain undiscovered and unnoticed until, placed in a position, the sun's rays are made to fall upon them, as with focal power, thus revealing both their nature and properties. It is so with the word of God. In itself of infinite worth and transcendent value,—containing no type, revealing no doctrine, enjoining no precept, unfolding no promise, and recording no fact, which does not occupy a position of importance and beauty of surpassing magnitude; yet, until the Sun of Righteousness shines upon it,—until seen in the relation which it sustains to Jesus,—it remains a "hidden mystery," its worth and beauty shaded from the eye.[7]

This metaphor communicates a couple of key components in Winslow's hermeneutic. He affirmed the intrinsic value of Scripture. As God's truth, the Bible is of "infinite worth." However, until each passage is "seen in the relation which it sustains to Jesus," the interpreter has not plumbed its riches. Winslow concluded that every passage, if it is to be hermeneutically faithful, must be interpreted in the light of the "Sun of Righteousness."

Both Testaments Testify to Christ. Another key aspect of Winslow's hermeneutic was his firm conviction concerning the unity of Scripture. He believed both the Old and New Testaments, from Genesis to Revelation, provide a united witness to Christ. He wrote, "The Bible is the Book of Jesus—it is a Revelation of Christ. Christ is the golden thread which runs through the

5. Winslow, *Glory of the Redeemer*, 71.
6. Winslow, *Glory of the Redeemer*, 72.
7. Winslow, *Glory of the Redeemer*, 2.

whole.... The Old Testament predicts the New, and the New fulfils the Old, and so both unite in testifying, 'Truly, this is the Son of God!'"[8]

Because he viewed Christ as the hermeneutical key to the Bible, Winslow engaged in Christ-centered interpretation of Old Testament texts. As noted above, he employed this practice in two sermon series printed for publication, one from the Joseph narrative in Genesis and the other from Psalm 130.[9] The opening words to his sermon series through the Joseph narrative illustrate his approach. He proclaimed:

> The Word of God is as a garden of fruit and flowers—luscious with the sweetness, penciled with the beauty, and fragrant with the perfume of—*Christ*. All its shadows, types, and prophecies, all its doctrines, precepts, and promises testify of Him. Search the Scriptures in whatever part, or view them from whatever stand-point you may, of *Christ* they speak, and to *Christ* they lead.[10]

Additionally, he called Psalm 130 a "Christ-unfolding Psalm."[11]

Winslow's Christ-centered hermeneutic was not limited to the Old Testament. It was comprehensive in scope because he applied it to the various genres of both Testaments. Many preachers think they are preaching "Christian" sermons because they have their Bible open but ultimately fail to do so because they do not preach Christ. This pitfall applies to Old and New Testament texts. Thus, he exhorted, "Aim to unravel Jesus in the types, to grasp Him amid the shadows, to trace Him through the predictions of the prophet, the records of the evangelist, and the letters of the apostles."[12] No matter what part of Scripture Winslow expounded, his purpose was to expound the riches of Christ.

The Hermeneutic of Jesus. Winslow grounded his Christ-centered hermeneutic in the words of Scripture. He developed his conclusions from the words of Christ to the Pharisees in the gospel of John and Christ's conversation with two disciples on the Emmaus road as recorded in Luke's gospel. Reflecting on John 5:39, he wrote: "Of these Scriptures He is the Alpha and the Omega— the substance, the sweetness, the glory—the one, precious, absorbing theme. Listen to His own words, 'Search the Scriptures, for these are they which

8. Winslow, *Emmanuel, or Titles of Christ*, 119e.

9. Winslow, *Patriarchal Shadows,* and *Soul-Depths & Soul-Heights: Sermons on Psalm 130* (London: John F. Shaw, 1874; repr., Edinburgh: Banner of Truth, 2006).

10. Winslow, *Patriarchal Shadows*, 3.

11. Winslow, *Soul-Depths*, vii.

12. Winslow, *Glory of the Redeemer*, 343.

testify of me.' Moses wrote of me—David sang of me—seers prophesied of me—evangelists recorded my life—apostles expounded my doctrine."[13] Moreover, in a devotional reflection on Luke 24:27, Winslow winsomely suggested, "The Old and the New Testament Scriptures of truth do for Christ what Pilate and Herod did against Him—they confederate together. They unite in a holy alliance, in a sublime unity of purpose, to show forth the glory of the incarnate God."[14] When Winslow engaged in Christ-centered interpretation, he believed he was following the hermeneutic of Jesus. To interpret the Scriptures differently is to ignore the example of Jesus and "lower the character of the Bible."[15]

In sum, Winslow viewed Christ-centered interpretation as the means for understanding Scripture rightly. Apart from viewing God's Word through the lens of Christ, the various parts will not make sense. He explained, "I cannot sufficiently reiterate the averment that the Bible can only be clearly understood as it is studied in the light of the Sun of Righteousness, with one intent and aim only to know the Lord Jesus Christ, of whom the Old and the New Testament unitedly testify."[16] With this instruction Winslow also shepherded his people.[17]

Winslow's Convictions Concerning Christ-Centered Preaching

The way a minister handles the text exegetically will necessarily influence his preaching. Winslow's hermeneutic naturally surfaced in his sermons. In a meditation on the cross of Christ he declared, "'We preach Christ crucified,' is the echo of every true minister of Christ."[18]

---

13. Winslow, *Precious Things*, 265.

14. Octavius Winslow, *Morning Thoughts, or, Daily Walking with God: A Portion for Each Day in the Year* (London: John F. Shaw, 1858; repr., Grand Rapids: Reformation Heritage Books, 2003), 730.

15. Winslow, *Glory of the Redeemer*, 341.

16. Octavius Winslow, *The Tree of Life: Its Shade, Fruit, and Repose* (London: John F. Shaw, 1868), 78e.

17. As a pastor, Winslow gave practical instruction to his congregants concerning how to read Scripture: "To the question often earnestly propounded—'What is the best method of reading, so as to understand the Scriptures?' I would reply—Read them with the one desire and end of learning more of Christ, and with earnest prayer for the teaching of the Spirit, that Christ may be unfolded in the Word." *Glory of the Redeemer*, 342.

18. Winslow, *Foot of the Cross*, 99. Concerning Christ-centered preaching, Winslow was undoubtedly influenced by his mother. She wrote to him in a letter: "Remember, my dear O[ctavius], the more your sermons are filled with Christ, from first to last, the more will Christ honour your ministry. There is no preaching like it. Never be afraid of not finding something new to say of Him. The Holy Ghost will supply you with matter as you go on. Never doubt

The Importance of Christ-Centered Preaching. The significance of Christ-centered preaching in the power of the Holy Spirit held great weight for Winslow. He considered it to be "the only divinely appointed instrument of destroying false religion, overthrowing error, and converting the soul, and the only one God Himself will acknowledge and the Holy Spirit bless."[19] He went as far as describing the cross as an "effectual weapon" that the minister wields to dethrone the work of Satan.[20] In another place he wrote, "We feel no hesitation in attributing all that is erroneous in doctrine, depressed in vital Christianity, low in the spirituality of the Church, lax in the walk of religious professors, to a defective and shallow knowledge of Christ and His work—of the Saviour and of his salvation."[21] With these words, he explained the comprehensive effects of preaching Christ. The church's health rests on her knowledge of Jesus.

Winslow also instructed preachers to employ a Christ-centered preaching because eternity is at stake. The proclamation of Christ is the message of salvation.[22] He boldly declared, "All other preaching—preaching which has not Christ crucified for its beginning, its center, and its end, is solemn trifling with souls and with eternity—a splendid impertinence, a burlesque of the gospel, a dishonor to God, the murder of souls, whose blood, staining our garments, God will require at our hands."[23] Winslow did not hold back his convictions when it came to the significance of Christ-centered preaching.

Because of his convictions concerning the importance of Christ-centered preaching, he warned younger ministers of the shame that comes with failing to proclaim Christ. Speaking of the negligent preacher, he said:

---

it, never fear. The whole Bible points to Christ, and you must make it all bear upon the same subject—Christ the sum and substance of the whole. In Him, God and the sinner meet, and they can meet nowhere else. All the promises are in Christ Jesus, and we must get into Christ before we can get at the promises; and then they are all yea and amen to us." *Life in Jesus*, 115.

19. Winslow, *Tree of Life*, 121a.

20. Winslow, *Tree of Life*, 150.

21. Octavius Winslow, *"Is the Spirit of the Lord Straitened?" A Plea for a National Baptism of the Holy Ghost with Incidents of American Revival* (London: John F. Shaw, 1858), 23.

22. Winslow wrote of Paul and Silas's message in Acts 16: "They at once preached to him Jesus—they uplifted the cross—directed his eye to the Crucified—brought him to the Savior. 'Believe in the Lord Jesus Christ, and you shall be saved.' What a marvelous announcement! How suitable, how simple the remedy! This was all they prescribed. Not a word about election, or baptism, or church, or reformation. The one instrument of healing was *faith*; and the one Object of that faith, the Lord Jesus Christ." Octavius Winslow, *Born Again, or, From Grace to Glory* (London: John F. Shaw, 1864), 193–94.

23. Winslow, *Foot of the Cross*, 151.

And with what overpowering truth and conviction does, perhaps, the appalling fact flash upon the mind, "Christ crucified has not been the central truth of my ministry—the Alpha and Omega, the first and the last, the all in all, of my preaching!" He discovers that he has preached himself, and not his Master; that he has exalted himself, and not his Lord; that he has sought his own glory, and not Christ's: he has increased, but Jesus has decreased.[24]

Winslow promoted the glory of Christ in his weekly preaching. Though he was completely persuaded of the need for Christ-centered preaching, sadly, many in his day remained unconvinced.

The Lack of Christ-Centered Preaching. Winslow lamented how many did not preach Christ-centered messages. He wrote, "Is there not in the present day a sad declension in the setting forth of the Lord Jesus Christ?… We verily and solemnly believe that the pulpits of our land are awfully guilty here; that the modern preaching of the Gospel is not formed on the model of the apostles."[25] Winslow identified human knowledge, moralistic preaching, and brilliant eloquence as misguided substitutes. He believed this failure led to a decline in piety, spirituality, and service. He warned: "The cross of Jesus is the very soul of Christianity; all is death where Jesus is not. Grace decays, piety languishes, and formality takes the place of the power of the Gospel, where the person and the work of Christ are slighted, undervalued, or denied."[26] For these reasons, Winslow resolved to preach Christ consistently and convincingly. His zeal for Christ-centered preaching is observed in an exhortation to his fellow ministers. He exclaimed with simplicity, "Are you a Christian minister? Beloved brother, behold your divine, invincible weapon! The Cross of Christ! Preach Christ, and Christ only!"[27] Jesus must be the nonnegotiable centerpiece of all preaching.

The Impetus for Christ-Centered Preaching. Winslow's reflection on what Christ-centered preaching meant to the apostle Paul explains why he desired to follow a similar course in his own ministry. He wrote:

---

24. Octavius Winslow, *Eminent Holiness: Essential to an Efficient Ministry* (London: Houlston & Stoneman, 1843), 44–45.

25. Octavius Winslow, *Personal Declension and Revival of Religion in the Soul* (London: John F. Shaw, 1841; repr., Edinburgh: Banner of Truth, 2000), 125.

26. Winslow, *Personal Declension*, 125.

27. Winslow, *Foot of the Cross*, 151.

The cross of Christ was in his view the grand consummation of all preceding dispensations of God to men—it was the meritorious procuring cause of all spiritual blessings to our fallen race—it was the scene of Christ's splendid victories over all His enemies and ours—it was the most powerful incentive to all evangelical holiness—it was the instrument which was to subjugate the world to the supremacy of Jesus—it was the source of all true peace, joy, and hope—it was the tree beneath whose shadow all sin expired, all grace lived—it was the spot at whose foot bloomed the loveliest flowers, sparkled the purest springs, and grew the sweetest fruit that made glad the city of God.[28]

In addition, as with his hermeneutic, Winslow discovered motivation for Christ-centered preaching in the ministry of Jesus Himself. He wrote:

It was one of the grand and peculiar characteristics of our Lord's preaching, that *He Himself was the great theme*. Without entrenching upon His Father's glory, or arrogating to Himself an honor not His own, He could embody in His teachings all the truth of which He himself was the subject. As He came down from heaven to reveal heaven, as He came from the bosom of His Father to unveil that bosom, as He was one with the Father, it was impossible that He could faithfully and fully proclaim His gospel unless He Himself were its one grand and holy theme.[29]

Winslow emulated the pattern of Paul and Jesus by keeping Christ as the centerpiece of his sermons.

The Content of Christ-Centered Preaching. Many people assume preaching Christ simply means mentioning Jesus in the sermon or merely preaching Christ's work on the cross in order to invite people to salvation. This was not the case for Winslow. His understanding of Christ-centered preaching accords with that of contemporary scholar Sidney Greidanus, who defines it as "preaching sermons which authentically integrate the message of the text with the climax of God's revelation in the person, work, and/or teaching of Jesus Christ as revealed in the New Testament."[30] Like Greidanus, Winslow believed preaching Christ meant preaching Him in a comprehensive manner.

---

28. Winslow, *Foot of the Cross*, 121–22.

29. Octavius Winslow, *The Man of God, or, Spiritual Religion Explained and Enforced* (London: John F. Shaw, 1865), 47.

30. Sidney Greidanus, *Preaching Christ from the Old Testament: A Contemporary Hermeneutical Method* (Grand Rapids: Eerdmans, 1999), 10.

In a sermon arguing for home missions, Winslow delineated four distinct qualities of Christ-centered preaching.[31] First and foremost, preaching Christ means proclaiming His deity. If this fundamental doctrine is lost, then the whole of Christian faith goes with it. He proclaimed, "Lower the dignity of Christ's person, and you reduce the Gospel system to a mere nihility."[32] Second, preaching Christ involves presenting Him in the greatness of His work. This includes preaching both His active obedience, which is imputed to those who believe, and His atoning death on the cross. Third, Christ must be preached gratuitously. Winslow declared, "There can be no true and lucid exhibition of the Gospel, unaccompanied with a distinct and emphatic statement of the *freeness* of its bestowment.... Affix to it a *price* to be paid, and trammel it with *conditions* to be performed by the sinner, and you obscure its beauty, neutralize its power, and consign the spiritual bankrupt over to the blackness of darkness of despair."[33] Finally, preaching Christ must be attended by the supernatural work of the Holy Spirit. Without His regenerating and sanctifying influences, all is in vain. Though not an exhaustive list, these features explain much of what it means to preach Christ crucified.

Lest it be thought Winslow only articulated his view of preaching Christ crucified in the missionary context, he also expounded what it means to preach Christ in a chapter titled "I Am Jesus."[34] In a similar manner, he highlighted the deity of Christ and His work on the cross as foundational components. However, on this occasion he added other characteristics including preaching Christ in His fullness, His compassion, and His second coming.[35] It is important to note that in both cases he makes a strong connection between the deity of Christ and His atoning sacrifice. He asserted:

> I marvel not that men who deny the Godhead of Christ deny also the sacrifice of Christ; the one stands or falls with the other. If my Savior be but a mere creature; if He be but a man like myself; if He be not everlastingly and essentially God; then I can have no confidence in His death. The saving efficacy of the death of Christ—the obedience of Christ—the sacrifice of Christ—the blood of Christ—the power of Christ to save— all springs from the Godhead of Christ.[36]

---

31. The following information is taken from Winslow, *Christ, The Theme*, 37–59.
32. Winslow, *Christ, The Theme*, 39.
33. Winslow, *Christ, The Theme*, 56.
34. See Winslow, *Tree of Life*, 115–27e.
35. Winslow, *Tree of Life*, 121–27e.
36. Winslow, *Tree of Life*, 122e.

These two examples help provide insight into the Christological content of his preaching. No matter what topic or text he preached, he did more than simply mention Jesus at the end of the sermon.

Winslow's Christ-Centered Preaching in Practice
If Winslow employed a Christ-centered hermeneutic as the means to his Christ-centered preaching, the question remains: What did this look like in practice? In reading Winslow, for the most part, it does not seem that he tried to find Christ under every "proverbial rock" or in every phrase of the Old Testament. Rather, he worked out his hermeneutic in several different ways. In order to understand his approach, an evaluation of four sermons will be offered, three from the Old Testament and one from the New Testament.[37]

This analysis of his sermons utilizes terminology from Greidanus's method for christocentric preaching. He identifies seven "ways of preaching Christ" from the Old Testament: redemptive-historical progression, promise-fulfillment, typology, analogy, longitudinal themes, New Testament references, and contrast.[38] While Greidanus's method supplies a framework for moving from the Old Testament to the New Testament exegetically, I will also provide examples demonstrating how Winslow also preached Christ when applying the text.

Ways of Preaching Christ: "A Full Christ for Empty Sinners"—Genesis 42:25.
The first sermon comes from Genesis 42:25, titled, "A Full Christ for Empty Sinners."[39] It records the story of Joseph sending his brothers back to Canaan with provisions for their journey. The narrative reads, "Then Joseph commanded to fill their sacks with corn, and to restore every man's money into his sack, and to give them provision for the way: and thus did he unto them." There are at least two ways Winslow preached Christ in this sermon in order to expound the narrative's "great gospel truths."[40] With the first point of his sermon, Winslow utilized the way of analogy. He did so by noting the parallel between how God worked through Joseph as a brother and how Christ is the brother of all who believe in Him. Winslow instructed, "Keep in view the fact, that Christ is our

---

37. These were selected as representative from an analysis of more than seventy-five sermons.

38. Greidanus, *Preaching Christ*, 234–77. Greidanus believes good christocentric interpretation and preaching will first understand the passage in its own historical context before understanding it in its canonical and redemptive historical contexts (227–34).

39. Winslow, *Patriarchal Shadows*, 47–65.

40. Winslow, *Patriarchal Shadows*, 48.

brother, that as our Brother He is at the head, yes, that He is *the Head,* of all spiritual blessings, and you will be provided with a key to the gospel interpretation of this part of the story, so striking and instructive in its teaching."[41] However, this was not the primary way he preached Christ in this sermon.

Winslow primarily utilized the way of typology. Contemporary scholar Jim Hamiliton defines typological interpretation as "canonical exegesis that observes divinely intended patterns of historical correspondence and escalation in significance in the events, people, or institutions of Israel, and these types are in the redemptive historical stream that flows through the Bible."[42] In this vein, Winslow called Jesus our "true Joseph," "our spiritual Joseph," and "our gospel Joseph."[43] When considering his conclusions, it is important to realize he viewed Joseph as a type of Christ at nearly every turn.[44] One of the most prominent ways he presented Joseph as a type of Christ was with respect to the forgiveness and provision he extended toward his brothers.[45]

---

41. Winslow, *Patriarchal Shadows,* 48 (emphasis original). Though Winslow may have viewed this as a legitimate type, it seems that the way of analogy would be more fitting when considering Greidanus's method, though it is difficult to draw a sharp distinction. The way of analogy finds "parallel situations" between the Old Testament and New Testament. Here, in the brother analogy, there is a parallel "between what God is and does for Israel and what God *in Christ* is and does for the church." Greidanus, *Preaching Christ,* 263–64.

42. James Hamilton offers this definition of typological interpretation: "Typological interpretation is canonical exegesis that observes divinely intended patterns of historical correspondence and escalation in significance in the events, people, or institutions of Israel, and these types are in the redemptive historical stream that flows through the Bible." James M. Hamilton, "Was Joseph a Type of the Messiah? Tracing the Typological Identification between Joseph, David, and Jesus," *The Southern Baptist Journal of Theology* 12, no. 4 (Winter 2008): 53.

43. In this series, he referred to Joseph as "our true Joseph" seventeen times, "our spiritual Joseph" five times, and "our gospel Joseph" once. This was not an uncommon practice for Winslow. In his preaching and writings he called Jesus the true Aaron, the true Levi, the true Joshua, the true David, our spiritual Jonah, one greater than the prophet Isaiah, the true bread, and the true tabernacle.

44. At the beginning of the series Winslow explained, "Committing ourselves to the teaching of God's Word, we are about to search for Christ among patriarchal shadows. Joseph, by general agreement, and fitted to be in the most essential incidents of his history, is a personal and remarkable type of the Lord Jesus Christ. It is true we have no express declaration of this in Scripture; nevertheless, if the history of Joseph, as recorded by Moses in Genesis, be compared with the history of the Lord Jesus Christ, as recorded by the evangelists in the gospels, the analogy will be found complete. Indeed, it would seem impossible to take the most cursory survey of his eventful and chequered life, and not see *the Lord Jesus foreshadowed in each circumstance as it passes in review before the spiritual and reflective mind." Patriarchal Shadows,* 4, emphasis added.

45. Winslow viewed Joseph's brothers as a type of the church. For example, just as the brothers came to Joseph in desperate need and empty handed, so the church must

In reflecting on how Joseph blessed his brothers even though they sold him into slavery, Winslow announced, "These brethren had injured him. Yet he forgives all, forgets all, and returns them a blessing for their wrong. Now that they are in distress and need, the ocean of his love rolls over all the past, and hides and obliterates it forever. What a type of Jesus! Though we have sinned against Him, crucified Him, wronged Him a thousand times over, yet He loves us still."[46] Although some would debate this interpretation, it seems to stay within the flow of redemptive history.[47]

Though Winslow utilized typological interpretation in a faithful manner at times, there were also instances when he stretched the text's meaning by engaging in what Greidanus calls "typologizing."[48] For example, when he explained Joseph filling his brothers' empty sacks with corn, Winslow saw an illustration of the fullness of Christ.[49] More specifically, he focused on Christ as the church's Mediator:

> Behold, then, our true Joseph! It was the good pleasure, the sovereign will, the gracious purpose of the Father, that all the treasures of His love, all the riches of His grace, all the fullness of the covenant should be placed in the hands of Christ, to be dispensed by Him according to the collective and individual necessities of His Church.

---

approach Christ in the same way to experience His full provision. See *Patriarchal Shadows*, 48–54.

46. Winslow, *Patriarchal Shadows*, 63.

47. It appears Dennis Johnson would approve of such interpretation because the suffering of Joseph and the rescue that comes from his hand stays within the "broad outline" of redemptive history as fulfilled in Christ. He writes, "In fact, we do have warrant for seeing Joseph's ordeal and its beneficial outcome, at least in broad outline, as foreshadowing the suffering of Jesus and the rescue that flows from it. Joseph is a key figure in the covenantal history traced by Stephen in Acts 7. First in Joseph, then in Moses, then in the prophets generally, and finally, climactically, in the Righteous One himself, a repeated pattern appears: Although God's people consistently reject the leaders and spokesmen sent by God, he patiently preserves their lives through the very deliverers whom they have spurned. Without invoking *typos* terminology, Stephen traced a pattern (*typos*) embedded in redemptive history, which had reached its climactic expression in the eschatological appearance of the Righteous Servant, Jesus." *Him We Proclaim: Preaching Christ from All the Scriptures* (Phillipsburg, N.J.: P&R, 2007), 215. For another treatment favoring Winslow's approach, see Hamilton, "Was Joseph a Type," 52–77. One highly respected Old Testament scholar who remains skeptical of this type of Christ-centered interpretation is Walt Kaiser. For a short discussion of some of his concerns, see Walter Kaiser Jr., *The Majesty of God in the Old Testament: A Guide for Preaching and Teaching* (Grand Rapids: Baker, 2007), 15–19.

48. Greidanus believes expositors "typologize" by "overextending the use of typology by searching for types in rather incidental details in the text." *Preaching Christ*, 97.

49. Winslow, *Patriarchal Shadows*, 55.

And in what does this fullness consist? A fullness of dignity to atone, a fullness of life to quicken, a fullness of righteousness to justify, a fullness of virtue to pardon, a fullness of grace to sanctify, a fullness of power to preserve, a fullness of compassion and sympathy to comfort, and a fullness of salvation to save poor sinners to the uttermost; in a word, all fullness; a fullness commensurate with need of every kind, with trial of every form, with sorrow of every depth, with sin of every name, with guilt of every hue, yes, with every conceivable and possible necessity in which the children of God may be placed; fullness of grace here, and fullness of glory hereafter; a fullness which the Church on earth will live upon; and boast of until time be no more; a fullness which will be the delight and glory of the Church in heaven to behold, until eternity shall end. In whom could all this fullness be enthroned? In a mere creature? Preposterous thought![50]

Though his Christology was sound, Winslow pressed the details of the narrative and went beyond the bounds of what most would consider careful and accurate typological interpretation. This tendency surfaces in other sermons in his Joseph series. For example, he interpreted Joseph's statement in Genesis 45:13, "And ye shall tell my father of all my glory in Egypt," as shadowing forth Christ's glory in heaven. Interestingly, one contemporary reviewer questioned some of Winslow's interpretative decisions.[51]

Winslow's Christ-centered preaching provided the dominant note during his series of fifteen sermons through the Joseph narrative. He referred to Jesus and the gospel in these sermons more than five hundred times.[52] Winslow also consistently referred to the narrative's "gospel interpretation" and "gospel teaching."[53] Again, though Winslow's expositions through Genesis were not limited to preaching Christ by way of typology, it was the dominant method.

Ways of Preaching Christ: "Contrition and Confession"—Psalm 130:3. We can also see Winslow's Christ-centered methodology in his treatment of Psalm 130:3 ("If thou, LORD, shouldest mark iniquities, O Lord, who shall

---

50. Winslow, *Patriarchal Shadows*, 56–57.

51. This reviewer wrote, "The author considers Joseph as a remarkable type of Christ, and runs an interesting, and in some points we think a somewhat fanciful, parallel between them." "Criticism on Books: Practical Religion," in *The American Presbyterian and Theological Review*, ed. Henry B. Smith and J. M. Sherwood 1 (July 1863): 518.

52. This number was gathered through utilizing a searchable PDF file of this work which can be accessed online: http://grace-ebooks.com/library/Octavius%20Winslow/OW_The%20Fullness%20of%20 Christ.pdf.

53. For examples, see *Patriarchal Shadows*, 48, 179.

stand?"), which reveals other ways he preached Christ from all of Scripture. The title of his sermon was "Contrition and Confession," and his aim was to unpack "the holiness of God, and the contrition and confession of the believer."[54] Winslow demonstrated five ways to preach Christ from this text.

The first way Winslow preached Christ was by utilizing a longitudinal theme. Longitudinal themes trace the development of motifs that ultimately culminate in Christ. This is similar to the redemptive-historical way, which undergirds the six other ways and identifies how the storyline from creation to new creation centers in Christ. In this sermon, Winslow explicitly tied the doctrine of God's holiness to the work of Christ, declaring that the most significant demonstration of God's holiness is seen in the substitutionary death of Christ on the cross. He then went on to explain how either the sinner or the substitute must absorb the wrath of God.[55]

A second way could be termed the way of application. As he exhorted his hearers to practice confession and repentance, he told them these actions should be accomplished through Jesus. He declared:

> You have nothing to do with your sins—past, present, or to come—but to mortify the root, to combat vigorously their ascendancy, and to wash constantly in the divine laver of Christ's atoning blood, confessing daily and hourly sins, with the hand of faith laid upon the head of the sacrificial Lamb thus walking before God with a quickened, tender, purified conscience, desiring in all things to please him.[56]

Winslow often proclaimed Christ by applying the truth of the text in light of Christ's person and work.

The third way Winslow preached Christ was by focusing on the teaching of the Savior through the way of New Testament reference. In expounding what it means to live with a contrite heart, he appealed to the words of Jesus in the Sermon on the Mount: "Blessed are they that mourn" (Matt. 5:4).

As a fourth way, Winslow again made a typological reference by appealing to the priestly ministry of Aaron. He declared that Jesus is "our true Aaron" who "made a full atonement for the 'iniquity of our holy things.'"[57]

Finally, Winslow concluded the sermon by pointing to Christ as the solution of the text, because it is only through "the Great Sin-Bearer" that man

---

54. Winslow, *Soul-Depths*, 32.
55. Winslow, *Soul-Depths*, 35–36.
56. Winslow, *Soul-Depths*, 37–38.
57. Winslow, *Soul-Depths*, 44.

is able to stand before a holy God.[58] This is what Greidanus calls the way of contrast.[59] This sermon provides a great example of the diverse ways Winslow proclaimed Christ to his hearers.

Ways of Preaching Christ: "Broken Cisterns"—Jeremiah 2:13. During a visit to Scotland, Winslow preached a sermon titled "Broken Cisterns."[60] This sermon expounded the doctrine found in Jeremiah 2:13: "My people have committed two evils; they have forsaken me the fountain of living waters, and hewed them out cisterns, broken cisterns, that can hold no water." In addition, this sermon also displayed a few different ways of preaching Christ.

The first time he expounded Christ from this text, Winslow combined the techniques of longitudinal theme and New Testament reference. After explaining how the Father is an infinite fountain of life, Winslow declared, "The same figure will apply to the Lord Jesus Christ. It is a most expressive one. He thus appropriates it to himself—'Jesus stood and cried, saying, "If any man thirst, let him come unto me and drink"' [John 7:37]. And in another place he describes the water which he gives, as 'living water'" [John 4:10].[61] Thus, Winslow explained how this Old Testament truth is displayed in Jesus as evidenced in the New Testament.

Winslow also preached about the broken cistern of self-righteousness. After arguing that the works of the law are a cistern that will never satisfy, he employed the method of contrast by pointing to Jesus as the fulfillment of the law. He explained, "The law is a 'broken cistern;' it holds no sweet waters of salvation, it gives out no streams of peace. But the Lord Jesus is the living fountain. He is the 'end of the law for righteousness to every one that believeth.'"[62] In this example, he again employed the use of New Testament reference to point to Christ.

Finally, in his closing exhortations, Winslow again demonstrated how Jesus is the applicational solution for the passage through the method of contrast. He exhorted: "Turn every loss of creature-good into an occasion of greater nearness to Christ. The dearest and loveliest creature is but a cistern—an inferior and contracted good. If it contains any sweetness, the Lord

---

58. Winslow, *Soul-Depths*, 44.
59. This way sometimes "begins with the problems encountered in the Old Testament and leads to the solution in Jesus Christ." Greidanus, *Preaching Christ*, 272.
60. Winslow, *Glimpses of the Truth*, 156–85.
61. Winslow, *Glimpses of the Truth*, 159–60.
62. Winslow, *Glimpses of the Truth*, 161.

put it there.... Jesus loves you far too much to allow another, however dear, to eclipse and rival him."[63] In preaching from the Old Testament, Winslow utilized various tools to point to and preach about the person and work of Jesus. This was true for his preaching from New Testament texts as well.

Ways of Preaching Christ: "Saved By Hope"—Romans 8:24–25. The final sermon demonstrating Winslow's Christ-centered methodology is based on Romans 8:24–25.[64] This passage reads, "For we are saved by hope: but hope that is seen is not hope: for what a man seeth, why doth he yet hope for? But if we hope for that we see not, then do we with patience wait for it." This exposition demonstrates two ways of preaching Christ from a New Testament text.

The first way Winslow preached Christ could be called the doctrinal way. He explained how believers are "saved by hope" in that they are saved into a renewed condition of hope. He then taught that the instrument of the believer's salvation is faith, and that faith must constantly look to Christ. He declared, "We cannot keep our eye too exclusively or too intently fixed on Jesus. All salvation is in Him, all salvation proceeds from Him, all salvation leads to Him, and for the assurance and comfort of our salvation we are to repose believingly and entirely on Him. Christ must be all: Christ the beginning, Christ the center, and Christ the end."[65] Here he expounded the doctrinal content of the passage as it relates to Christ.

He also preached Christ as the object of the believer's hope.[66] In this way, Winslow moved from doctrinal explanation to practical application. With his typical exhortative and eschatological style, Winslow preached:

> For the consummation of this hope, then, let us diligently labor, meekly suffer, and patiently wait. Living beneath the cross, looking unto Jesus, toiling for Jesus, testifying for Jesus, and cultivating conformity to Jesus, let us "be always ready to give a reason of the hope that is in us"; and be always ready to enter into the joy and fruition of that hope, the substance and security of which is—"Christ in you the hope of glory."[67]

As he exhorted his hearers, he instructed them to pursue Christ as the means of exercising hope that would produce a faithful witness and enable them to

---

63. Winslow, *Glimpses of the Truth*, 180–81.

64. This sermon was chosen for analysis because it does not specifically refer to Christ in the text unlike many sermons from Romans 8.

65. Winslow, *No Condemnation*, 236.

66. Winslow, *No Condemnation*, 238.

67. Winslow, *No Condemnation*, 241.

enter the joy of His presence. Preaching Christ as the doctrinal content and practical application of the text serves as a foundational model for preaching Christ-centered sermons. Such preaching keeps the gospel central and honors the apostolic pattern of christocentric preaching.

In considering Winslow's convictions concerning Christ-centered preaching, it is fair to question whether there are potential dangers. Even orthodox believers can become modalists in practice, via their worship and preaching.[68] Was this the case with Winslow? Did his Christ-centered approach push his doctrine of the Trinity to the periphery? The following section will argue that Winslow's Christ-centered preaching was motivated by his Trinitarian theology.

Winslow's Trinitarian Motivation for Christ-Centered Preaching

One might assume a preacher who emphasizes Jesus' life and ministry would possibly neglect or demote the Father and the Spirit. Concerning Winslow's ministry, such an assumption would be false. Winslow called the doctrine of the Trinity "a doctrine upon which the entire superstructure of Christianity rests."[69] An assessment of Winslow's Trinitarian theology reveals that his Christ-centered preaching was indeed rooted in an orthodox understanding of the triune God. In other words, his Trinitarian theology both informed and motivated his Christ-centered preaching. This is perhaps most clearly seen in his view of the ordering of the Godhead and their roles in redemptive history.[70]

According to Winslow, Scripture unfolds a particular order within the Godhead as displayed in redemptive history. The Father, Son, and Spirit relate to one another in a particular way as they bring saving grace to fallen man. Winslow explained, "If it is the office of Jesus to lead us to the Father,

---

68. Wayne Grudem has supplied a good definition of modalism. Modalists believe "God is not really three distinct persons, but only one person who appears to people in different 'modes' at different times." *Systematic Theology* (Grand Rapids: Zondervan, 1994), 242.

69. Octavius Winslow, *Our God* (London: John F. Shaw, 1870; repr., Grand Rapids: Reformation Heritage Books, 2007), 72.

70. Ordering refers to the way the persons of the Godhead relate to one another. It highlights the distinction of roles while preserving their equality of essence. Grudem is helpful when he writes, "When Scripture discusses the way in which God relates to the world, both in creation and in redemption, the persons of the Trinity are said to have different functions or primary activities. Sometimes this has been called the 'economy of the Trinity,' using *economy* in an old sense meaning 'ordering of activities.'... The 'economy of the Trinity' means the different ways the three persons act as they relate to the world and to each other for all eternity." *Systematic Theology*, 248–49.

it is equally the office of the Spirit to lead us to Jesus. We only spiritually and savingly know the Father through the Son, and the Son by the Spirit."[71] This conviction was central to his Trinitarian theology. He believed such a view of the Godhead in the economy of salvation was indispensable. This is why he said, "And thus we learn the existence and necessity of the Trinity in the economy of grace. No system of theology is complete, and no hope of salvation is sure, that excludes this essential doctrine of the Christian faith."[72] Thus, he argued that God's salvific work, which culminates in Christ, has an inherently Trinitarian shape. Winslow's theology of the Trinity viewed Jesus as the hinge on which the revelation of the triune God turns.[73]

Jesus Reveals the Father

Because Jesus is the means by which we understand the person of God the Father, Winslow maintained that preaching should center in Him. Winslow's simple argument was if you want to know God the Father, look at Jesus the Son.[74] As Emmanuel, God with us, Jesus brings God near. He wrote, "Come to Jesus, look at Jesus, listen to Jesus, and realize that in so doing you approach to, gaze upon, and hear the voice of, God your Father in heaven."[75] He placed a tremendous emphasis on Christ's role of revealing the Father. He declared, "Jesus came into this world as much to reveal God as to save man."[76]

Winslow set the Son's mission of revealing the Father in its cosmic scope.[77] He held that God created man to enjoy unending, unhindered fellowship in His glorious presence, but tragically, because of the fall, man could no longer behold the glory and character of God. The heart of God was veiled to humanity, and man could not know God or save himself through his own effort. Thus, Deity had to reveal Himself. This happened in the incarnation

---

71. Winslow, *Our God*, 143.

72. Winslow, *Our God*, 143–44.

73. This is not to say that God did not reveal Himself prior to the incarnation of Christ. It simply affirms that Jesus is the centerpiece of God's redemptive plan.

74. In the language of John 1:18, Jesus explained the Father to the world. The Greek word is ἐξηγήσατο, which means "to set forth in great detail, expound." William Arndt, Frederick Danker, and Walter Bauer, *A Greek-English Lexicon of the New Testament and Other Early Christian Literature*, 3rd ed., s.v. "ἐξηγέομαι" (Chicago: University of Chicago Press, 2001), 349.

75. Octavius Winslow, *Words of Divine Comfort* (London: John F. Shaw, 1872), 8th Day.

76. Octavius Winslow, *The Ministry of Home, or, Brief Expository Lectures on Divine Truth* (London: William Hunt and Co., 1868), 38.

77. In reading Winslow's sermons, it is encouraging to find that he often explained the doctrine under consideration in its canonical context. By doing so, he allowed biblical theology to inform his preaching.

of Christ.[78] Winslow explained, "The great object of Christ's mission to our world was to make God known to man in all the glory of His being and harmony of His perfection."[79] From His incarnation until His ascension, Jesus revealed the glory of the Father in every step. Regarding the life of the Son, Winslow wrote, "Therein we trace the love, the grace, the glory of our Heavenly Father, and can read in a new light, and interpret with increased meaning and brightness, our Lord's own precious words, 'He that has seen Me has seen the Father.'"[80]

According to Winslow, Jesus was equipped to reveal the Father because they were completely united in essence and purpose. Winslow proclaimed the divine nature of Christ from his understanding of John 10:30:

> This doctrine then, we unhesitatingly declare. Christ in his absolute Deity, we fearlessly preach. We proclaim it as Jesus himself proclaimed it. Touching his union with the Father, we can admit not the slightest inferiority. "I and the Father are one." As a delegated God, we repel the absurdity—as a created Saviour, we heed not the dream. He is God absolute, or an impostor—He is Divine, supremely, or Christianity is a fable—He is Deity itself, or we are lost![81]

To separate Christ from the essence of the Godhead would be tantamount to destroying the Godhead and denying the divinity of both the Father and the Son.[82] Not only do the Father and the Son share the same nature, they also share a common purpose: they work together for man's redemption. He preached, "There was a perfect concurrence of the Father's will, and mind, and heart, with the work, abasement, and glory of Jesus. It was by the determinate counsel and foreknowledge of the Father that Jesus was delivered unto death."[83] In all Christ accomplished through His birth, life, death, resurrection, and ascension, He worked in perfect harmony with the Father.

Consequently, Winslow's understanding of the mutual relations of the Godhead led to equally high views of the Father and the Son. He understood it was never the purpose of the Son to steal glory from the Father. On the contrary:

---

78. See Octavius Winslow, *Divine Realities, or, Spiritual Reflections for the Saint and Sinner* (London: John F. Shaw, 1860), 70–71.

79. Winslow, *Emmanuel, or Titles of Christ*, 9e.

80. Winslow, *Patriarchal Shadows*, 147.

81. Winslow, *Christ, The Theme*, 44–45.

82. Winslow, *Sympathy of Christ*, 131.

83. Winslow, *Patriarchal Shadows*, 146.

In seeking the glory of God supremely, our Lord pleased not Himself. If ever there was the single eye, it beamed in Christ. He had no separate kingdom, swayed no rival scepter, wore no divided crown separate from His Father. All that He embarked in, did, and taught converged to one common center, pointed to one single aim, terminated in one great end—the glory of God![84]

Winslow knew many in his day harbored "hard thoughts" toward the Father.[85] They believed the finished work of Christ on the cross *procured* the love of the Father rather than *revealed* it. Thus, the magnificence of God's saving work was limited to the Son and divorced from the Father. This misinterpretation upset Winslow, because he was "jealous for the Father's glory."[86] He expounded:

> So wont are we to fix our admiring and adoring gaze upon the incarnate Son—so wont to entwine our exclusive affection around him who for us "loved not his life unto the death," as to come short of the stupendous and animating truth, that all the love, grace, and wisdom which appear so conspicuous and so resplendent in salvation, have their fountainhead in the heart of God the Father![87]

For all of his Christ-centeredness, Winslow never demoted the Father in his preaching.[88] Man's worship belongs to the Father and the Son.[89]

The Spirit Reveals the Son

Winslow's Trinitarian doctrine was not limited to the relationship between the Father and the Son. He was equally concerned about the person and work of the Holy Spirit.[90] Winslow wholeheartedly affirmed the deity of the

---

84. Winslow, *Sympathy of Christ*, 374. He went on to add, "His whole soul was swallowed up in God. 'I seek not my own glory,' was a declaration of unselfishness which found a living expression in every action of His life" (375).

85. Winslow, *Glimpses of the Truth*, 156.

86. Winslow, *Glimpses of the Truth*, 157.

87. Winslow, *Glimpses of the Truth*, 156.

88. In a sermon preached from Genesis 45, Winslow declared, "The exalted and endeared views you have of Jesus should be associated with like views of God; every high conception you have of the love and glory of the Son, ought equally to be a high conception of the love and glory of the Father." *Patriarchal Shadows*, 146–47.

89. For more on the relationship between the Father and the Son, see Octavius Winslow, *The Lord's Prayer: Its Spirit and Its Teaching* (London: John F. Shaw, 1866; repr., Stroke-on-Trent, U.K.: Tentmaker Publications, 2003), 13–25.

90. Significantly, one of his first publications was a work on the Holy Spirit. See Octavius Winslow, *The Inquirer Directed to an Experimental and Practical View of the Holy Spirit*

Spirit along with the dignity and worship that belonged to Him as an equal member of the Godhead.[91] According to Winslow, the Holy Spirit, like Jesus, possesses a specific role when it comes to the work of God in redemptive history. He explained, "If, as we have endeavored to show, we only really see God's light as it is revealed in Christ, it follows as a truth equally conclusive, that we only truly know Christ as He is made known to us by the Spirit."[92] For this reason also, preaching must center in Jesus because He is the one whom the Spirit reveals and glorifies.

The primary role of the Spirit is to highlight the person and work of the Son. In many respects, the Spirit takes on a modest ministry. He is modest in that He points to and reveals Jesus rather than promotes His own dignity and worth.[93] Contemporary theologian Graham Cole captures this when he writes, "The magnificence of the Spirit lies in [His] self-effacement or divine selflessness. For this reason believers are rightly called 'Christians' not 'Pneumians.'"[94] This understanding reflects why Winslow said, "It is especially the office of the Spirit to make us acquainted with the Lord Jesus. *"He shall testify of me,"* is the gracious promise of the Saviour. All that we truly, spiritually, and savingly know of the Lord Jesus is the result of the Holy Spirit's teaching."[95] In sum, he believed that "the great work of the Spirit is to glorify Christ."[96]

The Spirit's work of testifying to Christ is especially observed in His applying the work of salvation to sinners. The Spirit was sent to lead men to Christ.[97] Winslow said of this, "The Spirit of Christ is essentially a missionary Spirit."[98] He expounded the essential work of the Spirit as follows:

(London: John F. Shaw, 1840; repr., *The Work of the Holy Spirit: An Experimental and Practical View* [Edinburgh: Banner of Truth, 2003]).

91. Winslow argued for the deity of the Spirit by appealing to His names, attributes, and works. *Work of the Holy Spirit*, 11–30.

92. Winslow, *Our God*, 143.

93. Winslow, *Patriarchal Shadows*, 34–35.

94. Graham Cole, *He Who Gives Life: The Doctrine of the Holy Spirit* (Wheaton, Ill.: Crossway, 2007), 284. J. I. Packer agrees: "The New Testament writers...saw the Spirit's post-Pentecostal task as essentially that of mediating the presence, word, and activity of the enthroned Christ. It is by grasping this basic New Testament perspective that we get the Spirit in focus." *Keep in Step with the Spirit: Finding Fullness in Our Walk with God*, rev. ed. (Grand Rapids: Baker, 2005), 45.

95. Winslow, *"Is the Spirit,"* 20–21.

96. Winslow, *Glory of the Redeemer*, 338.

97. Winslow, *No Condemnation*, 117–18.

98. Winslow, *No Condemnation*, 120.

As far as the work of our dear Lord becomes available in the personal salvation of the believer, it depends solely upon the life-giving influence of God the Holy Spirit. Complete as is the righteousness, efficacious as is the blood, and all-sufficient as is the grace of Christ, yet apart from the especial, effectual, and Divine operation of the Spirit upon the heart, they would remain to us as a robe unworn, a fulness untouched, a "fountain sealed." Thus, there is a beautiful relation, a sweet harmony, between the atoning work of Jesus and the official work of the Holy Spirit—"He will glorify me."[99]

In affirming the close relationship between the Spirit and the Son in the work of redemption, Winslow was careful to observe distinctions as well in the economy of grace. Jesus provided the perfect sacrifice through His sinless obedience, thus atoning for man's sin and satisfying divine justice on the cross. The Spirit reveals and applies that finished work. To confuse the two would dishonor both the Son and the Spirit.[100]

Another important component in Winslow's Christ-centered preaching involves the Spirit's work of illumination when people encounter the Scriptures. Many times, during the introduction to his sermon, Winslow prayed for such illumination. For example, "Oh, may the Holy Spirit be our teacher and revealer, opening to our understandings and applying to our hearts these scriptures of truth that so manifestly and decidedly testify of Jesus!"[101] He prayed for this illumination because he believed that

it is the office of the blessed and eternal Spirit to unfold, and so to glorify, Jesus in the Word. All that we spiritually and savingly learn respecting Him, through this revealed medium, is by the sole teaching of the Holy Spirit, opening up this word to the mind. He shows how all the luminous lines of Scripture truth emanate from, return to, and center in, Christ—how all the doctrines set forth the glory of His person, how all the promises are written in His heart's blood, and how all the precepts are embodied in His life.[102]

---

99. Winslow, *Glory of the Redeemer*, 339.

100. Winslow explained the distinction in their work, writing, "The work of the Spirit is, not to atone, but to reveal the atonement; not to obey, but to make known the obedience; not to pardon and justify, but to bring the convinced, awakened, penitent soul to receive the pardon and embrace the justification already provided in the work of Jesus. Now, if there is any substitution of the Spirit's work for Christ's work,—any undue, unauthorized leaning upon the work within, instead of the work without, the believer, there is a dishonor done to Christ, and a consequent grieving of the Holy Spirit of God." *Personal Declension*, 136–37.

101. Winslow, *Patriarchal Shadows*, 28.

102. Winslow, *Glory of the Redeemer*, 341–42.

Winslow depended on the work of the Holy Spirit to reveal and apply the saving work of Christ. In a reciprocal manner, he possessed confidence the Spirit would honor his ministry as he preached Christ and Him crucified.

The Triune Work of Redemption

Not only did Winslow see a distinct, Christ-centered order within the Godhead regarding the work of redemption, he also proclaimed their unified work. He viewed Christ's work on the cross as a means of studying the "grand manifestation of the Three people in the Godhead."[103] Winslow held that the triune God appears most glorious and "like Himself" in the light of salvation.[104] He proclaimed, "The *Father's* love appears in sending his Son— the *Son's* love in undertaking the work—the *Holy Spirit's* love in applying the work. Oh, it is delightful to see how, in working out the mighty problem of man's redemption, the Divine Three were thus deeply engaged!"[105] He continued, "With which of these could we have dispensed? All were needed—and had one been lacking, our salvation had been incomplete, and we had been eternally lost."[106] Thus, Winslow emphasized the absolute necessity of all three members working together in salvation.

According to Winslow, there was not the slightest step in the grand plan of redemption that did not involve the work of all three persons. Christ's work on the cross "fulfilled the eternal purpose and counsel of the Triune Jehovah."[107] Added to that, the triune God will bring the believer securely to a glorious eternity. He explained, "In bringing to glory the Church they thus have saved, the sacred Three are solemnly pledged."[108] From beginning to end, the triune God works in complete harmony to bring about man's salvation.

He also believed this doctrine was intensely practical. He aimed at an "experimental acquaintance" with the doctrine in hopes it would produce holy living.[109] In light of what God has accomplished for man, he concluded man's deepest devotion should be given back to God. He wrote:

> And how animating and sanctifying is the thought that, when thus dedicating ourselves to the Triune God, rendering to each divine person the

---

103. Winslow, *Foot of the Cross*, 124.
104. Winslow, *Glimpses of the Truth*, 75.
105. Winslow, *Glimpses of the Truth*, 75.
106. Winslow, *Glimpses of the Truth*, 75.
107. Winslow, *Glory of the Redeemer*, 143.
108. Winslow, *Glimpses of the Truth*, 75.
109. Winslow, *Our God*, 111.

most unquestioning faith, the warmest love, the divinest worship, and
the most dutiful obedience, it is because we recognize three distinct
people in the One Godhead, and look for rich and inestimable blessings
flowing from, the love of God the Father, through the merits of God the
Son, and by the power of God the Holy Spirit.[110]

As Winslow articulated, everything in the believer's life should come under
sway of the triadic pattern: from the Father, through the Son, by the Holy Spirit.

In reflecting on Winslow's Trinitarian understanding of redemptive history it should be concluded that his Trinitarian theology both motivated and
justified his Christ-centered preaching. As he said, "Remember God's order:
Christ leads you to the Father, and the Holy Spirit leads you to Christ."[111]
This understanding does not create any distinction in equality, divinity, or
importance between the Father, Son, and Spirit. It simply highlights how the
triune God has revealed Himself in time and space. This is why Winslow's
preaching centered on the person and work of the Son.

Conclusion

As the above analysis shows, Winslow's Christ-centered hermeneutic clearly
influenced his pulpit ministry. An examination of four representative sermons demonstrated some of the various ways he preached Christ. Further
consideration of his works showed Winslow's Christ-centered preaching was
not divorced from healthy Trinitarian theology. On the contrary, the doctrine of the Trinity provides sufficient motivation and justification for the
task, because redemptive history culminates in Christ and His work on the
cross. The Son reveals the Father. The Spirit reveals the Son. God's order is
centered in Christ. For these reasons, Winslow exhorted his fellow ministers:

> Oh, whatever you do, preach Christ! Preach Him in His Godhead—
> preach Him in His manhood—preach Him as the Revealer of the
> Father—preach Him in His finished work—preach Him in His personal
> beauty—preach Him in His love, grace, and sympathy—preach Him as
> the all in all of the soul bound to His judgment-seat—preach Him scrip-
> turally and intelligently, lovingly and winningly; in the pulpit, out of
> the pulpit, living and dying, oh, raise high the cross of Christ![112]

110. Winslow, *Emmanuel, or Titles of Christ*, 5–6e.
111. Winslow, *Our God*, 144.
112. Winslow, *Foot of the Cross*, 151.

5

PREACHING TO THE HEART

As stated in the introduction, Winslow believed "the religion of the Lord Jesus is valuable only as its power is experienced in the heart."[1] According to Winslow, experimental preaching is preaching to the heart for life transformation. Preachers must address the heart because the heart is where change happens. Jesus explained this in Luke 6:43–45. If the heart is good, a person's life will be fruitful and God-glorifying. Conversely, if the heart is not infused by grace and truth, it will not produce the fruit God desires. As Paul Tripp notes, the role of the heart is of utmost significance: "This is the principle of inescapable influence: Whatever rules the heart will exercise inescapable influence over the person's life and behavior."[2] This understanding drove Winslow to preach to the heart.

Experimental Christianity is truth applied in daily living. Winslow valued it as a necessity: "We must be experimental Christians, if Christians at all. A bare notionalist, a mere theorist, an empty professor of religion, is a fearful deception."[3] He believed anything less than an experimental application of God's Word is sub-Christian. Winslow was also convinced the church in his day lacked a deep spirituality because of a deficient emphasis on experimental Christianity. He argued, "In order then thus to strengthen the tone of spirituality among the churches, experimental and practical

---

1. Octavius Winslow, *The Inquirer Directed to an Experimental and Practical View of the Atonement* (London: John F. Shaw, 1839; repr., *Atonement and the Cross* [Stoke-on-Trent, U.K.: Tentmaker, 2008]), 7. For a more detailed description from Winslow regarding experimental Christianity, see the introduction of this work. Moreover, because of Winslow's intense focus on experimental Christianity, a deeper study of his theology of the Christian life could prove a beneficial topic for future research.

2. Paul Tripp, *Instruments in the Redeemer's Hands: People in Need of Change Helping People in Need of Change* (Phillipsburg, N.J.: P&R, 2002), 68.

3. Octavius Winslow, *The Precious Things of God* (London: James Nisbet, 1860; repr., Ligonier, Pa.: Soli Deo Gloria, 1993), 271.

religion must be more frequently and earnestly insisted upon."[4] He desired to see the church move toward greater maturity, and this is why he employed an experimental methodology.

This chapter begins by examining Winslow's understanding of experimental Christianity and preaching. The goal of experimental preaching will then be assessed by looking at Winslow's doctrine of progressive sanctification and convictions on preaching for holistic change. Finally, material from Winslow's sermons will be presented. In addition to his doctrinal and Christ-centered preaching, six other elements comprised his experimental methodology: application, discrimination, interrogation, illustration, exhortation, and persuasion. These elements enabled him to accomplish his intention of applying doctrine to the hearts of his hearers.

The Theory of Experimental Preaching

According to Winslow, experimental Christianity lies at the heart of Christianity and Christian ministry.[5] He wrote, "The Lord will have His people, and especially the ministers of His gospel, experimentally acquainted with His truth."[6] Notably, Winslow's first two major works addressed experimental Christianity. Both *The Inquirer Directed to an Experimental and Practical View of the Atonement* and *The Inquirer Directed to an Experimental and Practical View of the Holy Spirit* deal with how these great and foundational doctrines touch the everyday life of the believer.[7] Winslow's view of experimental Christianity can be summarized by the following phrases: doctrine to life, experienced power, personal devotion, and authentic living.

---

4. Winslow, *Atonement and the Cross*, 8.

5. Much of this section will unpack Winslow's understanding of experimental Christianity in general. However, his view of experimental Christianity naturally influenced and surfaced in his pulpit ministry. Thus, it is valid to glean insights from his various theological writings in order to ascertain what he meant by experimental Christianity and the implications it holds for his preaching.

6. Octavius Winslow, *Evening Thoughts, or, Daily Walking with God: A Portion for Each Evening in the Year* (London: John F. Shaw, 1859; repr., Grand Rapids: Reformation Heritage Books, 2005), 236.

7. See Octavius Winslow, *The Inquirer Directed to an Experimental and Practical View of the Atonement* (New York: M. W. Dodd, 1838); and Octavius Winslow, *The Inquirer Directed to an Experimental and Practical View of the Holy Spirit* (London: John F. Shaw, 1840; repr., Edinburgh: Banner of Truth, 2003).

Doctrine to Life

Winslow sought to display the relevance of every doctrine he proclaimed.[8] He was not content if his hearers walked away with only a cognitive understanding of the text. Instead, his goal was life transformation. Some preachers focus on doctrine to the neglect of practical application, failing to recognize the inextricable link between God's truth and Christian living. However, experimental preaching applies doctrine to life.[9] This concept is foundational to every other aspect of experimental Christianity and preaching. The following material further emphasizes how experimental preaching for Winslow is grounded in doctrine and centered in Christ.[10]

Grounded in Doctrine. Strong doctrinal preaching and textual exposition are essential to experimental preaching. Winslow believed a proper understanding of Bible doctrine must lead to holy living.[11] He never raised a false dichotomy between the head and the heart and consistently emphasized "the close and important, yet much forgotten connection, which exists between a clear, spiritual perception of God's truth, and a holy, humble, and close walk with God. The two can never be separated."[12] Winslow structured his preaching around the inextricable connection between doctrine and precept. Citing Paul's epistles, he exclaimed, "How significantly and indissolubly interwoven are the doctrines and the precepts of the Bible! Who can study devoutly the Pauline epistles addressed to the Ephesian and Colossian churches, and not be profoundly impressed with this truth?"[13] According to Winslow, you cannot have one without the other.

He also recognized a natural relationship between the doctrines, precepts, and promises of Scripture: "Doctrine is the basis of precept, and

---

8. For example, see Octavius Winslow, *The Glory of the Redeemer,* 8th ed. (London: John F. Shaw, 1865; repr., Pittsburgh: Soli Deo Gloria, 1997). Throughout this work Winslow demonstrates the experimental nature of christological truths such as His deity, eternality, glory, resurrection, and second coming.

9. As noted in the introduction, contemporary homiletician Joel Beeke defines experimental or "experiential" preaching as preaching that "addresses the vital manner of how a Christian experiences the truth of Christian doctrine in his life." "Experiential Preaching," in *Feed My Sheep: A Passionate Plea for Preaching,* 2nd ed. (Lake Mary, Fla.: Reformation Trust, 2008), 53.

10. This section reiterates the material in chapters 3 and 4 while giving greater attention to how doctrinal and Christ-centered preaching must be declared experimentally.

11. For more on Winslow's doctrinal preaching, see chapter 3 of this work.

12. Winslow, *Atonement and the Cross,* 25.

13. Octavius Winslow, *The Nightingale Song of David: A Spiritual and Practical Exposition of the Twenty-Third Psalm* (London: John F. Shaw, 1876), 23–24.

precept is the handmaid of promise. Built up in the divine doctrines, the
believer will study to walk in the holy precepts; and walking in the precept,
he may fully expect a fulfillment of the promise."[14] Believers should love
the precepts of Scripture in order to apply the doctrines and experience the
promises of God.[15]

When believers fail to apply doctrine, this reveals a weak experience of
truth. Winslow explained, "When there is a real experience of the power of
the doctrines, there will be a love of the precept. You will desire to be sanctified, as well as justified—to have your heart purified, and your life molded
by the holiness of the truth."[16] Believers should value carrying out the commands of Scripture as highly as they value knowing the doctrines. Winslow
believed mature Christians understand how doctrine and application work
together. He wrote, "The word reveals God, and an experimental knowledge
of God confirms the truth of the word; the one thus establishing the other."[17]
In a similar manner, one's lack of applying the precepts will have a proportionate effect on his or her ability to understand and feel the importance of
biblical doctrine. Winslow said, "A distant and careless walk not only veils
the mind to the glory of the truth, but hardens the heart to the power of the
truth."[18] Experimental preaching provides the essential link between understanding doctrine and living life to God's glory.

Centered in Christ. Experimental preaching must also be centered in Christ.[19]
Just as Winslow viewed Christ as the hermeneutical center of the Bible, so he
regarded Jesus as the experimental center of the Christian life. Christ should
be the great doctrinal truth preached in every sermon so that believers grow
spiritually. He wrote, "The character and the degree of our spiritual knowledge begins and terminates in our knowledge of Christ. *Christ* is the test of
its reality, the measure of its depth, and the source of its growth."[20] Jesus is
the beginning and end of experienced truth.

---

14. Winslow, *Nightingale Song*, 24.

15. Winslow prayed, "Lord, make me as intensely to love the precepts, as I firmly believe
the doctrines, and earnestly plead the promises of Your word." *Nightingale Song*, 24.

16. Winslow, *Precious Things*, 265–66.

17. Octavius Winslow, *Grace and Truth* (London: John F. Shaw, 1949), 27e.

18. Winslow, *Atonement and the Cross*, 25.

19. For more on Winslow's Christ-centered preaching, see chapter 4 of this work.

20. Octavius Winslow, *Divine Realities, or, Spiritual Reflections for the Saint and Sinner*
(London: John F. Shaw, 1860), 218.

The authenticity and intensity of the believer's walk flow from his relationship with Christ. Winslow believed this reality touched every truth of God's Word:

> The more simply and entirely the believing soul lives on Christ, the more enlarged, experimental, and practical will be his ideas of all truth. The central fact of the Bible is, Christ crucified. From this, as their centre, all the lines of truth diverge, and to this, as by a common attraction, they all again return. To know Christ then—to know Him as dwelling in the heart by His own Spirit—is to have traversed the great circle of spiritual truth.[21]

That is why Winslow stressed the importance of beholding the glory of Christ. He called it "the very soul of experimental Christianity."[22] Winslow also believed only those who belong to God can behold His glory by faith. He explained, "To see the Redeemer's glory, the eye must be spiritual; a spiritual object being only discerned by a spiritual organ."[23] Beholding the glory of Christ gives believers a proper view of God and a proper view of self. They no longer see glory in themselves but delight in adoring thoughts of God. Winslow argued, "If you are advancing in an experimental, sanctifying acquaintance with the Lord Jesus, you are advancing in that knowledge which Paul thus estimates, 'I count all things but loss for the excellency of the knowledge of Christ Jesus my Lord.'"[24] Experimental preaching is nothing less than Christ-centered preaching.

Experienced Power
Another key aspect of experimental Christianity and preaching is experienced power. Echoing 1 John 1:1–3, Winslow said experimental Christians "will not testify of an unknown, unfelt, and inexperienced Savior."[25] He argued that truth must be experienced with power in the soul and that it is often acquired in the school of affliction.

---

21. Winslow, *Evening Thoughts*, 530.
22. Winslow, *Glory of the Redeemer*, 110.
23. Winslow, *Glory of the Redeemer*, 110.
24. Winslow, *Divine Realities*, 218.
25. Winslow, *Evening Thoughts*, 236. 1 John 1:1–3 says, "That which was from the beginning, which we have heard, which we have seen with our eyes, which we have looked upon, and our hands have handled, of the Word of life; (for the life was manifested, and we have seen it, and bear witness, and shew unto you that eternal life, which was with the Father, and was manifested unto us;) that which we have seen and heard declare we unto you, that ye also may have fellowship with us: and truly our fellowship is with the Father, and with his Son Jesus Christ."

Power in the Soul. Winslow taught that it is not enough simply to know God's Word. The experimental believer desires to know "its quickening, sanctifying, comforting power."[26] When truth enters the heart and works effectually from the inside out, the believer can then claim he has truly tasted the religion of Jesus. Winslow powerfully wrote:

> The real value of any truth to a child of God is the *conscious power of that truth in his own soul.* The Bible is designed to be an experimental and a practical book. It deals not in abstract truth, in mere theoretical teaching, but in revelations intended by its Divine Author to address themselves to the judgment, thus finding an inlet to the conscience and the heart, and becoming a leaven of holiness in the soul, diffusing its influence through the entire moral and intellectual man. We repeat the observation, that any one truth is valuable to the Christian in proportion to his personal and experimental acquaintance with its nature and, effects. And here it is impossible to resist the solemn remark—*how far an individual may go in an intellectual subscription to, and a theoretical reception of, vital and essential truth, and yet be utterly ignorant of its renewing and sanctifying power in his soul!* (emphasis added).[27]

A surface knowledge of the Scripture does not produce a powerful life, but when the truth is worked deep into the heart by the Spirit of God, the conscience and heart become engaged and the soul experiences the "conscious power" of God's truth.

When the power of God's truth works in the soul, it produces conformity to the divine image. This is why Winslow said, "There cannot possibly exist genuine piety apart from experimental truth, and in proportion to the deep experience of the truth, will be the depth of spirituality."[28] This proportionate relationship between the deep experience of truth and one's spirituality touches every facet of the Christian life. For example, Winslow said this about God's love: "The love of God will become a motivating power in our lives to the extent that we experience it in our souls. The outward holy life of a believer is the result of an inward principle of love to God."[29] The same conclusions could be drawn concerning hope, faith, joy, compassion, generosity, kindness, or any other godly virtue.

---

26. Winslow, *Precious Things*, 271.

27. Octavius Winslow, *The Inner Life: Its Nature, Relapse, and Recovery* (London: John F. Shaw, 1850), 249–50.

28. Winslow, *Atonement and the Cross*, 8.

29. Octavius Winslow, *Our God* (London: John F. Shaw, 1870; repr., Grand Rapids: Reformation Heritage Books, 2007), 15.

Experimental Affliction. Winslow wrote much about trials.[30] Throughout his life, he learned many lessons in God's school of affliction. Winslow was only seven years old when his father died, and three of his children died suddenly.[31] As a pastor, Winslow encouraged others to go to the source of his own comfort in affliction, God's Word. He wrote, "The Bible is the book of the afflicted. We fly to it in times of correction. Then it is we read it more attentively, counsel with it more closely, understand it more clearly, relish it more sweetly, and receive it as the engrafted Word into the heart more experimentally."[32] He also thought affliction aids one's understanding of Scripture.[33] Times of trial and affliction are often the means by which God grants seasons of significant growth and enables His people to experience His power at work within them in deeper ways.[34]

In spite of the value Winslow placed on preaching and writing, he argued there are times when God uses the school of suffering to teach His people what they could never learn in a book or a sermon.[35] He wrote hyperbolically,

---

30. See Octavius Winslow, *Midnight Harmonies, or, Thoughts for the Season of Solitude and Sorrow* (New York: Robert Carter & Brothers, 1853). He wrote that book "as a tribute of heartfelt sympathy to those who may be passing through a season of anxiety and trial" (vi). See also "The Preciousness of Trial" in *Precious Things*, 74–112; "Trial, A Help Heavenward" in *Help Heavenward: Guidance and Strength for the Christian's Life-Journey* (London: James Nisbet & Co., 1869; repr., Edinburgh: Banner of Truth, 2000), 66–79; and "The Weaned Child," in *The Bow in the Cloud: Springs of Comfort in Times of Deep Affliction*, ed. William Bacon Stevens (Philadelphia: Hubbard Brothers, 1871; repr., Birmingham, Ala.: Solid Ground Christian Books, 2007), 140–53.

31. See chapter 1 for this information and other examples of trials Winslow endured.

32. Octavius Winslow, *Born Again, or, From Grace to Glory* (London: John F. Shaw, 1864), 224.

33. Reflecting on the words of David in Psalm 119:71, Winslow stated that affliction illuminates the Bible "as though a new book had been composed, another constellation in the spiritual hemisphere had burst upon the telescope of faith." *Precious Things*, 272.

34. Winslow's thoughts on experimental affliction are reminiscent of Martin Luther's reflection on what makes a good theologian. Taking his cue from Psalm 119, Luther says that three things make a good theologian: *oratio* (prayer), *mediatio* (meditation), and *tentatio* (some translate suffering). Concerning *tentatio* he wrote, "This is the touchstone which teaches you not only to know and understand, but also to experience how right, how true, how sweet, how lovely, how mighty, how comforting God's Word is, wisdom beyond all wisdom.... For as soon as God's Word takes root and grows in you, the devil will harry you, and will make a real doctor of you, and by his assaults will teach you to seek and love God's Word. I myself (if you will permit me, mere mouse-dirt, to be mingled with pepper) am deeply indebted to my papists that through the devil's raging they have beaten, oppressed, and distressed me so much. That is to say, they have made a fairly good theologian of me, which I would not have become otherwise." See *Martin Luther's Basic Theological Writings*, ed. Timothy F. Lull (Minneapolis: Augsburg Fortress, 1989), 66–67.

35. Winslow, *Grace and Truth*, 87e.

"We know more of the Lord Jesus through one sanctified affliction than by all the treatises the human pen ever wrote."[36] He also believed God uses trial to sanctify and deepen the believer's experience of Him. Thus, he exhorted, "Welcome whatever makes you more acquainted with God; despise nothing that will deepen your intimacy with God in Christ. Welcome the cross, though it may be heavy; welcome the cup, though it may be bitter.... Receive it as an advantage sent to you from your Father; receive it as a heavenly message to your soul."[37] Winslow viewed affliction as the means God often uses to put the believer in a position to receive more of Himself.

Personal Devotion

Additionally, Winslow's experimental preaching aimed at the personal application of God's truth. It is not surprising his preaching was often direct and confrontational. If a person does not experience the truth personally, Winslow would say to him, "You know nothing of it." In his own words, "We know so much of divine truth, my reader, as we have in a measure a personal experience of it in our souls. The mere speculatist and notionalist in religion is as unsatisfactory and unprofitable as the mere theorist and declaimer in science. For all practical purposes both are but ciphers."[38] A statement like this provides great insight into the shape and purpose of Winslow's ministry. His writings and sermons possess a strong devotional tone.[39]

"Holy Egotism." In the opening of his work *Our God*, Winslow noted Martin Luther's love for the personal pronouns of Scripture. Concerning them he wrote, "This may be termed the 'holy egotism' of the Bible, and it recognizes and teaches an important truth—the believer's personal appropriation to himself of the doctrines, precepts, and promises of God's Word."[40] An example of Winslow's emphasis on "holy egotism" is observed in his meditation on Psalm 31:15: "My times are in thy hand." In light of the psalmist's words, he declared, "We deal too timidly with our individuality—with the truth of God as individuals—with Jesus as individuals—with the covenant of

---

36. Winslow, *Help Heavenward*, 69.
37. Winslow, *Evening Thoughts*, 237.
38. Winslow, *Divine Realities*, 218.
39. Joel Beeke called *Our God* "devotional writing at its finest." Foreword to *Our God*, by Octavius Winslow (London: John F. Shaw, 1870; repr., Grand Rapids: Reformation Heritage Books, 2007, vii). *Our God* is a work on certain moral perfections of God.
40. Winslow, *Our God*, ix.

grace as individuals—with our responsibility as individuals."[41] There is not one blessing of the gospel God's people should fail to claim.

Winslow believed one of the indicators of a declining state of grace and loss of passion is a decrease in the personal enjoyment of religion.[42] When a person is devoted in an intimate, affectionate manner, he or she savors the things of God with great delight. On the other hand, the person who has lost personal communion with God fails to experience His power. By focusing on the benefits of their personal relationship with God, believers discover deeper intimacy with God.

Devotional Ownership. By practicing sincere, personal devotion to God, Winslow knew believers could avoid a fake and contrived spirituality. The alternative is to live off the spirituality of others. Winslow warned, "See that your religion is your own—the personal, vital experience of your own heart. Nothing is easier, more deceptive, or more fatal than to make a religious profession, adopt a religious ceremonial, imitate the experience, and quote the language of others."[43] He went on to say, "A *borrowed or a counterfeit religion* is of all religions the most ensnaring and dangerous. Do not go to the grave clad in the religious habiliments of others, but robed in Christ's true and joyous garments of salvation, 'girded with the golden girdle' of truth, holiness, and love."[44] Only through a personal relationship with God can the believer experience true Christianity.

Authentic Living

Experimental preaching is also designed to elicit sincere faith. Winslow understood many people think they are believers but are really hypocrites. He saw no gray area when it comes to a person's spiritual condition. He wrote, "A soul is either living or dead. The artificial representation of life is no more real life than a painted sun is the real sun, or than a corpse under powerful galvanic shocks is a living body."[45] Winslow's strong language provides a clue as to the seriousness with which he engaged this subject.

An example of his concern for authentic spirituality can be observed in his work *The Inner Life.* He published it to address "the religious professors of

41. Winslow, *Divine Realities,* 37.

42. See Octavius Winslow, *Personal Declension and Revival of Religion in the Soul* (London: John F. Shaw, 1841; repr., Edinburgh: Banner of Truth, 2000), 15–16.

43. Winslow, *Our God,* 145.

44. Winslow, *Our God,* 146.

45. Winslow, *Inner Life,* 2.

the day."[46] Winslow lamented what he saw in the "religious world," observing that many masquerade as Christians but do not bear the fruit of authentic godliness.[47] He said, "It is impossible for a truly spiritual mind to resist the conviction, or close the eye to the fact, that *inward vital godliness* by no means keeps pace with the *profession* of Christianity which almost universally prevails."[48] Winslow encountered many counterfeit Christianities in his day. Some of the more prominent deceptions included mere profession, mere intellectual assent, and formalism.[49]

More Than Mere Profession. One of Satan's works is to muddy the lines between true and false religion, between mere profession and authentic discipleship. Winslow understood this and battled against nominal Christianity. He wrote, "It is one of the ever-working schemes and master strokes of the prince of darkness—and too successful is his exploit—to annihilate in the view of man, the essential difference which God's holy word draws between the mere external profession of Christianity, and its internal and vital possession."[50] Winslow also believed experimental Christianity involves action and commitment. He argued:

---

46. Winslow, *Inner Life*, iv.

47. Winslow explained the origin of this writing: "The subject of this work suggested itself to the author's mind during a visit to the metropolis. His close communion, at that time, with what is called the 'religious world,' forced upon his mind the painful conviction, that while religious profession was greatly on the increase—and never more so in the higher classes of society than at the present—vital godliness was in proportion on the decline; that while—to speak commercially—the quantity of religion was increasing, its quality was deteriorating. The vast number whose Christian profession was avowed—whose religious character was recognized—whose theological creed was sound—whose conversation was pious—whose sacred observances were rigid—whose benevolence was applauded—whose zeal was admired—who prided themselves upon their eloquent preacher, and their favorite religious author; but who yet were living in the world, and living as the world, and living to the world—deeply and painfully saddened him. The question frequently arose in his mind—'Where is the salt? Where are the really living souls? Where are those who know what true conversion is? Who are following Christ, and are living for God? Where are the possessors of the true spiritual life?' Alas! the world has become so like the Church, and the Church so closely resembles the world; the one so religious, and the other so carnal; an unskilled eye may be deceived in searching for the essential points of difference. Nor this alone. Even among those in whose souls it would be wrong, no, impossible, to deny the existence of spiritual life, how few are found who really seem for themselves to know it!" *Inner Life*, iv–v.

48. Winslow, *Inner Life*, 1.

49. It should be noted that these categories often overlap in his writings. For example, the mere professor may also acquiesce to the truth intellectually without it bearing fruit in his life.

50. Winslow, *Inner Life*, 73.

To have outwardly professed Christ, what is easier? To speak respectfully of him; to bow the head at the mention of his name; to have assented to his doctrines, and ably and successfully defended his institutions, nothing less difficult. It costs a man nothing to do all this. There is no cross in it; and what is a man's religion if he extracts from it the cross? There is no love to Christ influencing, impelling the soul; and what value are all inferior motives? There is no singleness of eye to God's glory; and what if self only be the idol which the heart sets up, and before which it burns its daily incense? But O, to have Christ in the heart!—this, this is the truth of God experienced. Call you it enthusiasm? Blessed enthusiasm! We exult in it, we glory in it. Let the formalist, let the man of notional religion, let the mere professor call it what he may, deride it as he will; we admire the grace, and adore the love, and extol the power, which has formed "Christ within us the hope of glory."[51]

Winslow despised a Christianity that costs nothing because it is devoid of Jesus. He believed that the remedy for the "professor" resides in Christ, because He invigorates and enables the disciple to live life to God's glory.

More Than Intellectual Assent. Another expression of false Christianity involves those who merely assent to the truth intellectually but fail to experience it in their hearts. Winslow was not impressed by professing Christians who could unfold their system of theology with great precision and eloquence if it was not accompanied by good works. He wrote, "One grain of the truth experienced in the heart is more valuable and precious than the whole system in the head only."[52] The tragedy of the person who can articulate the finer points of theology but only possesses head knowledge is his own self-deception. Winslow explained:

In attempting to describe the case of a mere professor of the Gospel, we will commence with his religious creed. Herein, we fear, lies his deepest self-deception. He is, perhaps, a profound theologian, is well schooled in the "five points" of divinity, is an acute reasoner, a skillful debater, and an able and vigilant defender of the outposts of Christianity. He can subscribe fully to the Thirty-nine Articles, to the Westminster Confession, and to the general truths of revelation. He has no doubt of the divinity of the Bible, his creed is well balanced, and his general views of truth would be considered evangelical and orthodox. And yet, thus far may he proceed in the deepest self-deception. With all this "form

---

51. Winslow, *Atonement and the Cross*, 26.
52. Winslow, *Evening Thoughts*, 236.

of knowledge," this lodgment of the truth in the understanding, this subscription of the intellect to the doctrines of revelation, he is an utter stranger to that heart-transformation, that inward illumination of the Holy Spirit, without which the soul is spiritually dead, the heart is unrenewed and unholy, and the whole moral man is unfit for the kingdom of heaven. In short, we have here the case of one who, while his judgment assents to the truth, his heart entirely rejects it. The Gospel is to him a thing of intellectual subscription, and not of heart experience. Not a single truth of the Bible has become an element of life and holiness in his soul.[53]

These direct words reveal the danger and folly of mere intellectual assent to the truths of God. Winslow claimed such assent is worth nothing.[54]

More Than Formalism. Another deceptive form of false religion Winslow identified is formalism. Like the Pharisees of Jesus' day, formalists wear only the outer garb of Christianity. They perform Christian duties and look great externally, but like the professor and the notionalist, they are strangers to the transforming power of truth. Winslow confronted such persons with the gospel. He challenged: "Your talking respectfully of Jesus will avail you nothing; your church memberships, your liberality, your irreproachable deportment, your spotless morality, your regular attendance on the sanctuary, all, all are vain without the justifying righteousness of the God-man upon you."[55]

He warned formalists by pointing them to the scrutiny of God's final judgment. He exhorted his readers to examine and see if they possessed saving grace. Any means the formalist pursues apart from Christ will not prepare him for God's just judgment no matter how great his religious fervor.[56] He admonished, "It is not the talking about religion, or ministers, or churches, nor an outward zeal for their prosperity, that either constitutes or indicates a truly spiritual man. And yet how much of this in our day passes current for the life of God in the soul?"[57] Winslow's writings are filled with such warnings to mere professors, notionalists, and formalists who lack the Spirit's salvific and sanctifying work.

---

53. Octavius Winslow, *Glimpses of the Truth As It Is in Jesus* (Philadelphia: Lindsay & Blakiston, 1856), 201.

54. Winslow, *Our God*, 53.

55. Winslow, *Atonement and the Cross,* 70.

56. Winslow, *Glory of the Redeemer,* 410.

57. Winslow, *Personal Declension,* 19.

The Goal of Experimental Preaching: Sanctification

As stated above, Winslow believed the goal of experimental preaching is life transformation. He made the relevance of every doctrine clear so his hearers might be sanctified. Winslow's doctrine of progressive sanctification informs his experimental preaching for the sake of change.

Winslow's Doctrine of Progressive Sanctification

Winslow's doctrine of progressive sanctification is foundational to understanding the goal of experimental preaching.[58] What is progressive sanctification? Winslow said, "Sanctification is a conformity to the image and the example of Christ. The more the believer is growing like Jesus, the more he is growing in holiness."[59] Progressive sanctification is vitally important for two significant reasons. First, it enables the believer to see God clearly. Winslow said, "There is no vision of God either present or future, save through the medium of holiness."[60] Second, it prepares and frees him for good works. Winslow explained, "We are not more eminently useful, because we are not more eminently holy."[61] When teaching the doctrine of sanctification, he expounded man's problem, God's solution, and encouraged believers toward an increasing advance in holiness.

Man's Problem: Indwelling Sin. Jeremiah 17:9 says, "The heart is deceitful above all things, and desperately wicked: who can know it?" In reflecting on this verse, Winslow wrote about the heart of man apart from grace: "Do not trust in it, it is treacherous; expect nothing truly good from it, it is a depth of undiscovered depravity. Is this harsh language? Are these sentiments revolting to you? I speak but the truth of God when I say that your heart, in its present unrenewed state, is your worst enemy."[62] Additionally, Winslow recognized indwelling sin does not disappear after regeneration. On the contrary, our sinfulness is all the more exposed by the gospel. This is true for every saint. He warned, "Sin dwells in the heart of the most deeply sanctified, is ever at work in the most eminent Christian; and it has been

---

58. Winslow clearly referred to sanctification as "progressive." See Octavius Winslow, *Lights and Shadows of Spiritual Life* (London: John F. Shaw, 1876; repr., *The Spiritual Life* [Stoke-on-Trent, U.K.: Tentmaker Publications, 1998]), 15.

59. Winslow, *Holy Spirit*, 117.

60. Winslow, *Help Heavenward*, 16.

61. Winslow, *Glory of the Redeemer*, 122.

62. Winslow, *Holy Spirit*, 36.

truly remarked, that the best of saints have need to be warned against the worst of sins."[63]

Indwelling sin, or the flesh, constantly battles the new man. Winslow's words were instructive when he wrote, "The contest is for supremacy. The great question at issue is, 'which shall reign in the believer—sin or holiness, nature or grace, Satan or God?' Oh, what a fiery conflict is this!"[64] He also believed the world and Satan both work against the Christian's progress in sanctification. The world appeals to the flesh in order to draw the believer away from holiness. Sensual pleasures, creature comforts, intellectual pursuits, and worldly applause encourage the downfall of the child of God.[65] Satan aggressively pursues the demise of God's children.[66] How is the believer to advance in holiness under such duress? To answer that question, Winslow turned to the gospel.

The Gospel's Cure: Mortification. The only way for the believer to deal with indwelling sin is by putting it to death. This happens by the power of the Holy Spirit. Winslow explained the mortification of sin by pointing to Romans 8:13, which says, "For if ye live after the flesh, ye shall die: but if ye through the Spirit do mortify the deeds of the body, ye shall live."

Winslow believed sanctification involves heart transformation rather than behavior modification. He argued that sin must be mortified at its root: "Outward sins may be cut off, and even honestly confessed and mourned over, while the concealed principle, the root of the sin, is overlooked, neglected, and allowed to gather strength and expansion."[67] This is the essence of how the believer should pursue holiness. He wrote, "True sanctification is a daily mortification of the root of sin in the heart—the continual destruction of the principle."[68] If the root is not addressed, the consequences are momentous. With the flavor of John Owen, Winslow wrote, "What is your predominant sin?—lay the axe at its root. Seek its death and destruction, or it will be death

---

63. Winslow, *Inner Life*, 55.
64. Winslow, *Glory of the Redeemer*, 82–83.
65. Winslow, *Inner Life*, 144–45.
66. See Octavius Winslow, *The Lord's Prayer: Its Spirit and Its Teaching* (London: John F. Shaw, 1866; repr., Stroke-on-Trent, U.K.: Tentmaker Publications, 2003), 48. There Winslow explains that Christ came to destroy the works of Satan in the world and in the believer's soul. He lists three primary means by which Christ dethrones His enemy: conversion, sanctification, and affliction.
67. Winslow, *Atonement and the Cross*, 79.
68. Winslow, *Holy Spirit*, 132.

and destruction to you, as long as it prevails."[69] The believer must be killing sin, and he must do so by the Spirit.[70]

One of the chief ways the Spirit kills sin in the believer's life is by exalting Jesus. While Winslow promoted the use of means in the process of sanctification, he held that the reading of the Word, solitude, and confession of sin were useless apart from the work of Christ on the cross. That is why he wrote, "One sight of a crucified Savior imparted by the Holy Spirit will more effectually weaken the power of indwelling sin than all other means combined. O the might of the cross! O the virtue of the blood! O the power of the grace of Jesus to crucify, cleanse, and subdue our iniquities!"[71] The cross of Christ must motivate the believer's pursuit of holiness. More frequent looks to Christ should generate greater progress in sanctification. Winslow understood sanctification to be one of God's great designs in the cross. He wrote:

> If to view God in Christ is a comforting truth, it is also a sanctifying truth. Why has God revealed Himself in Jesus? To evince the exceeding hatefulness of sin, and to show that nothing short of such a stupendous sacrifice could remove it consistently with the glory of the Divine nature, and the honor of the Divine government. Each sin, then, is a blow struck at this transcendent truth. The eye averted from it, sin appears a trifle; it can be looked at without indignation, tampered with without fear, committed without hesitation, persisted in without remorse, gloried in without shame, confessed without sorrow. But when Divine justice is seen drinking the very heart's blood of God's only Son in order to quench its infinite thirst for satisfaction; when God in Christ is seen in His humiliation, suffering, and death, all with the design of pardoning iniquity, transgression, and sin, how fearful a thing does it seem to sin against this holy Lord God! How base, how ungrateful, appears our sin in view of love so amazing, of grace so rich, and of glory so great! Cultivate a constant, an ardent thirst for holiness. Do not be discouraged, if the more intensely the desire for sanctification rises, the deeper and darker the revelation of the heart's hidden evil. The one is often a consequent of the other; but persevere. The struggle may be painful, the battle

---

69. Winslow, *Inner Life*, 57. In light of such a statement and the immense respect he had for John Owen as evidenced in his writings, there is little doubt that Winslow had read Owen's *Mortification of Sin* and his classic statement, "Be killing sin or sin will be killing you." See John Owen, *The Works of John Owen*, ed. William H. Goold (Edinburgh: Johnstone & Hunter, 1850–1855; repr., Edinburgh: Banner of Truth, 1991), 6:9.

70. For more on the Spirit's work in sanctification, see chapter 2. See also "The Sanctification of the Spirit" in Winslow, *Holy Spirit*, 105–36.

71. Winslow, *Inner Life*, 59.

may be strong, but the result is certain, and will be a glorious victory, *victory,* through the blood of the Lamb![72]

According to Winslow, the process of sanctification must be gospel-centered. He also believed sanctification should be a constant advance.

Sanctified Advance. Winslow encouraged disciples to constantly pursue greater maturity in Christ.[73] He exhorted, "Again we would urge—seek high attainments in holiness. Do not be satisfied with a low measure of grace, with a stunted religion, with just enough Christianity to admit you into heaven."[74] He communicated the church's lack of progress in holiness through "mathematical" language. Reflecting on 1 Peter 1:5–9, Winslow explained, "We are, at best, but dull scholars in the science of spiritual arithmetic. We have imperfectly learned one of its first rules, that of adding grace to grace.... The movement is to be progressive, the course onward; each day, if possible, augmenting the measure of our grace, and adding to the number of the Spirit's graces."[75] Winslow challenged Christians to fulfill God's design for their lives by pursuing Christlikeness with great purpose and passion. Simply put, "[God] is glorified in the progressive holiness of His people."[76] One could summarize Winslow's conclusions concerning progressive sanctification by saying the Spirit mortifies the root of sin by wielding a gospel axe.

Preaching for Change

Winslow believed pastors should work to see every member of their church grow in godliness.[77] If preaching for change is the goal of experimental preaching, then three key components accomplish the task. They include striving for holistic change, preaching for faith, and preaching to the affections.

---

72. Winslow, *Glory of the Redeemer,* 69–70.

73. Winslow encouraged people to strive for the greatest measures of holiness. He wrote, "Thus we must be careful of supposing that there is any eminence in the divine life to which other saints have attained that is unattainable by us—that there is any sacred height in grace, holiness, and assurance they reached to which we may not ascend, or that there is any knowledge of Christ, any conformity to His likeness, any communion with Him experienced by others that cannot be our experience, too." *Our God,* 149–50.

74. Winslow, *Holy Spirit,* 132.

75. Winslow, *Grace and Truth,* 27e.

76. Winslow, *Glory of the Redeemer,* 317.

77. See Winslow, *Nightingale Song,* 26.

Striving for Holistic Change. Experimental preaching aims at holistic change in God's people. For example, it is not enough to stir the affections without confronting the conscience, nor is it enough to inform the intellect without persuading the will. True experimental preaching does not stop short of comprehensive change in the heart. Winslow said:

> The religion of Christ is essentially and intensely experimental in its character. There is nothing in it theoretic, speculative, or ideal. Its history is true, its facts are authentic, its doctrines are divine. It appeals to the intellect, and takes it captive; it enters the heart, and finds a home. It blends with every faculty of the mind, entwines with every passion of the soul, and is absorbed with our entire mental, moral, and spiritual being.[78]

If this is true of Christianity, then it should also be true of Christian preaching. D. Martyn Lloyd-Jones, one of England's greatest preachers in the twentieth century, agreed with Winslow's conclusions. He said, "Preaching is that which deals with the total person, the hearer becomes involved and knows that he has been dealt with and addressed by God through this preacher."[79] The experimental preacher is after holistic change.[80]

Preaching for Faith. Winslow also maintained preaching for change means preaching for faith, so that hearers might experience both conversion and maturity in Christ. According to Winslow, preaching for conversion is the pastor's great work. He declared, "Our great work is to bring men to Christ. We are truly wise, only as we are 'wise to win souls'; and our attainments are really to secure this end.... Oh how criminally do we lose sight of this, as an immediate, legitimate, and glorious end of our preaching!"[81] In other words, a preacher should always be concerned with the salvation of souls. Winslow said anything less is criminal. At the same time, Winslow was also careful to

---

78. Octavius Winslow, *The Tree of Life: Its Shade, Fruit, and Repose* (London: John F. Shaw, 1868), 3e.

79. D. Martyn Lloyd-Jones, *Preaching and Preachers* (Grand Rapids: Zondervan, 1971), 56.

80. Lloyd-Jones also argued that the preacher "is there—and I want to emphasise this—to do something to those people; he is there to produce results of various kinds, he is there to influence people. He is not there to influence a part of them; he is not only to influence their minds, or only their emotions, or merely to bring pressure to bear upon their wills and to induce them to some kind of activity. He is there to deal with the whole person; and his preaching is meant to affect the whole person at the very centre of life. Preaching should make such a difference to a man who is listening that he is never the same again." *Preaching and Preachers*, 53.

81. Octavius Winslow, *Eminent Holiness: Essential to an Efficient Ministry* (London: Houlston & Stoneman, 1843), 70.

warn people not to make "a Christ of their faith."[82] In other words, he knew some people were prone to viewing *faith* as the object of salvation rather than Jesus. He declared, "Divine and precious as it is, faith is but the path that leads us to the King."[83] Faith does not save, but it is the gracious instrument by which we apprehend more of God.

Winslow also believed preaching for faith involves preaching for life change. Faith embraces God's truth and puts it into practice. Winslow viewed faith as precious because it enables God's people to see Him and trust Him in every area of life. He wrote:

> Faith is the optical faculty of the regenerate, it is the spiritual eye of the soul. Faith sees Christ, and as Christ is seen His excellence is recognized; and as His excellence unfolds, so He becomes an object of endearment to the heart! Oh, how lovely and how glorious is Jesus to the clear, far-seeing eye of faith! Faith beholds Him the matchless, peerless One; His beauty eclipsing, His glory outshining, all other beings! Faith sees majesty in His lowliness, dignity in His condescension, honor in His humiliation, beauty in His tears, transcendent, surpassing glory in His cross![84]

Winslow saw an inextricable link between a person's experience of truth and his faith. He said, "The exact measure of our faith is the extent of our experimental knowledge of God."[85] This also places a great responsibility on the hearer.

Just as Winslow had a theology of preaching, he also had a theology of hearing. It is safe to assume he would insist that experimental preaching must have experimental listening because it is the means the Lord uses to give faith. Of Lydia's conversion in Acts 16, Winslow wrote, "Her heart was opened to hear the Word of the Lord. In the language of Bunyan, the 'eargate' was first assailed. 'Faith comes by hearing.' There are many individuals who refuse even outwardly to listen to the message God sends to them. Like the *deaf adder*, sinners stop their ears to the voice of the charmer, charm he ever so wisely, lest they should hear with their ears and be converted and be saved."[86] Additionally, Winslow believed refusing to hear God's Word with

---

82. Winslow, *Precious Things*, 58.
83. Winslow, *Precious Things*, 58.
84. Winslow, *Precious Things*, 18.
85. Winslow, *Grace and Truth*, 26e.
86. Octavius Winslow, *The Ministry of Home, or, Brief Expository Lectures on Divine Truth: Designed Especially for Family and Private Reading* (London: William Hunt and Co., 1868), 52–53.

humility dishonors Him and grieves His Spirit.[87] For these reasons, preachers must preach for faith and hearers must listen with humility.

Preaching to the Affections. As stated earlier, God desires more than intellectual assent to His truth. Winslow referred to experimental Christianity as "the religion of the heart."[88] He believed good experimental preaching must engage the head *and* heart:

> But the truth as it is in Jesus demands more than the mere assent of the understanding. It does not, indeed, bypass the province of reason, nor set aside the aid of the intellectual powers of man; but, while it appeals to this tribunal, and exacts its homage and its belief—carrying triumphant the noblest and loftiest powers of the soul—it enters the heart, and there puts forth its mightiest power, achieves its greatest triumph, receives its profoundest love and conviction, claiming and securing the affections for Christ.[89]

God desires for people to love Him with their minds and affections. Winslow maintained that God's people must feel the truth, that they taste its realness. He said, "Blessed are they who feel, and who feel daily, that they are indeed 'risen with Christ,' and who find every new perception of this great truth to act like a mighty lever to their souls."[90]

Winslow was not afraid to assert that one's emotions should be involved in the pursuit of Christ. He wrote, "We must acknowledge that the religion of Jesus is the religion of sensibility; that there is no godly repentance without feeling, and no spiritual contrition apart from deep emotion."[91] At the same time, he kept a healthy balance between the heart and the head. He believed "the heart must, so to speak, discourse with the head—there must be a communication, a harmony of the intellect and the affections in the religious training of the soul."[92] He was after a balanced approach between what the mind grasps and what the heart feels in everyday experience.

When preachers strive for holistic change by preaching for faith and preaching to the affections, they strive to make an impression in order to make

---

87. Winslow, *Glory of the Redeemer,* 240.
88. Winslow, *Atonement and the Cross,* 24.
89. Winslow, *Born Again,* 4–5.
90. Winslow, *Inner Life,* 252.
91. Winslow, *Inner Life,* 168.
92. Winslow, *Nightingale Song,* 61.

the knowledge of Christ "live" in the hearts of their hearers.[93] God uses those impressions to move people to action. This is the goal of experimental preaching.

The Practice of Experimental Preaching

After considering Winslow's convictions as to the nature and goal of experimental preaching, the question remains: How did he accomplish this homelitically? A study of Winslow's sermons reveals eight essential elements in his experimental preaching. Two have already been discussed in detail: experimental preaching must be grounded in doctrine and centered in Christ. Six other elements consistently present in his experimental preaching include application, discrimination, interrogation, illustration, exhortation, and persuasion.[94] As he preached for change by applying doctrine to life, these elements often intersected.[95]

Applicatory Preaching

In many ways, application was the foundational element for Winslow's experimental homiletic.[96] In large part, the other elements serve as means

93. In the same spirit, D. Martyn Lloyd-Jones made this the aim of his ministry. In reflecting on the preaching of Jonathan Edwards, he wrote, "The first and primary object of preaching is not only to give information. It is, as Edwards says, to produce an impression. It is the impression at the time that matters, even more than what you can remember subsequently.... [Preachers] are not merely imparters of information.... The business of preaching is to make such knowledge live." *The Puritans: Their Origins and Successors* (Edinburgh: Banner of Truth, 1987), 360.

94. Material from the following sections will rely primarily on Winslow's sermons. Most insights will be drawn from five of his sermon series compiled in the following works: *Patriarchal Shadows of Christ and His Church: As Exhibited in Passages Drawn from the History of Joseph and His Brethren* (London: John F. Shaw, 1863; repr., Grand Rapids: Sovereign Grace Treasures, 2005). These sermons are from Genesis 41–47; *Soul-Depths & Soul-Heights: Sermons on Psalm 130* (London: John F. Shaw, 1874; repr., Edinburgh: Banner of Truth, 2006); *No Condemnation in Christ Jesus: As Unfolded in the Eighth Chapter of the Epistle to the Romans* (London: John F. Shaw, 1853; repr., Edinburgh: Banner of Truth, 1991); *Glimpses of the Truth*; and *The Inner Life*. These last two sermon compilations are from various passages of Scripture.

95. In an insightful statement, Beeke says that experiential preaching is "preaching that seeks to explain in terms of biblical truth how matters ought to go, how they do go, and the goal of the Christian life." "Experiential Preaching," 54. Taking his categories, it is easy to see how the following six elements of Winslow's preaching fit into Beeke's scheme. *Discrimination* and *interrogation* address how matters are going in the present. *Application, exhortation,* and *persuasion* explain how matters ought to go in the future and work toward the goal of the Christian life. *Illustration* could fit under any of these categories.

96. In his classic work on preaching, *The Art of Prophesying*, William Perkins defined *application* as "the skill by which the doctrine has been properly drawn from Scripture in

of applying the text.[97] It has been said, "A sermon that lacks application may be good teaching, but it is not preaching."[98] Winslow would wholeheartedly agree. He wrote, "Were we to select a single word from the Bible which we would desire to be distinctly, prominently, and constantly before the eye of the believer, it would be—obedience."[99] In a sermon on the fullness of Christ, Winslow declared, "Let obedience to Christ in everything be the distinctive badge of your discipleship."[100]

Winslow held that God's work was just as necessary for *applying* the truth as it was for *understanding* the truth. At the beginning of a sermon on spiritual decline, he prayed on behalf of himself and the congregation, "May the Holy Spirit be our teacher! May we be kept from unprofitable speculation, and from all trifling with a case so desperate, and with a theme so momentous! May an unction from the Holy One impart a searching, personal, and sanctifying application of the truth to our hearts!"[101] This prayer emphasizes Winslow's concern for sanctification through the application of God's Word.

At times Winslow reserved the bulk of application for the end of the sermon while at other times he scattered the application throughout.[102] One example of declaring the "practical influence" primarily at the sermon's conclusion is found in a message titled "Eternal Glorification" from Romans 8:30.[103] In light

---

ways which are appropriate to the circumstances of the place and time and to the people in the congregation." *The Art of Prophesying with the Calling of the Ministry*, rev. ed. (Edinburgh: Banner of Truth, 2002), 54.

97. For example, Winslow utilized *interrogation* with the hope that people would consider how they can better display the truth in their life. He also used exhortation to encourage his hearers with specific points of application.

98. Joel Beeke, *Living for God's Glory: An Introduction to Calvinism* (Lake Mary, Fla.: Reformation Trust, 2008), 260.

99. Winslow, *Glory of the Redeemer*, 328. Winslow emphasized that obedience leads to holiness and happiness. He went on to say, "It involves every covenant mercy, and it is the great secret of all holiness, and therefore of all happiness" (328).

100. Winslow, *Patriarchal Shadows*, 25.

101. Winslow, *Inner Life*, 46–47.

102. When reserving the bulk of the application for the sermon's end, Winslow followed the Puritan model of explaining the text, unpacking the doctrine, and then giving the "uses" or practical application. See Lloyd-Jones, *Puritans: Their Origins*, 381–82. In the instances where he scattered the application throughout, Winslow followed the style espoused by Charles Bridges, who said, "The method of perpetual application, therefore, *where the subject will admit of it*, is probably best calculated for effect." *The Christian Ministry with an Inquiry into the Causes of Its Inefficiency* (London: R. B. Seely and W. Burnside, 1830; repr., Edinburgh: Banner of Truth, 2006), 275.

103. Winslow, *No Condemnation*, 339. Even in this sermon Winslow applied the doctrinal truth in a few brief statements throughout the body of the sermon before his conclusion.

of the believer's future state, he encouraged his hearers to (1) make their call-ing and election sure, (2) mature in sanctification, and (3) labor hard for Christ in the present. Of the latter he declared, "How should the prospect of certain glory stimulate us to individual exertion for Christ! What a motive to labour! With a whole eternity of rest, how little should we think of present toil and fatigue for the Saviour!"[104] An example of his applying the text throughout the sermon is found in a sermon titled "Christian Love."[105] There, Winslow expounded the different characteristics of Christian love and brought points of application concerning each characteristic, including striving for unity, avoid-ing offense, forgiveness, forbearance, avoiding rash judgments, sympathy, and faithfulness. His pointed application helped congregants leave the sanctuary equipped to put the truth into practice.

Discriminating Preaching

The discriminating preacher is the preacher who knows his audience well. Discriminating preaching draws a distinction between different types of hearers and helps hearers discern where they stand before God.[106] Are they saints or sinners? Are they hypocrites or genuine disciples? Are they imma-ture or growing believers?[107] In Winslow's words, discriminatory preaching "separate[s] the precious from the vile."[108]

Winslow believed discriminating preaching presses hearers to deal more closely with their souls. He also maintained this was one of the chief characteristics of Christ's preaching. Citing the example of the Pharisees withdrawing after hearing the preaching of Jesus, he wrote:

> If there were any one feature in our Lord's ministrations more pecu-liarly impressive than another, it was the discriminating character that

---

104. Winslow, *No Condemnation*, 342.

105. Winslow, *Patriarchal Shadows*, 183–88.

106. Again, it is likely that Winslow was heavily influenced by his Puritan predecessors in the task of discriminatory application. J. I. Packer has argued that "strength of application was, from one standpoint, the most striking feature of Puritan preaching, and it is arguable that the theory of discriminating application is the most valuable legacy that Puritan preach-ers have left to those who would preach the Bible and its gospel effectively today." *A Quest for Godliness: The Puritan Vision of the Christian Life* (Wheaton, Ill.: Crossway, 1990), 288.

107. William Perkins identified seven categories of hearers. They include: (1) Unbelievers who are both ignorant and unteachable; (2) the teachable, but ignorant; (3) the knowledge-able, but proud; (4) the humbled; (5) the believing; (6) those who have fallen back; and (7) both believers and unbelievers. See *Art of Prophesying*, 56–63. Because of the obvious influence the Puritans had on Winslow, it would be surprising if he had not read Perkins's book.

108. Winslow, *Glimpses of the Truth*, 29.

marked them. No one, on hearing him, could retire without the deep conviction that he was the man whose moral image Jesus had been drawing, and in such true and vivid resemblance, as to compel him to acknowledge the faithfulness of the portrait. There was no personality, no harshness, no unnecessary keenness in his reproof, no exaggeration of coloring, nothing overdrawn; but such a simple, faithful, scriptural dealing with human conscience, as either compelled his hearers to submit to his authority, and rank themselves among his followers, or to retire, silenced, self-accused, and self-condemned.[109]

Winslow's discriminating preaching helped his hearers identify where they stood spiritually.

In a sermon on "The Nature and Manifestations of the Inner Life," Winslow addressed several groups consecutively. First, he addressed those who do not possess spiritual life in Christ. He declared, "You are all life, all nerve, all animation, all ardor, all activity, all excitement, all hope, to whatever is noble, and intellectual, and refined, and enterprising, of earth; but all death, all insensibility, all indifferent, all languor, all hopeless, to every thought and feeling and consideration of the great things that relate to your state beyond the grave. Is this wise, is this rational, is this sane?"[110]

After addressing unbelievers, Winslow "turn[ed] to the living."[111] In doing so, he addressed believers in different stages of Christian experience. He encouraged those who were anxious concerning whether or not they possessed the divine life by declaring, "Sit not brooding over your mournful condition, in fruitless lamentation, but rise, and go to Jesus. Take to him the stone-like heart, the corpse-like soul. Tell him that you want to feel more, and to weep more, and to love more, and to pray more, and to live more."[112] In a similar manner, he encouraged the afflicted with Christ-centered truth:

> You are, perhaps, *a severely tried, a sorely tempted, a deeply afflicted believer.* But cheer up! You have Christ living in you, and why should you yield to despondency or to fear? Christ will never vacate his throne, nor relinquish his dwelling. You have a suffering Christ, a humbled Christ, a crucified Christ, a dying Christ, a risen Christ, a living Christ, a triumphant Christ, a glorified Christ, a full Christ, dwelling in you by his Spirit. Yes! and you have, too, a human Christ, a feeling Christ, a sympathizing Christ, a tender, loving, gentle Christ, spiritually and

---

109. Winslow, *Personal Declension*, 146.
110. Winslow, *Inner Life*, 32. This sermon is included in appendix 2 of this work.
111. Winslow, *Inner Life*, 35.
112. Winslow, *Inner Life*, 37.

eternally reposing in your heart—why, then, should you fear the pressure of any need, or the assault of any foe, or the issue of any trial, since such a Christ is in you?[113]

These last two examples demonstrate how Winslow's Christ-centered preaching worked seamlessly as an aspect of his experimental preaching. Winslow went on to address the mournful and those searching for spiritual life.[114] Experimental preaching is preaching that discerns and addresses the various needs of the congregation.

Interrogating Preaching

The third element of Winslow's experimental preaching was interrogation. Winslow was an interrogating preacher. He liked to ask penetrating questions. He believed self-examination is one of the most important spiritual disciplines, though it was one of the most neglected in his day. Concerning the exhortation in 2 Corinthians 13:5 to "examine yourselves," Winslow wrote, "Alas! how is this precept overlooked! How few are they who rightly and honestly examine themselves! They can examine others, and speak of others, and hear for others, and judge of others; but themselves they examine not, and judge not, and condemn not."[115] Those who neglect this discipline reap serious spiritual consequences.[116]

Winslow's sermons reveal his view of the pulpit as a place for preachers to hold up the mirror of the Word in order to help the congregation examine themselves. Thus, he peppered his sermons with searching questions. His approach can be summarized as loving confrontation. While preaching Galatians 2:20 he declared, "Then let me ask and press upon you the personal and searching question, has the law of God been brought into your conscience with that enlightening, convincing, and condemning power, as first to startle you from your spiritual slumber, and then to sever you from

---

113. Winslow, *Inner Life*, 38.

114. Winslow, *Inner Life*, 39–41. Winslow's identification of the different types of people also surfaced in his writing. In direct and bold terms he wrote, "Scoffing infidel! polluted sensualist! Sordid miser! groveling worldling! proud pharisee! deceived professor! you are to stand before the judgment-seat of Christ. What will your scepticism, what will your carnal joys, what will your money, what will your fame, what will your own works, and what will your empty lamp do for you then?" *Glory of the Redeemer*, 256. Another example is discovered when Winslow addresses the rich and the powerful with the gospel according to their own unique life situation. *Glory of the Redeemer*, 166–70.

115. Winslow, *Inner Life*, 13–14.

116. Winslow, *Inner Life*, 14.

all hope or expectation of salvation in yourself?"[117] Another example demonstrates how he often stacked his questions. In the following inquiry, he asked his hearers to inspect how they measured up to the words of Paul, "Yet not I, but Christ liveth in me" (Gal. 2:20). He asked pointedly, "Judge your spiritual condition, dear reader, by this characteristic of the inner life. Is it yours? Has there been this renunciation of your sinful self, and of your righteous self? Has the Spirit of God emptied you? Has the grace of God humbled you? Has the life of God crucified you? Are you as one in whom Christ lives, walking humbly with God?"[118] One final example of his interrogating style for the purpose of examination comes from a sermon on "Spiritual-Mindedness" from Romans 8:6. After speaking of the necessity of spiritual life in the soul, he then questioned:

> Dear reader, is this your condition? Have you the life of God in your soul? Have you passed from death unto life? Is the fruit you bear the result of your engrafting into Christ? You attend upon the service of the sanctuary; you visit the abodes of the wretched: you administer to the necessities of the poor; you are rigid in your duties, and zealous in your charities; but does it all spring from faith in Christ, and from love to God? Is it from life, or for life? Oh! remember, that the spiritual-mindedness which the Bible recognizes, of which God approves, has its root in the life of God in the soul![119]

These questions were the means Winslow consistently used to confront the conscience of his hearers.[120]

Winslow also utilized interrogatives to encourage his hearers. Concerning the believer's assurance of the divine life, he declared, "The life of God in the soul evidences itself by its actings. Are you sensible of your sinfulness? Do you love the atoning blood? Is Jesus precious to your soul? Do you delight in God, and in retirement for communion with Him? Then for your encouragement we remind you, that these are not the actings of a soul lying in a state of moral death, nor are these the productions of a soul still unregenerate."[121] These questions were designed to bring comfort rather than conviction.

---

117. Winslow, *Inner Life*, 8.

118. Winslow, *Inner Life*, 23.

119. Winslow, *No Condemnation*, 74.

120. Lloyd-Jones is again helpful. Much like Winslow, he believed that preaching must confront people with the truth in a direct and heart-searching manner. He wrote, "If people can listen to us without becoming anxious about themselves or reflecting on themselves we have not been preaching." *Preaching and Preachers*, 56.

121. Winslow, *Glimpses of the Truth*, 235.

By interrogating his hearers with piercing questions, Winslow helped them evaluate their lives and encouraged them with God's truth. It was a key weapon in his arsenal of experimental preaching.

Illustrating Preaching

Another aspect of Winslow's experimental preaching involved how he often preached in pictures. To say Winslow was an illustrative preacher does not mean he illustrated sermons in the same manner as many contemporary homileticians.[122] Rather than telling stories about life situations, Winslow used word pictures.[123] In a sermon from Psalm 130:5 on waiting for the Lord, Winslow spoke of the worthlessness of waiting on man. With vivid, picturesque language he declared, "We build upon the creature, hang upon it, wait for it, until we wring the last drop from it as from a sponge, and nothing is left but emptiness and dryness. Oh, if but half the time we have spent in waiting on, and in waiting for, man—and at last finding him but a wounding reed and a broken cistern—had been spent in waiting upon and for the Lord, how much more successful and how much happier we should have been!"[124] This example demonstrates how Winslow crafted his own word pictures and also alluded to imagery from Scripture.

In his effort to promote holistic change in his hearers, it seems he painted word pictures to inform the mind, stir the affections, and persuade the will through sensate language. His preaching demonstrates the multifaceted value of using illustrations. A sermon titled "No Condemnation" demonstrates his illustrative style. In the opening sermon of his series through Romans 8, Winslow set verse 1 in the context of chapter 7 by using vivid language. He declared, "Lifting them from the region of conflict and cloud, he places them upon an elevation towering above the gloom and strife of the battle-field,

---

122. Bryan Chapell defines the understanding that many preachers have of sermon illustrations when he writes, "Illustrations are 'life-situation' stories within sermons whose details (whether explicitly told or imaginatively elicited) allow listeners to identify with an experience that elaborates, develops, and explains the scriptural principles." *Using Illustrations to Preach with Power*, rev. ed. (Wheaton, Ill.: Crossway, 2001), 21. While many preachers may lean in the direction of Chapell's definition, Jim Shaddix and Jerry Vines provide a more comprehensive understanding: "Illustrations are mental photographs that illumine the ideas of our messages." Jim Shaddix and Jerry Vines, *Power in the Pulpit: How to Prepare and Deliver Expository Sermons* (Chicago: Moody, 1999), 190.

123. For further study of the use of word pictures, see Jack Hughes, *Expository Preaching with Word Pictures with Illustrations from the Sermons of Thomas Watson* (Ross-Shire, U.K.: Christian Focus, 2001).

124. Winslow, *Soul-Depths*, 66.

around whose serene, sunlight summit gathered the first dawning of eternal glory."[125] He went on to explain the meaning of "condemnation" by painting a picture of the man under its sentence:

> "Condemnation" is a word of tremendous import; and it is well fairly to look at its meaning, that we may the better understand the wondrous grace that has delivered us from its power. Echoing through the gloomy halls of a human court, it falls with a fearful knell upon the ear of the criminal, and thrills with sympathy and horror the bosom of each spectator of the scene. But in the court of Divine Justice it is uttered with a meaning and solemnity infinitely significant and impressive. To that court every individual is cited. Before that bar each one must be arraigned. "Conceived in sin, and shaped in iniquity," man enters the world under arrest—an indicted criminal, a rebel manacled, and doomed to die. Born under the tremendous sentence originally denounced against sin: "In the day that you eat thereof you shall surely die;" or, "You shall die the death," he enters life under a present condemnation, the prelude of a future condemnation. From it he can discover no avenue of escape. He lies down, and he rises up—he repairs to the mart of business, and to the haunt of pleasure, a guilty, sentenced, and condemned man. "Cursed is every one that continues not in all things which are written in the book of the law, to do them," is the terrible sentence branded upon his brow. And should the summons to eternity arrest him amid his dreams, his speculations, and his revels, the adversary would deliver him to the judge, the judge to the officer, and the officer would consign him over to all the pangs and horrors of the "second" and "eternal death." "He that believes not, is condemned already." My dear reader, without real conversion this is your present state, and must be your future doom.[126]

This example reveals how Winslow utilized word pictures, which often led to direct application. The active listener would surely picture himself in the court of divine justice with "condemnation" branded upon his brow upon hearing Winslow's vibrant depiction. Finally, he described the present condition of those in Christ:

> A present discharge from condemnation must produce a present joy. Open the iron-bound door of the condemned cell, and by the dim light that struggles through its bars read the sovereign's free pardon to the

---

125. Winslow, *No Condemnation*, 2.

126. Winslow, *No Condemnation*, 3–4. The use of the phrase "dear reader" makes it obvious that Winslow edited these "extemporaneous ministrations" for publication by both shortening their length in most or all cases and by changing his terminology where appropriate (v).

felon, stretched, pale and emaciated, upon his pallet of straw; and the radiance you have kindled in that gloomy dungeon, and the transport you have created in that felon's heart, will be a present realization. You have given him back a present life; you have touched a thousand chords in his bosom, which awake a present harmony; and where, just previous; reigned in that bosom sullen, grim despair, now reigns the sunlight joyousness of a present hope. Christian! there is now no condemnation for you! Be yours, then, a present and a full joy.[127]

These examples give an idea of how Winslow preached in pictures with the goal of arresting the attention and moving the affections of his hearers.

Exhortative Preaching

The Bible uses many terms to describe the task of preaching, and several of those communicate the idea of exhortation.[128] To aid the application of the text, Winslow packed his sermons with encouragement and exhortation. Winslow's exhortation took two forms: explicit and implicit.

His explicit exhortation was often direct, both challenging and encouraging his hearers. As a means of urging his hearers to apply the text, Winslow often concluded his sermons with a flurry of exhortative instruction. His sermon on "Spiritual-Mindedness" provides such an instance. He concluded his sermon by urging his hearers:

> How great and exalted the heavenly calling of the Christian! *Aim to walk* worthy of it. *Debase it not* by allying it with a carnal mind. *Impair not* your spiritual life by enchaining it to spiritual death. *Let the friendships* which you cultivate, and the relationships of life which you form, be heavenly in their nature, and eternal in their duration. *Seek to please* God in all things. *Rest not* where you are, even though you may have attained beyond your fellows. *Let your standard* of heavenly-mindedness be not that of the saints, but of Christ. *Study not* a copy, but the Original. High aims will secure high attainments. He is the most heavenly, and the happiest, who the most closely resembles his Divine Master. *Be much* in your closet. There is no progress in spiritual-mindedness apart from much prayer; prayer is its nourishment, and its element. But *leave not* your religion there; let it accompany you into the world. While careful not to carry your business into your religion—thus secularizing and

---

127. Winslow, *No Condemnation*, 7–8.

128. See Peter Adam, *Speaking God's Words: A Practical Theology of Expository Preaching* (Downers Grove, Ill.: IVP, 1996), 75–76. He finds the words "call, denounce, warn, rebuke, command, give judgment, encourage, appeal, urge, ask" as pointing to the concept of exhortation.

degrading it—*be careful* to carry your religion into your business—high integrity, holy principle, godly fear—thus imparting an elevation and sanctity to all its concerns. *Be the man of God* wherever you are. *Let these solemn words* be held in vivid remembrance—"I have created you for my glory. I have formed you for my praise. You are my witnesses, says the Lord" (emphasis added).[129]

In such a short space, Winslow provided no fewer than thirteen exhortations to his listeners. His exhortative style also reveals the depth of passion with which he preached.[130]

In another sermon on "Hoping in the Lord," Winslow exhorted his hearers to see the vanity of this world and the value of eternity with God. This time he set up his exhortation with a declarative statement: "Oh, the folly of building the hope of happiness below God, out of Christ, and this side of heaven! Chase no longer the phantom, the dream, the shadow of human hope, of earth-born good; but acquaint yourself with God, seek Christ, and fix your thoughts, your affections, your whole being, upon the world of stern and solemn reality which time is rapidly speeding you."[131]

Winslow also practiced implicit exhortation. The dominant note of his implicit exhortation was to instill hope, often by closing his sermons with an eschatological thrust. While many of his sermons through the Joseph narrative possess this element, his eschatological preaching is most clearly observed in *Soul-Depths and Soul-Heights*. Eight of the nine sermons in that series contain this implicit eschatological exhortation at the conclusion of the sermon. For example, in a sermon titled "Prayer Out of Soul Depths," Winslow encouraged his hearers by implicitly encouraging them to look toward their eschatological hope. He announced, "Soon the soul-desponding saint will ascend from the lowest depths of earth to the loftiest height of heaven. Long before the body springs from the dust, your soul, O believer, will have taken its place amid the blood-ransomed throng, clustering in shining ranks around the throne of God and the Lamb."[132] In the aforementioned sermon "Hoping in the Lord," Winslow urged, "Fight on, toil on, hope on, soldier of

---

129. Winslow, *No Condemnation*, 86–87.

130. For example, note his exhortative instruction on prayer: "Oh, see that your hours of converse with Jesus are not rudely invaded! Go at morning's dawn, at mid-day's turmoil, at evening's shade, yes, in the still hour of night…and, draw near to the Mighty One, the Compassionate One, the All-seeing One, and tell the Savior all! Oh, cultivate sacred retirement." *Patriarchal Shadows*, 92.

131. Winslow, *Soul-Depths*, 44–45.

132. Winslow, *Soul-Depths*, 29.

Christ, laborer for Jesus, tried and suffering one! Soon you shall put off your travel-stained garments, unclasp your dust-covered sandals, lay down your pilgrim-staff; and, attired in glory-robes, enter the palace, and feast your eyes upon the beauty of the King forever."[133] Here Winslow combined both explicit and implicit exhortation. This type of eschatological preaching offered hope and encouragement to his hearers.

Persuasive Preaching

The final element of Winslow's experimental preaching was his persuasive style. He sought to convince the reason and move the will by the use of persuasion. In typical fashion, Winslow did not hesitate to set the truth before his hearers plainly and boldly:

> You reject the Rock of Ages, refuse the sheltering pavilion of the Savior's cross, and despise the offers of his grace, where, then, when the tempest leaps forth in all its maddening fury, will you flee? Yet how calmly you tread upon the very brink of ruin, how sportively you sail along the very edge of the vortex, how content and happy to course your way to the bar of a holy and a just God, through a world of disease and casualty and death, without one anxious thought to obtain deliverance, or one earnest struggle to escape your doom![134]

Additional evidence of his persuasive preaching is observed in a sermon where he utilized a couple of rhetorical devices to sustain his argument. As he began to press his audience to seek the inward witness of the Holy Spirit, he said, "Here I must hold you."[135] Shortly thereafter he continued his argument saying, "From this I cannot release you."[136] He used these rhetorical approaches to gain his audience's attention and encourage them to make a decision for the truth.

Two final examples are discovered in his sermons from Genesis. In the first, titled "A Full Christ for Empty Sinners," he reiterated his main point in order to persuade his hearers to respond to the gospel. He declared:

> Keep this truth constantly in view—a full Christ for an empty sinner. With no other will He have dealings; the rich He will send away empty, the poor He will send away full. The only sinner whom He rejects is he who comes with a price. His salvation is for the lost—His blood is for the guilty—His grace is for the poor. Come now—come as you are—come

133. Winslow, *Soul-Depths*, 108.
134. Winslow, *Inner Life*, 34.
135. Winslow, *Inner Life*, 97.
136. Winslow, *Inner Life*, 99.

though you have been a thousand times before; yours shall be all the blessing—His all the praise.[137]

He also sought to encourage saints with the use of persuasion. In a sermon titled "Christ's Knowledge of His People," Winslow preached on the matter of faith: "Dear heart, cheer up! you shall never be lost! Jesus has spoken it, and it is enough. He says, 'Him that cometh unto me,'—no qualifications, no limitations, as to the amount of guilt, or the multitude of sins, or the degree of faith—simply, 'him that cometh;'—take Christ at His word; come to Him as you are, and He will in no wise discourage or reject you."[138] Winslow utilized persuasion because he desired to see believers and unbelievers changed.

The Intersection of Experimental Elements

As stated earlier, these elements of experimental preaching often intersect. A few examples reveal how Winslow merged these elements in his preaching. In "Full Christ for Empty Sinners," Winslow declared, "Sinner! will not your rebellion, your unbelief, your impenitence give way before this matchless love? Bow the knee, bend the heart, and crown Him with your faith, your love, your life!"[139] In these two short sentences you find the elements of discrimination ("sinner"), interrogation ("will not...?"), persuasion ("before this matchless love") and exhortation ("Bow the knee, bend the heart"). Furthermore, in a sermon meditating on Habakkuk 3:19 titled "Soul Heights," Winslow primarily employed interrogation and exhortation when he proclaimed: "Is this the life you are living, my reader? is this the mere existence in which you vegetate? Rise to a higher life, a nobler purpose, a more glorious end! Don't you know that, 'we must all appear before the judgment seat of Christ, to give account of the deeds done in the body'? That 'every one must give account of himself to God'?"[140] There are hints of persuasion in this example as well.

Finally, several experimental elements can be observed in the conclusion of a sermon titled "The Righteousness of the Law Accomplished in the Believer." In light of Christ having fulfilled the law, Winslow declared:

Christian! Christ's whole obedience is yours. What can sin, or Satan, or conscience, or the law itself allege against you now? Be humble, and

---

137. Winslow, *Patriarchal Shadows*, 64.
138. Winslow, *Patriarchal Shadows*, 44.
139. Winslow, *Patriarchal Shadows*, 63.
140. Winslow, *Soul-Depths*, 124.

mourn over the many flaws and failures in your obedience; yet withal rejoice, and glory, and make your boast in the fullness, perfection, and unchangeableness of that righteousness of the Incarnate God which will place you without fault before the throne. Sinner! if the righteousness of the law is not fulfilled in you now, that righteousness will be exhibited in your just condemnation to all eternity! Flee to Christ Jesus, the end of the law for righteousness to every one that believes.[141]

With these final words, Winslow practiced discrimination, interrogation, exhortation, and persuasion. By intersecting these elements, Winslow invited his hearers to pause and consider how they should apply the truths of the text. This is the essence of experimental preaching.

Conclusion

Winslow's experimental preaching was based on convictions concerning the nature and demands of the Christian life. Fundamentally, he believed every truth and doctrine of God's Word should be applied by the believer. Moreover, his understanding of progressive sanctification and the purpose of preaching for holistic change naturally influenced his pulpit practice. Winslow preached to the heart by grounding his sermons in sound doctrine and centering them in Christ, as well as employing application, discrimination, interrogation, illustration, exhortation, and persuasion. These eight elements demonstrate how Winslow accomplished his experimental method.

---

141. Winslow, *No Condemnation*, 52.

WINSLOW'S EXPERIMENTAL HOMILETIC FOR TODAY

Even if Winslow exhibited a fruitful and influential ministry in his day, a valid question remains: What does he have to say to pastors and church leaders today? I believe Winslow has much to say if we will listen. He provides a wealth of instruction for twenty-first-century pastors, beginning with his theology of preaching and extending through various features of his experimental preaching.

The following eight suggestions are offered as humble proposals for applying his homiletic today. They will explore the relevance of Winslow's homiletic for a theology of preaching, doctrinal preaching, Christ-centered preaching, and other sermonic elements related to experimental preaching. In addition, observations and insights from the contemporary church will be compared with Winslow's approach.

Winslow's Significance for a Theology of Preaching

Winslow first teaches us that *today's preachers should ground their preaching methodology in a robust theology of preaching*. Peter Adam believes "preaching suffers nowadays from an uncertain theological base."[1] Whether preachers realize it or not, their methodology emanates from certain theological convictions, or the lack thereof. Some preachers believe in expository preaching and make the explanation and application of Scripture the trademark of their ministry.[2] Others begin with "felt needs" and speak to what they perceive are the contemporary issues of their hearers.[3] Some even wish

---

1. Peter Adam, *Speaking God's Words: A Practical Theology of Expository Preaching* (Downers Grove, Ill.: IVP, 1998), 9.

2. For a classic work on expository preaching, see Haddon Robinson, *Biblical Preaching*, 2nd ed. (Grand Rapids: Baker, 2001).

3. Some of today's preachers follow the homiletic of Harry Emerson Fosdick, who advocated a "felt needs" approach to preaching over against expository and topical methodologies in the early twentieth century. Fosdick wrote, "People come to church with every kind of

to redefine or "re-imagine" the preaching task. Doug Pagitt believes preaching, which he labels in a derisive manner as "speaching," should transition into what he calls "progressional dialogue."[4] Each of these diverse methodologies arises from particular convictions regarding the nature of sin, man, Scripture, salvation, preaching, and other key doctrines.

Winslow grounded his experimental homiletic in a vigorous theology of preaching. He would agree with John Stott, who says, "The essential secret is not mastering certain techniques but being mastered by certain convictions. In other words, theology is more important than methodology."[5] Additionally, Winslow believed preaching is a glorious assignment that involves speaking for God. His understanding accords with John Piper, who declares: "Preaching is not conversation. Preaching is not discussion. Preaching is not casual talk about religious things. Preaching is not simply teaching. Preaching is the heralding of a message permeated by the sense of God's greatness and majesty and holiness."[6]

Preachers should also enter their task with a sense of gravity because salvation is at stake. Therefore, they should "never give the impression that preaching is something light or superficial or trivial."[7] David Wells pinpoints the persona of many pulpits with the following diagnosis by contrasting the contemporary pulpit with that of the Puritans: "If the spirit of Puritanism

---

difficulty and problem flesh is heir to. A sermon is meant to meet such needs—the sins and shames, the doubts and anxieties that fill the pews. *This is the place to start*, with the real problems of the people." "Preaching as Personal Counseling," in *The Company of Preachers: Wisdom on Preaching, Augustine to the Present*, ed. Richard Lischer (Grand Rapids: Eerdmans, 2002), 398 (emphasis added). Two well-known preachers who put this methodology into practice are Rick Warren and Bill Hybels. For example, Warren writes, "Today preaching to felt needs is scorned and criticized in some circles as a cheapening of the gospel and a sell-out to consumerism. I want to state in this in the clearest way possible: Beginning a message with peoples [sic] felt needs is not some modern approach invented by 20th century marketing! Its [sic] the way Jesus always preached." "A Primer on Preaching Like Jesus, Part One," *CBN.com* (n.d.), http://www.cbn.com/spirituallife/churchandministry/warren_preach_like_jesusa.aspx.

4. Pagitt says progressional dialogue "involves the intentional interplay of multiple viewpoints that leads to unexpected and unforeseen ideas. The message will change depending on who is present and who says what."*Preaching Re-Imagined* (Grand Rapids: Zondervan, 2005), 52.

5. John Stott, *Between Two Worlds: The Art of Preaching in the Twentieth Century* (Grand Rapids: Eerdmans, 1982), 32.

6. John Piper, "Preaching As Expository Exultation for the Glory of God," in *Preaching the Cross*, by Mark Dever, J. Ligon Duncan III, R. Albert Mohler Jr., et al. (Wheaton, Ill.: Crossway, 2007), 104–5.

7. D. Martyn Lloyd-Jones, *Preaching and Preachers* (Grand Rapids: Zondervan, 1971), 98.

is best represented graphically by a preacher in an elevated pulpit, the arm raised in vigorous punctuation on the truth of God, that of modern evangelicalism today is probably best represented by the ubiquitous happy face, a bright smile beckoning smiles in return."[8] Winslow approached the pulpit in the spirit of the Puritans. He preached with great earnestness and joy.[9] Such a biblical approach would serve today's church well.

Moreover, *today's preachers should also incorporate a healthy theology of Word and Spirit in their pulpit ministry*. Winslow had a deep theology of the Word and Spirit as it relates to preaching. He knew the Spirit of God works with the Word of God to bring regeneration, illumination, anointing, and sanctification. Arturo Azurdia and Greg Heisler are two contemporary homileticians who have emphasized the necessity of the Holy Spirit's ministry in the preaching task. Azurdia highlights the role of the Spirit in pointing to Christ. Revealing and glorying Christ "is the holy ambition of the Spirit of God."[10] Heisler lists ten ways the Holy Spirit is at work in preaching: (1) the inspiration of the Word; (2) the conversion of the preacher; (3) the call of the preacher to preach the Word; (4) the character of the preacher to live the Word; (5) the illumination of the Scripture in study; (6) empowering the preacher in delivery; (7) glorifying Christ through the preached Word; (8) opening the hearts of those who hear; (9) applying the Word to the listeners' lives; and (10) producing lasting fruit in the lives of Spirit-filled believers.[11] For all of these reasons, preachers need to seek the Spirit's blessing for their preaching ministries through a healthy view of the Word and Spirit.

---

8. David Wells, *God in the Wasteland: The Reality of Truth in a World of Fading Dreams* (Grand Rapids: Eerdmans, 1994), 28. Wells's words have proved prophetic. One of the "faces" of the "evangelical church" today is Joel Osteen. Osteen pastors Lakewood Church in Houston, whose weekly attendance averages more than thirty thousand. He has been nicknamed "the Smiling Preacher." See Susan Schindehette, "'The Smiling Preacher,'" *People.com* (June 6, 2005), http://www.people.com/people/article/0,,20147762,00.html.

9. Piper highlights how a theology of preaching should also impact one's delivery of the sermon: "O brothers, do not lie about the value of the gospel by the dullness of your demeanor. Exposition of the most glorious reality is a glorious reality. If it is not expository *exultation*—authentic from the heart—something false is being said about the value of the gospel. Don't say by your face or by your voice or by your life that the gospel is not the gospel of the all-satisfying glory of Christ. It is." "Preaching As Expository," 115.

10. Arturo Azurdia, *Spirit Empowered Preaching: Involving the Holy Spirit in Your Ministry* (Ross-shire, U. K.: Mentor, 2007), 49.

11. Greg Heisler, *Spirit-Led Preaching: The Holy Spirit's Role in Sermon Preparation and Delivery* (Nashville: B&H Academic, 2007), 4.

Winslow's Significance for Doctrinal Preaching

Winslow's homiletic also teaches us that *today's preachers should not shrink back from preaching the great doctrines of the faith.* Winslow's experimental preaching reveals the importance of doctrinal preaching. Many people in the pews today are biblically and theologically illiterate. Robert Hughes and Robert Kysar argue that preachers can "no longer...take for granted a fundamental understanding of the basics of the faith."[12]

Wells is also right when he contends that "the evangelical Church has cheerfully plunged into astounding theological illiteracy."[13] If preachers fail to expound doctrine, they do so to the church's detriment. Wells is again insightful when he writes, "A church that is neither interested in theology nor has the capacity to think theologically is a church...for whom Christian faith will rapidly lose its point, and this is already well underway within evangelicalism."[14] Pastors and preachers who do not take heed to such warnings run the risk of becoming increasingly irrelevant. Sermons strong in doctrinal content provide a needed remedy for this danger. People need to know the great doctrines of God, Christ, man, sin, and salvation.

Additionally, growth in biblical and theological knowledge is necessary because the spirituality of God's people depends upon it. Experimental Christianity builds off of doctrinal truth. David Clark writes, "Intellectual knowledge is highly prized as the means to spiritual knowledge of God."[15] Winslow understood this and grounded his experimental preaching in the great doctrines of the faith. Today's preachers should view themselves as theologians who are obligated to restore an appreciation for deep theological truth that affects daily living.

Winslow's Significance for Christ-Centered Preaching

Today's preachers should strive to demonstrate how every passage of Scripture points to Christ in a biblically faithful manner. Winslow's Christ-centered

---

12. Robert G. Hughes and Robert Kysar, *Preaching Doctrine for the Twenty-First Century* (Minneapolis: Fortress, 1997), 1.

13. David Wells, *No Place for Truth, or, Whatever Happened to Evangelical Theology?* (Grand Rapids: Eerdmans, 1993), 4.

14. David Wells, "The Theologian's Craft," in *Doing Theology in Today's World*, ed. John Woodbridge and Thomas McComiskey (Grand Rapids: Eerdmans, 1991), 191–92. Osteen provides an example in this area as well. In a 2005 interview, he said, "I'm not necessarily going to teach you doctrine.... I know what I'm called to present—a message of hope." Schindehette, "'The Smiling Preacher.'"

15. David Clark, *To Know and Love God: Method for Theology* (Wheaton, Ill.: Crossway, 2003), 210.

preaching, which flowed from his Christ-centered hermeneutic, should also contribute to today's conversation concerning the legitimacy of preaching Christ from all of Scripture. Much contemporary preaching reduces the text to moralistic instruction lacking grace and divorced from Christ and Him crucified. Daniel Akin is right when he says, "Call it what you will, preaching that does not exalt, magnify, and glorify the Lord Jesus is not Christian preaching.... We are not Jewish rabbis or scribes. Good and faithful exposition will be christological in focus. It will carefully interpret each text in the greater context of the grand redemptive storyline of Scripture showing Jesus as the hero of the Bible."[16] Pastors today, even those with a vibrant Christology, should heed his warning and instruction.

In recent days, however, there has been a resurgence of Christ-centered preaching among evangelicals. Several homiletics professors have published important works promoting the practice.[17] This resurgence is not without historical precedent. Its roots go back to the earliest days of apostolic and patristic preaching.[18]

Those who advocate Christ-centered preaching, however, should consider a potential theological hazard connected with the practice.[19] This hazard involves the doctrine of the Trinity. It is possible that Christ-centered preaching can degenerate into something less than what accords with biblical Trinitarianism. Robert Letham has argued that pastors in the Western church should beware of becoming modalistic in their worship of God. He suggests, "In the West, the Trinity has in practice been relegated

---

16. Daniel Akin, "Axioms for a Great Commission Resurgence," in *The Great Commission Resurgence: Fulfilling God's Mandate in Our Time*, ed. Chuck Lawless and Adam W. Greenway (Nashville: B&H Academic, 2010).

17. For an introduction to Christ-centered preaching, see Bryan Chapell, *Christ-Centered Preaching: Redeeming the Expository Sermon* (Grand Rapids: Baker, 1994); Edmund Clowney, *Preaching Christ in All of Scripture* (Wheaton, Ill.: Crossway, 2003); Graeme Goldsworthy, *Preaching the Whole Bible as Christian Scripture: The Application of Biblical Theology to Expository Preaching* (Grand Rapids: Eerdmans, 2000); Sidney Greidanus, *Preaching Christ from the Old Testament: A Contemporary Hermeneutical Method* (Grand Rapids: Eerdmans, 1999); and Dennis Johnson, *Him We Proclaim: Preaching Christ from All the Scriptures* (Phillipsburg, N.J.: P&R, 2007). Johnson's work, in particular, provides a comprehensive and practical resource that addresses the history of Christ-centered interpretation and preaching, provides a defense against criticisms, and supplies a practical approach for the task.

18. For a good historical summary of Christ-centered preaching, see Johnson, *Him We Proclaim*, 98–125.

19. For the biblical and historical arguments for the practice, see the works listed in footnote 17, particularly Johnson and Goldsworthy.

to such an extent that most Christians are little more than practical modalists."[20] Practical modalists are guilty of emphasizing one person of the Trinity to the neglect or exclusion of the other two persons. For example, while many Pentecostals may exercise an imbalanced view of the Spirit, many evangelicals are guilty of crossing into a "Jesus only" Christianity. For those employing a Christ-centered methodology of preaching, Letham's critique should be taken seriously. A healthy understanding of the doctrine of the Trinity should govern our preaching to ensure that the Father, Son, and Spirit receive the worship they deserve. Winslow modeled such an approach. His Trinitarian theology actually provided the motivation and justification for his Christ-centered messages.

Although Winslow's sermons were not always exegetically flawless, he provides several key insights for preachers who desire to preach the gospel from all of Scripture in a biblically faithful manner. First, while remaining faithful to the original context of Scripture, preachers should seek to preach the whole Bible as Christian Scripture. It is unacceptable to proclaim a text without setting it within the grand storyline of redemptive history. Jesus is the fulfillment of God's plan to reconcile man to Himself. This is what Greidanus means when he says, "The unity of redemptive history implies the *christocentric* nature of every historical text. Redemptive history is the history of Christ: He stands at its center, but no less at its beginning and end."[21] Ed Clowney made an even stronger point concerning preaching each text in light of Scripture's metanarrative. Tim Keller reflects on his teaching: "Ed Clowney points out that if we ever tell a particular Bible story without putting it into *the* Bible story (about Christ), we actually change the meaning."[22] Therefore, preachers who seek to preach the whole counsel of God should do so recognizing that the "Bible is, from its commencement to its close, a record of the Lord Jesus."[23]

Secondly, preachers should ground their sermons in a robust theology of the Trinity. It may be feared that few consistently articulate an accurate

---

20. Robert Letham, *The Holy Trinity: In Scripture, History, Theology, and Worship* (Phillipsburg, N.J.: P&R, 2004), 407.

21. Sidney Greidanus, *Sola Scriptura: Problems and Principles in Preaching Historical Texts* (Eugene, Ore.: Wipf & Stock, 2001), 135.

22. Tim Keller, "Advancing the Gospel into the 21st Century: Acts 13–19," *City Reaching* (blog), keynote address at the Mission America Coalition National Leadership Forum meeting (October 2003), http://cityreaching.com/floating154.php.

23. Octavius Winslow, *The Precious Things of God* (London: James Nisbet, 1860; repr., Ligonier, Pa.: Soli Deo Gloria, 1993), 263.

portrayal of the Trinity. Letham contends, *"Chief of all, the Trinity must be preached and must shape preaching.* Preaching is the high point of worship. Not only must the Trinity be preached, but *all* preaching must be shaped by the active recognition that the God whose word is proclaimed is triune. A Trinitarian mind-set must become as integral to the preacher as the air we breathe."[24] In a day when biblical and theological illiteracy is so prevalent, the doctrine of the Trinity cannot be assumed.

Thirdly, as exemplified in Winslow, a healthy understanding of the triune God as He has revealed Himself in redemptive history should provide motivation for Christ-centered preaching. This is important because it seems most homileticians make biblical and historical arguments for Christ-centered preaching. While this should be commended, a theological argument based on the revelation and work of the Godhead in redemptive history bolsters the case.

Winslow's Significance for Other Experimental Elements

Winslow's experimental approach also exposes several other weaknesses in modern preaching. Many of today's pulpits lack some or many of the elements found in Winslow's methodology. More specifically, preachers should incorporate applicatory, discriminatory, interrogating, exhortative, and persuasive elements more regularly in their preaching.

Today's preachers should make a commitment to preach sermons that clearly apply truth to the lives of their hearers. Winslow's practice of experimental preaching provides an exemplary model of applying doctrine to life. He understood mere intellectual assent to the truth is not real Christianity. Followers of Christ must apply God's Word. Just as Winslow lamented the fact that experimental preaching waned in his day, Joel Beeke believes the modern pulpit suffers from the same problem. He writes: "How different experiential preaching is from what we often hear today. The Word of God too often is preached in a way that will not transform listeners because it fails to discriminate and fails to apply. Such preaching is reduced to a lecture, a demonstration, a catering to what people want to hear, or the kind of subjectivism that is divorced from the foundation of Scripture."[25] John MacArthur actually believes application is not the preacher's job. In answering the question concerning why he does not include application in his sermons, MacArthur replied:

---

24. Letham, *Holy Trinity*, 423.
25. Joel Beeke, *Living for God's Glory: An Introduction to Calvinism* (Lake Mary, Fla.: Reformation Trust, 2008), 256.

It's not for me to do that. Application belongs to the Spirit of God. All I'm interested in is explanation and its implications. And the power comes in the implication and the Spirit of God takes the implications of what I've said tonight, all these things I've said, I don't need to say all kinds of little scenarios to you and paint all kinds of little individual circumstances. All I need you to know is this is what the Word of God says and the implications are powerfully brought to bear with authority on your life and I exhort you to respond to those implications, it is the Spirit's work to drive those implications into direct and personal application.[26]

To be fair, MacArthur's approach is concerned with the truth being applied to the hearer's life. At the same time, to say that application is not the preacher's job seems to undercut the very nature of experimental preaching.[27] At its best, experimental preaching addresses the whole person and strives for holistic change through applying doctrine to life.

Today's preachers should recognize the spiritual diversity of their audience and practice discriminatory preaching. Wise preachers take into consideration the varied spiritual backgrounds of their hearers. They understand that they must preach to believers and unbelievers as well as the spiritually mature and those struggling in the faith. Tim Keller is one contemporary preacher who echoes Winslow in this area. Keller advocates the need to address both believers and unbelievers with the gospel in every sermon. Concerning the need to craft sermons for the ear of unbelievers, he writes:

It is hard to overstate how ghettoized our preaching is. It is normal to make all kinds of statements that appear persuasive to us but are based upon all sorts of premises that the secular person does not hold. It is normal to make all sorts of references using terms and phrases that mean nothing outside our Christian sub-group.... As you write

---

26. John MacArthur, "Why Doesn't John MacArthur Add Much Application to His Sermons?" *Grace to You Blog,* n.d., http://www.gty.org/Resources/Sermons/GTY117. The poor punctuation in this paragraph has been retained from the online source. Interestingly, MacArthur has advocated the use of application elsewhere in his writings: "I prefer to say that all of a sermon should be applicable. If I preach the Word of God powerfully and accurately, everything I say should apply. Obviously, not all will apply to everyone in the same way, but it is my intent to speak what is life-changing for all." *Rediscovering Expository Preaching* (Dallas: Word, 1992), 343.

27. Hershael York and Bert Decker oppose MacArthur's view when they write, "Nothing in the Bible is purely academic—knowledge for the sake of knowledge with no practical value. *Everything* in the Bible has a practical value that we must discern and apply to our lives. Our sermons, therefore, need to be saturated not only with the content of the text, but also with a practical application for our hearers." *Preaching with Bold Assurance: A Solid and Enduring Approach to Engaging Exposition* (Nashville: Broadman & Holman, 2003), 77.

the sermon imagine a particular skeptical non-Christian in the chair listening to you. Add the asides, the qualifiers, the extra explanations necessary. Listen to everything said in the worship service with the ears of an unbelieving heart.[28]

Keller provides practical advice to preachers who desire to preach with greater discrimination. Preaching must be strong in applying principles of contextualization and address the various groups present as effectively as possible. It must consider those who are struggling and doubting, skeptics and atheists, the moral and immoral, new believers and the spiritually mature.

Today's preachers should utilize interrogatives in order to confront the conscience of their hearers.[29] In *The Imperative of Preaching*, John Carrick notes the value of using interrogatives. He believes most homileticians overlook the importance of searching interrogatives. He writes, "Remarkably...many homileticians do not deal with the interrogative at all, and even those who do deal with this issue have given no detailed, extended treatment of the subject."[30] Carrick recognizes three types of useful questions in preaching: analytical, rhetorical, and searching. He calls the searching question the most valuable in preaching because "it is personal; it is pointed; it searches and probes the hearts of men and has a very significant awakening tendency."[31] While Winslow primarily utilized the searching question to confront his hearers' consciences, he used analytical and rhetorical questions as well.[32]

Experimental preaching is analogous to an interrogation room. Preachers should utilize penetrating questions that turn hearers in on themselves and lead them to ask: "Is this true of me? How do I need to change?"

---

28. Tim Keller and J. Allen Thompson, *Redeemer Church Planting Manual* (New York: Redeemer Church Planting Center, 2002), 134.

29. The use of searching questions provides an interesting topic for future research on Winslow specifically and preaching in general.

30. John Carrick, *The Imperative of Preaching: A Theology of Sacred Rhetoric* (Edinburgh: Banner of Truth, 2002), 69.

31. Carrick, *Imperative of Preaching*, 66.

32. Nineteenth-century pastor J. Manning Sherwood noted this feature of dealing with man's conscience in the preaching of Jonathan Edwards. He believed it was his greatest asset in the pulpit. He wrote, "It was not his masterly metaphysics, his profound philosophy, his intellectual demonstrations, or his parade of learning, that made him such a giant in the pulpit;—there is a singular absence of these in his sermons [I would disagree with that comment]. But he got strait down upon the sinner's *conscience*, and there dealt his earnest blows with almost superhuman effect." "Bible Preacher," *The American National Preacher* 27 (September 1853): 214.

Interrogatives help people evaluate where they stand before God. Searching questions help them look in the mirror and identify what areas of repentance and growth in sanctification they need to pursue. Carrick explains, "Indeed, whereas there is often something intrinsically *comfortable* about the simple indicative, there is generally something intrinsically *uncomfortable* about the searching interrogative. Thus the whole tendency of the searching interrogative is that of producing *self-reflection* and *self-examination* in the hearer."[33] Thus, good questions promote the application of the Word. Interrogatives also help create what Lloyd-Jones called "the element of attack."[34] He believed this distinguished preaching from a lecture. Preachers would do well to consider the value of searching questions for their preaching.

Finally, *today's preachers should incorporate the elements of exhortation and persuasion as legitimate means of moving the will.* Exhortation and persuasion are also elements that distinguish the pulpit from the classroom. This is because preaching not only seeks to inform the mind; it desires to move the will. Exhortation seeks to press for a volitional response, and persuasion convinces the mind and will concerning the wisdom and plausibility of a particular course of action. That is why Winslow's experimental preaching incorporated both of these elements.

Peter Adam recognizes exhortation and persuasion as two key elements in good preaching.[35] He believes many of the verbs related to the ministry of the Word in the New Testament reveal the importance of exhortation and persuasion. Words such as "call, denounce, warn, rebuke, command, give judgment, encourage, appeal, urge, [and] ask" are exhortative in nature, while words such as "explain, make clear, prove, guard, debate, contend, refute, reason, persuade, convince, insist, defend, confirm, [and] stress" point to the need for persuasive preaching.[36] Today's preachers should regularly exhort and persuade their listeners to live out the truths of the gospel in every sermon.

---

33. Carrick, *Imperative of Preaching*, 79.

34. Lloyd-Jones, *Preaching and Preachers*, 79.

35. Adam, *Speaking God's Words*, 78.

36. Adam, *Speaking God's Words*, 76. The word "exhort" comes from the Greek word παρακαλέω, which can be translated "to urge strongly, appeal to, exhort, encourage, request, implore." William Arndt, Frederick Danker, and Walter Bauer, *A Greek-English Lexicon of the New Testament and Other Early Christian Literature*, 3rd ed. (Chicago: University of Chicago Press, 2001), s.v. "παρακαλέω." The word "persuade" comes from πείθω, which can be translated "to cause to come to a particular point of view, persuade, appeal to, win over." Arndt, Danker, and Bauer, *Greek-English Lexicon*, s.v. "πείθω."

Conclusion

Winslow's homiletic has much to say to contemporary preachers and homileticians. His robust theology of preaching and his emphasis on doctrinal and Christ-centered preaching provide foundational guidance. Moreover, the other experimental elements of application, discrimination, interrogation, exhortation, and persuasion provide quality examples for areas often neglected, to one degree or another, today. Winslow's writing and sermons provide a rich example of striving for holistic change by preaching *from* the heart *to* the heart.

The true beauty of experimental preaching is not simply that it works to achieve heart transformation. Most importantly, it brings God glory by keeping the person and work of the triune God at the center. Winslow believed everything in life is designed for the glory of God. He wrote, "The great and holy end is, 'the glory and praise of God.' God does nothing and permits nothing that shall not terminate in the manifestation of His glory."[37] His emphasis on experimental preaching will continue to glorify God if today's preachers are humble enough to learn from his example and put it into practice.

Since this work has aimed to introduce Octavius Winslow to today's church, it seems fitting to conclude with his own words concerning God's sovereign power to sustain the health of the church in the absence of ministers like him. Quoting the words of Jacob to his son Joseph in Genesis 48:21, he wrote:

> The Church of God is constantly called to mourn the departure of her ministers, her strong and distinguished pillars, her warm and zealous friends and supporters. And when thus a useful minister of Christ dies, when a prominent standard-bearer in the army of Christ falls, and when a strong pillar of the Church is removed by death, our hearts begin to fear and tremble, and we inquire, "Who will, or can, supply his place in the Church of God? Who will uplift that standard and wave it before the foe? Who will be able to carry on that important enterprise thus suddenly arrested? Who will fill this gap, battle for this principle, witness for this truth?" The answer is—"*God will be with you.*" "Enough, blessed Lord," we exclaim. "You take away ministers, remove earnest and zealous agents, and stern, strong pillars of the Church; but You live still, and will never leave Your Church destitute." Let this always comfort us when we hear of the removal by death of God's servants, the pillars of the Church, the witnesses of the truth, God will be with His Church,

---

37. Octavius Winslow, *Lights and Shadows of Spiritual Life* (London: John F. Shaw, 1876; repr., *The Spiritual Life* [Stoke-on-Trent, U.K.: Tentmaker, 1998], 83.

will guide His Church, will protect His Church, will lead her on from battle to battle, and from victory to victory, never leaving nor forsaking her in all times of trial, desertion, and bereavement. *"I die; but God will be with you."*[38]

---

38. Octavius Winslow, *The Man of God, or, Spiritual Religion Explained and Enforced* (London: John F. Shaw, 1865), 275–77.

APPENDIX 1

⁓

SERMON ON PSALM 130:3
CONTRITION AND CONFESSION[1]

If thou, LORD, shouldest mark iniquities, O Lord, who shall stand?
—PSALM 130:3

It is said—and we believe with truth—, that, to the eye of the miner, entombed deep in the heart of the earth, the heavens appear at noonday studded with myriads of the most brilliant planets, invisible at the same moment from the earth's surface. The phenomenon is easy of solution. It is *night* with the miner, in his depths; and the darkest night reveals wonders and splendors which the brightest day conceals. May not this simple fact furnish an apt illustration of our present subject? Some of the most glorious unfoldings of God's character and of Christ's beauty, of divine truth and lessons of the Christian life, are found in those 'soul-depths' we have been describing, not always experienced by believers who, for the most part, dwell but upon the surface of the divine life.

Not the least important is the subject of our present chapter—*the holiness of God, and the contrition and confession of the believer.* "If thou, LORD, shouldest mark iniquities, O Lord, who shall stand?" To the consideration of these points let us address ourselves, as the Holy Spirit shall aid us. The subject is solemn and important—the *most* solemn and important of all subjects. Right and deep views of sin lie at the root of correct and high views of God; and low thoughts of God inevitably engender low perceptions of sin.

---

1. This sermon was published in Winslow's book titled *Soul-Depths & Soul-Heights: Sermons on Psalm 130* (London: John F. Shaw, 1874; repr., Edinburgh: Banner of Truth, 2006), 32–46. All of the original wording, punctuation, paragraphing, and emphasis from the original have been retained in so much as they were by the publishers at Banner of Truth. I have made slight changes to the reprint of this sermon (e.g., the headings supplied by Banner of Truth have been omitted and some minor stylistic changes have been made). These two sample sermons were chosen as representative of Winslow's experimental preaching. The eight key elements of Winslow's experimental homiletic will surface throughout.

Dr. Owen, in his instructive exposition of this psalm, though somewhat verbose, thus forcibly puts the matter: "The generality of men make light work of sin; and yet in nothing does it more appear what thoughts they have of God. He that has light thoughts of sin had never great thoughts of God. Indeed, men's underrating of sin arises merely from their contempt of God. All sin's concernments place its relation unto God. And as men's conceptions are of God, so will they be of sin, which is an opposition to him. This is the frame of the most of men; they know little of God, and are little troubled about anything that relates unto him. God is not reverenced; sin is but a trifle; forgiveness a matter of nothing; whosoever will may have it for nothing. But shall the atheistical wickedness of the heart of man be called a discovery of forgiveness? Is not this to make God an idol? He who is not acquainted with God's holiness and purity, who knows not sin's deceit and sinfulness, knows nothing of forgiveness." The groundwork, then, of our present subject is, *the essential holiness of God,* upon which is based *the soul's godly sorrow for sin.* To these solemn points let us direct our devout attention.

The highest and most glorious perfection of God is *his essential holiness.* He would cease to be God could he cease to be *holy,* holiness being, not an accident, but an intrinsic perfection of his Being. It is the uniting bond of all his other perfections, imparting existence, cohesion, and beauty to all.

[Stephen Charnock observes:] "The nature of God cannot rationally be conceived without it. Though the power of God be the first rational conclusion drawn from the light of his works and wisdom, the next from the order and connection of his works, purity must result from the beauty of his works. God cannot be deformed by evil who has made everything so beautiful in his time. The notion of a God cannot be entertained without separating from him whatever is impure and bespotting, both in his essence and actions. Though we conceive him infinite in majesty, infinite in essence, eternal in duration, mighty in power, and wise and immutable in his counsels, merciful in his proceedings with men, and whatever other perfections may dignify so sovereign a Being: yet if we conceive him destitute of these excellent perfections, and imagine him possessed with the least contagion of evil; we make him but an infinite monster, and sully all these perfections we ascribed to him before; we rather own him a devil than a God. It is a less injury to him to deny his Being than to deny the purity of it. The one makes him no God, the other deformed, unholy, and detestable."

God is declared to be "glorious in holiness" (Ex. 15:11); so holy that it is said "he cannot look upon sin"; that is, cannot look upon it but with infinite hatred and abhorrence. "Thou art of purer eyes than to behold evil, and can not look on iniquity." He swears by his holiness. "Once have I *sworn by my holiness*, that I will not lie unto David." "The Lord will swear by his holiness." Holiness, as we have remarked, is the lustre and beauty of his Being. "How great is his beauty," because how perfect is his *holiness!* "Power is his arm; omniscience, his eye; mercy, his bowels; eternity, his duration; *holiness his beauty*." "The beauty of holiness."

Passing over the many exceptional proofs God has given of his hatred of sin, and his solemn determination to punish it—for example, the destruction of the old world by water, and that of the cities of the plain by fire; let us bend our thoughts to the most significant and appalling demonstration of his holiness the universe ever beheld, infinitely distancing and transcending every other—*the sufferings and death of his only and beloved Son*. The cross of Calvary exhibits God's hatred and punishment of sin in a way and to an extent which the annihilation of millions of worlds, swept from the face of the universe by the broom of his wrath, could never have done.

The Surety and Substitute of his elect church—bearing her sins, and exhausting her curse—divine law and justice exacted from him the utmost equivalent; the one, a perfect obedience, the other, the penalty of death. "Christ was once offered to bear the sins of many." "Who his own self bare our sins in his own body on the tree." "He was wounded for our transgressions, he was bruised for our iniquities." In all this we beheld a most awful display of God's hatred of sin. Finding the sins of the church upon Christ as its Surety, Substitute, and Savior, the wrath of God was poured out upon him without measure! To what other rational cause can we ascribe the profound emotion which these words describe: "My soul is sorrowful, even unto death." "And being in an agony…he sweat great drops of blood, falling down to the ground." "My Father, if it be possible, let this cup pass from me"?

He had never transgressed. "Holy, harmless, and undefiled," he was free from every taint of sin. Jesus had never broken God's law; but, on the contrary, "had done always those things which pleased him." And yet, pure and obedient though he was, God finding the sins of his people laid upon his Son, emptied upon his holy soul all the vials of his wrath due to their transgressions. Go, my soul, to Calvary, and learn how holy God is, and what a monstrous thing sin is, and how imperiously, solemnly, and holily bound Jehovah is to punish it, either in the person of the sinner, or in the person of a Surety.

Could the personal sinlessness of Christ exempt him from this terrible punishment? Could it in any measure lessen or mitigate the tremendous infliction of God the Father's wrath? Impossible! It was not Christ who was penally punished: it was the sins of his elect church, which he voluntarily and fully bore, punished in him. Never was the Son of God dearer to the Father than at the very moment that the sword of divine justice, flaming and flashing, pierced to its hilt his holy heart. But it was the wrath of God, not against his beloved Son, but against the sins which met on him when presenting himself on the cross as the substitutionary sacrifice and offering of his church. He "gave himself for us." What a new conception must angels have formed of the exceeding sinfulness of sin, when they beheld the flaming sword of justice quenched in the holy, loving bosom of Jesus! And in what a dazzling light does this fact place the marvellous love of God to sinners! Man's sin and God's love—the indescribable enormity of the one, and the immeasurable greatness of the other—are exhibited in the cross of Christ as nowhere else. Oh to learn experimentally these two great facts—sin's infinite hatefulness, and love's infinite holiness! The love of God in giving his Son to die; the love of Christ in dying; the essential turpitude and unmitigated enormity of sin, which demanded a sacrifice so Divine, so holy, and so precious!

> On the wings of faith uprising,
> Jesus crucified I see;
> While his love, my soul surprising,
> Cries, "I suffered all for thee."
>
> Then, beneath the cross adoring,
> Sin does like itself appear,
> When the wounds of Christ exploring,
> I can read my pardon there.
>
> Angels here may gaze and wonder
> What the God of love could mean,
> When that heart was torn asunder,
> Never once defiled with sin.

Nor this alone. In the cross of Christ we not only see the enormity of man's sin and the greatness of God's love, but in the atonement there offered the believing soul beholds the entire cancelling of all his transgressions, the complete blotting out of the thick cloud of all his guilt. Viewed in this light, as a penitent believer, you have nothing, in the sense of propitiation, to do with your sins. The work of propitiation is all done by Christ your Surety. "Whom God has set forth to be a propitiation for our sins"; and when this was done, "there remains no more sacrifice for sins." Christ's one offering of himself has forever perfected those who are sanctified. Cease, then, to look upon the great debt as though Jesus had not discharged it; upon the mighty bond, as though he had not cancelled it; upon your countless sins, as though his blood had not washed them all away.

You have nothing to do with your sins—past, present, or to come—but to mortify the root, to combat vigorously their ascendancy, and to wash constantly in the divine laver of Christ's atoning blood, confessing daily and hourly sins, with the hand of faith laid upon the head of the sacrificial Lamb thus walking as before God with a quickened, tender, purified conscience, desiring in all things to please him.

"If thou, LORD, shouldest mark iniquities, O Lord, who shall stand?" Contrition is the first feeling in David's experience which these words indicate. It was in the "depths" that this most holy grace was inspired. The believer has need to be brought into a very close knowledge of himself to learn what true and deep contrition for sin is. The deepest humiliation, the warmest tears, the most broken and contrite spirit, are not often found in the "high places" where the soul is privileged to walk. We must descend from the mount into the valley, and in the valley "lie low in a low place"—yes, the lowest; to learn the meaning and force of David's prayer: "O Lord, pardon mine iniquity; for it is great"; and of Job's acknowledgment: "I abhor myself, and repent in dust and ashes."

Oh, what a volume of meaning do these words contain, as they apply to our individual selves: "If thou, LORD, shouldest mark iniquities," my iniquities—the depravity of my nature, the sinfulness of my heart, the unrighteousness of my most holy things—my thoughts and imaginations, my words and actions, my covetousness, worldliness, and carnality; my low aims, selfish motives, and by-ends; O Lord, how could I stand?

In this light we must interpret David's contrite words; and thus interpreted, with what solemnity and self-application will they come home to every bosom in which throbs one pulse of spiritual life—in which glows one spark of divine love!

Cultivate, beloved, a holy contrition for sin. Subject your heart to the closest anatomy, your actions to the most searching analysis, your mental conceptions, motives, and words, to the most rigid and faithful scrutiny. This godly sorrow, and holy contrition, will preserve your heart pure and tender, your spirit lowly and watchful, your holy posture and place ever low beneath the cross.

An old divine thus appropriately discourses: "The merchant never allows a single day to elapse without taking an account of what he may have gained or lost in the course of it: let us do the same by our souls. Let not one evening pass over our heads without our examining how our spiritual account stands; let us enter into the inmost recesses of our heart, and ask ourselves, 'In what have I offended God during the day? Have I indulged in idle conversation? Have I sinned by neglecting to perform my duties? Have I tried too hardly the patience of any of my debtors? Have I tried too hardly the patience of any of my brethren? Have I injured the reputation of any one by my words? When I have seemed to take part in holy things, has not my mind been occupied with the affairs of this world? When the concupiscence of the flesh has presented its dangerous poisons to me, have I not voluntarily inclined my lips towards the cup?' And under whatever of these or other heads we may find ourselves on the debtor side, let us lament over our transgressions from our inmost souls, and labor to make up tomorrow what we may have lost today."

The effect of this holy scrutiny will be humble contrition, and that in its turn will be exceedingly bitter; nevertheless, the more bitter our repentance, the sweeter the fruit. It is said by naturalists that the bitterest flower yields the sweetest honey. Bitter in their bud, fruits gain sweetness as they advance to maturity; so it is with the exercises of penitence—they begin by being bitter, but they end by growing sweet.

Hence our dear Lord said, "Blessed are those who weep." What! are tears blessed? Is weeping sweet? Yes! Not the tears falling upon the coffin and the grave of loved ones of whom death has bereaved us; not the tears wept over ruined fortune, and lowered circumstances, and alienated friendship; but, blessed are they who weep over their sins, lament their backslidings, and mourn their spiritual lapses and willful wanderings from the straight and narrow road to heaven, as beneath the shadow of the cross.

Confession is another element of David's acknowledgment. "If thou, LORD, shouldest mark iniquities, O Lord, who shall stand?" These words involve a personal and *humble acknowledgment* of sin on the part of the psalmist. Confession of sin is a consequence of contrition for sin. No grace in the "royal penitent" was more conspicuous than the grace of *confession* to God. "I *acknowledged* my sin unto thee, and my iniquity have I not hid. I said, I will *confess* my transgressions unto the LORD." "I *acknowledge* my transgressions: and my sin is ever before me."

And here we touch upon a duty—no, a privilege—the most holy, spiritual, and sanctifying of the Christian life—*confession of sin* to God. What a significant and magnificent confession have we in these words: "If thou, LORD, shouldest mark iniquities, O Lord, who shall stand?" We cannot urge upon the reader a more spiritual, purifying, and comforting habit than this. It seems to involve every spiritual grace of the Christian character; an intelligent apprehension of sin, sincere repentance, deep humiliation, living faith, holy love, and a simple turning of the soul to Jesus.

Why is it that so many of God's saints travel all their days with their heads bowed like a bulrush? Why so few attain to the high standard of an *assured* interest in Christ? Why so many walk in the spirit of legal bondage, knowing little or nothing of their pardon, adoption, and acceptance? May it not, to a great degree, be traced to their lax habit of *confession of sin to God*? It is because they go day by day, and week by week, bearing along their lonely, dusty road, the burden of conscious sin and uncleansed guilt. Oh, the great secret of a pure, holy, and happy walk is in living close by God's confessional—is in going with the slightest aberration of the mind, with the faintest consciousness of guilt, and at once, with the eye upon the blood, unveiling and acknowledging it, without the slightest concealment or mental reservation, to God! So long as this holy privilege is neglected, guilt, like a corroding poison, an inflamed wound, a festering sore, eats as a canker into the very vitals of our peace and joy and hope.

This was David's testimony: "When I kept silence, my bones waxed old through my roaring all the day long. For day and night thy hand was heavy upon me: my moisture is turned into the drought of summer. I *acknowledged* my sin unto thee, and my iniquity have I not hid. I said, I will *confess* my transgressions unto the Lord; and thou *forgavest* the iniquity of my sin."

Do not suppose that, because contrition and confession were among the earliest exercises of your conversion, that there they ended. God forbid! They belong to each stage, and should trace every step of the Christian life. The close of that life is often marked by the deepest, holiest, and most evangelical sorrow for sin; the dying eye moistened with contrition's last and latest and most precious tear. What most endears the open Fountain? What leads us the most frequently and the most believingly to bathe in its ever-fresh, ever-flowing, ever-cleansing stream? What makes Jesus so precious? Oh, it is the daily, the constant habit of *confession*. We must ever remember that the Paschal Lamb was eaten with *bitter herbs*, and that those bitter herbs imparted a sweetness to the sacrificial offering. And thus it is that, the bitter herbs of repentance, blended with a holy confession of sin at the cross, impart a higher estimation of the atonement, an additional sweetness to the blood, and render the Savior more precious to the heart. Oh the peace, the repose, the light, which springs from the confession of sin to God, no imagination can conceive or words express!

A simple personal incident may illustrate the idea. Sauntering on one occasion through the "long-drawn aisles" of a Roman Catholic cathedral, my eye was arrested by one of the numerous dreary-looking "confessionals" which invariably obtrude from the walls of those foreign edifices. While musing upon the object, a young female in modest attire approached, and, prostrating herself at the feet of the ghostly priest, placed her mouth close to his ear as he bent his head to receive her confession. In a short time she arose, and with a flushed countenance, a beaming eye, and an air of conscious relief, passed me quickly on her way. She had unveiled the sacred, and perhaps guilty, secrets of her heart to the ear of the ghostly confessor, had received his "absolution," and retired from the church with the aspect of one from off whose soul a terrible weight of sin and terror had been removed. And, as in solemn reflection I gazed upon the melancholy spectacle, I thought—If such the soul-peace, such the mental relief, which confession to a poor sinful mortal induces—false though it be; what must be the divine, what the true repose and comfort of a humble, penitential, and unreserved confession of sin to God, through Christ Jesus!

Christian, do not carry the burden of your sin a single step further; the moment the consciousness of guilt and departure from God oppresses you, however apparently slight it may appear—a thought, a look, a passion, a word, an act—repair immediately to the feet of Jesus, disclose it without the slightest mental reservation, and, by a renewed application of atoning blood, seek its immediate and entire removal. Thus penitentially confessing and divinely absolved, you shall uprise from the feet of the great High Priest, exclaiming, with a lightened conscience and a praiseful heart, "I acknowledge my sin unto thee, and mine iniquity have I not hid. I said, I will confess my transgressions unto the LORD; and thou forgavest the iniquity of my sin" (Ps. 32:5).

"If thou, LORD, shouldest mark iniquities, O Lord, who shall stand?" The false and fatal idea of the ungodly is, that God does not "mark"—that is, does not notice or record "iniquity"—forgetting the solemn declarations of his own word: "The ways of man are before the eyes of the Lord, and he ponders all his goings." "The eyes of the Lord are in every place, beholding the evil and the good." Oh that these weighty declarations may sink deep into our hearts! The most holy saint of God needs them.

If the Lord should mark, ponder, chasten *the iniquity of our most holy things*—the double motive, the self-seeking end, the sinful infirmity, which attaches to our best and holiest doings, who of us could stand in his presence? All that we do for God, and for Christ, and for our fellows, is deformed and tainted by human infirmity and sin. A close scrutiny and analysis of our most saintly act would discover the leprosy of iniquity deeply hidden beneath its apparent loveliness and sanctity. How humbling, yet how true! We have need to weep over our tears, to repent of our repentances, to confess our confessions; and, when our most fervent prayer has been breathed, and our most self-denying act has been performed, and our most liberal offering has been presented, and our most powerful sermon has been preached, and our sweetest anthem has poured forth its music, we have need to repair to the "blood that cleanses from *all* sin," even the sins of our most holy things!

How instructive and impressive the type! "Thou shalt make a plate of pure gold, and grave upon it, like the engravings of a signet, HOLINESS TO THE LORD.... And it shall be upon Aaron's forehead, that Aaron may bear the iniquity of the holy things, which the children of Israel shall hallow in all their holy gifts; and it shall be always upon his forehead, that they may be accepted before the LORD" (Ex. 28:36–38). Thus has Christ, our true Aaron, made a full atonement for the "iniquity of our holy things"; and the mitre is always upon his head, that our persons and our offerings may be ever accepted before the Lord.

This brings us to the *answer* which the gospel supplies to the searching, solemn question: "If thou, Lord, shouldest mark iniquity, who shall stand?" The gospel reveals Christ as the Great Sin-Bearer of the sinner, and this is the answer of faith to the solemn, searching challenge. We can do nothing in the way of penitence, confession, and forgiveness until we see all our sins and iniquities—both those of our unconverted, and those of our converted life—laid upon Jesus. We must see him "wounded for our transgressions, and bruised for our iniquities." We must see him who knew no sin made a sin-offering for us; our sins put upon Christ, and, in return, his righteousness put upon us; Christ and the sinner thus changing places, the One assuming the sin, and the other receiving the righteousness. "For he hath made him to be sin for us, who knew no sin; that we might be made the righteousness of God in him" (2 Cor. 5:21). And now, when the question returns with personal force, "Should God mark my iniquities, how can I stand?" let faith, resting upon the divine word, answer, "Jesus is my Substitute: Jesus stood in my place: Jesus bore my sins: Jesus did all, suffered all, and paid all in my stead, and here I rest."

Oh, yes, the believing sinner, robed with the righteousness of Christ, stands now before the holy Lord God, freely and completely justified from all things; and will stand in the great day of the Lord without spot or wrinkle, when the heavens and the earth are fleeing before his face, and when the wicked are calling upon the rocks and the mountains to fall upon them, and hide them from the wrath of the Lamb; for the great day of his wrath will have come, and who shall be able to stand?

> When from the dust of death I rise
> To take my mansion in the skies,
> Even then shall this be all my plea,
> Jesus has lived and died for me.
>
> Bold shall I stand in that great day;
> For who aught to my charge shall lay?
> While through Thy blood absolved I am
> From sin's tremendous curse and shame.

"There is therefore now no condemnation to them which are in Christ Jesus,…who walk not after the flesh, but after the Spirit."

APPENDIX 2

~

SERMON ON GALATIANS 2:20
THE NATURE AND MANIFESTATIONS OF THE INNER LIFE[1]

I live; yet not I, but Christ liveth in me.
—GALATIANS 2:20

It is impossible for a truly spiritual mind to resist the conviction, or close the eye to the fact, that inward vital godliness by no means keeps pace with the profession of Christianity which almost universally prevails. A more alarming sign could scarcely appear in the moral history of the world. If the prevalence of a nominal Christianity be one of the predicted and distinct characteristics of the approaching consummation of all things—if it is to be regarded as the precursor of overwhelming judgments, and as immediately ushering in the coming of the Son of man, then who can contemplate the religious formalism which so generally exists among professing Christians without a feeling of sadness, and the excitement of alarm? Were we duly affected by the spectacle which we see around us, of multitudes substituting signs for things, symbols for realities, an external profession of Christ for the indwelling of Christ, the mere semblance of life for life itself, how should we, sympathizing with man, and jealous for the Lord, *sigh and cry*, as those who have God's mark upon their foreheads (Ezek. 9:4).

It seems but proper that, in a work called forth by this alarming state of the professing church, and designed to lay open that state in some of its scriptural and figurative delineations, we should commence with a consideration of the nature, properties, and actions, of the spiritual, or inner life, of the quickened soul. It is a self-evident truth, that the absence of spiritual life is but the existence of spiritual death. There is no link that unites the two

---

1. This sermon was published in Winslow's book *The Inner Life: Its Nature, Relapse, and Recovery* (London: John F. Shaw, 1850), 1–44. All of the original wording, punctuation, paragraphing, and emphasis from the original have been retained.

conditions. A soul is either living or dead. The artificial representation of life is no more real life than a painted sun is the real sun, or than a corpse under powerful galvanic shocks is a living body. The reader will therefore at once perceive that, in entering upon an inquiry into this state of religious formalism, it is of the greatest moment that we have a clear and distinct idea of that inward, deep, spiritual life, apart from which, with all his intellectual light, orthodox creed, and religious profession, a man is "dead in trespasses and in sins." I know of no words which more distinctly and beautifully bring out this subject than those of the apostle, in referring to his own experience—"I live; yet not I, but Christ liveth in me."

The first great truth which the passage suggests is, that every true believer in the Lord Jesus is the subject of an inward, spiritual life—*I live*. It is altogether a new and supernatural existence. The old and the natural state, as we have just affirmed, is a state of *death*. Death! it is a solemn word! Dead! it is an awful state! And yet how difficult to bring a man to a real belief and conviction of this his condition! And why? Because he is dead. No argument, no reasoning, no persuasion, however profound or affecting, can convince a corpse that it is lifeless. Equally impossible is it to convince the natural man that his soul is spiritually dead, and that before he can be a true expectant of heaven, an heir of glory, he must be *born again*, and so become the subject of a new and spiritual life. Indignant at the statement, he rejects, spurns, and deprecates the idea. The reason is, that in pressing home upon him the fact, we are met with death in the judgment, with death in the will, with death in the affections, with death in the whole soul. The original sentence under which every individual of the human family lies is thus recorded—"In the day that thou eatest thereof thou shalt surely die:" in the Hebrew, "Thou shalt die the death." Our parent disobeying this law, died, and in him, as their federal head, died every son and daughter of Adam. "You hath he quickened who were dead. He that hath the Son hath life, but he that hath not the Son of God hath not life." On another occasion Jesus said, "Let the dead bury their dead," i.e., let those who are spiritually dead bury those who are naturally dead. What an appalling condition! The spectacle of a dead body is solemn. The idea of natural death is awful. To see the eye that gleamed with bright intelligence fixed and glazed in death; the lips that spake so kindly, and that discoursed so profoundly,—sealed in unbroken silence; the countenance whose every feature was radiant with the light of intellect and love, cold and rigid,—how instinctively we shudder at the sight, and recoil from the touch! But with all the affecting and humiliating circumstances of our natural dissolution, what, in comparison, is this spectacle of a lifeless form of clay with that of the soul *dead in sin?* With all its intellectual greatness, its splendid genius, its powers of thought, its rich endowments, its varied acquisitions, its creative energies, its brilliant achievements, its religious creed and forms and observances its *name to live,*—it is yet spiritually dead. Dead to all that is worthy the name of life, dead to every lofty consideration and feeling, purpose and enterprise, in harmony with its creation, and parallel with its endless being. Dead as to any spiritual understanding of God, or knowledge of Christ, or transforming power of the Holy Spirit, or experience of those spiritual exercises, and sacred feelings, and hallowed emotions, and animating hopes, which belong to the soul made *alive to God.* The question is repeated,—what, with all its attendant circumstances, humiliating and affecting, is the spectacle of a lifeless body in contrast with the spectacle of a lifeless *soul?* We might almost reply— nothing. The dissolution of the body is not the destruction of the soul. The perishing of the material is not the annihilation of the immaterial. Death is not the end of our being; nay, it is not even an interruption of it. It is an event that befalls a man at a certain point of his existence, but it is a change of place and circumstance only, involving the suspension of his immortality—no, not for a moment. How infinitely more momentous, solemn, and appalling, then, is that spiritual state of man which links his future destiny to all the certain horrors of the *second death!* O that this might be a quickening truth, startling, an arousing reflection to the unconverted reader! What grand impertinences, what, mere non-entities, do all other considerations appear in contrast with this! You may lose and recover again everything else, but your soul. This, once lost, is irrecoverably and forever lost. And have you never paused and reflected upon the probability of your losing it? You are at this moment the subject of spiritual death; in the strong language of the Savior you are *condemned already*; and the last enemy, with the funeral pall of your soul in his hands, stands prepared to enshroud you within its dark folds, at the word of him "in whom you live, and move, and have your being." Does not this affect you, alarm you, arouse you? Spirit of God! who but yourself can quicken the soul? Who can convince of danger, convict of sin, and lead to Christ, but you? Speak but the word, and there shall be light. Touch but the soul, and it shall awaken. "Come from the four winds, O breath, and breathe upon these slain, that they may live."

But, with regard to the great truth before us, we again remark, that every truly gracious man is *a living soul.* He is in the possession of an inner, spiritual life. He can appropriate to himself the words of the apostle—*I live.* The first important characteristic of this spiritual life is its engrafting upon a state of death. The words of the apostle will explain our meaning, "For I through the law am dead to the law, that I might live unto God" [Gal. 2:19]. "I am crucified with Christ, nevertheless I live." Addressing the believing Colossians, he says, "You are dead, and your life is hid with Christ in God." The simple meaning of these declarations is—the living soul is dead to the law of God as an instrument of life, and to its works as a ground of salvation. It is dead, too, to the curse and tyranny of the law, and consequently to its power of condemning. To all this, the soul made alive by Christ, is dead with Christ. Thus is it most clear that a man, dead already, though he originally is, in trespasses and in sins, must morally die before he can spiritually live. The crucifixion with Christ must precede the living with Christ. He must die to all schemes and hopes of salvation in or by himself, before he can fully receive into his heart Christ as the life of his soul. This spiritual mystery, this divine paradox, the natural man cannot understand or receive; he only can, who is "born of the Spirit." Then let me ask and press upon you the personal and searching question, has the law of God been brought into your conscience with that enlightening, convincing, and condemning power, as first to startle you from your spiritual slumber, and then to sever you from all hope or expectation of salvation in yourself? If so, then will you know of a truth what it is, first, to die before you live. Dying to the law, dying to self, you will receive him into your heart who so blessedly declared, "I have come that you might have life, and that you might have it more abundantly." Thus is the life of God in the soul engrafted upon a state of death. "I am crucified with Christ, nevertheless I live."

The second view of this inner, spiritual life is, its supernatural character. It is above nature, and therefore all the power of nature cannot inspire it. Nature, we admit, can go far in imitating some of its characteristics, but nature cannot create the essential property or principle of this life. Nature can produce a semblance of faith, as in the case of Simon Magus; of repentance, as in the case of Judas; of hearing the word with joy, as in the case of Herod; it can even appear to taste the heavenly gift, and feel the powers of the world to come all this, and much more, can nature do, and yet be nature still. Here its power stops. There is that which it cannot do. It cannot counterfeit the indwelling of Christ in the sinner's soul. It cannot enable a man to say, "I live, and Christ lives in me." This infinitely transcends its mightiest power. Spiritual life, then, springs not from nature, and is therefore produced by no natural cause or means. It is from God. He it is who calls this new creation into being, who pencils its wonders, who enkindles its glories, and who breathes over it the breath of life. It is God's life in man's soul.

Thus the true Christian is one who can adopt the expressive and emphatic language of Paul—*I live*. Amplifying the words, he can exclaim, "*I live*—as a quickened soul. *I live*—as a regenerate soul. *I live*—as a pardoned sinner. *I live*—as a justified sinner. *I live*—as an adopted child. *I live*—as an heir of glory. *I live*, and I never lived before! My whole existence until now has been but as a blank. I never truly, really lived, until I died! I lived, if life it may be called, to the world, to sin, to the creature, to myself; but I never lived by Christ, and I never lived to God." O tremendous truth! O solemn thought! for a soul to pass away into eternity without having answered the great end of its creation—without having ever really lived! With what feelings, with what emotions, with what plea, will it meet the God who created it? "I created you," that God will say, "for myself, for my glory. I endowed you with gifts, and ennobled you with faculties, and clothed you with powers second only to my own. I sent you into the world to expend those gifts, and to employ those faculties, and to exert those powers, for my glory, and with a view to the enjoyment of me forever. But you buried those gifts, you abused those faculties, you wasted those powers, and you lived to yourself and not unto me; and now to yourself, and in everlasting banishment from my presence, you shall continue to live through eternity." Come from the four winds, O breath of the living God, and breathe upon the dead, that they may live! Avert from the reader so dire a doom, so fearful a catastrophe! And permit none, whose eye lights upon this solemn page, any longer to live to themselves, but from this moment and forever, gracious Savior! may they live for you—their solemn determination and their sublime motto this—*For me to live is Christ*.

But we are now conducted to a great and a most precious truth—the indwelling of Christ in the heart as constituting the spiritual life of the believer. "I live; yet not I, *but Christ liveth in me*." It is not so much that the believer lives, as that Christ lives in the believer. *I in them*. The Lord Jesus is *essential life*. Were it not for this, the doctrine of indwelling life would be but a dream. With what authority of tone, and with what sublimity of language, has he affirmed this idea, "I am the resurrection and the life: he that believeth in me, though he were dead, yet shall he live." Can thought be more grand, or words be more intelligible? "With Thee is the fountain of life." Couple together these two passages, and what demonstrative proof do they afford to the doctrine of the essential Deity of the Savior. How could he be the *Resurrection and the Life*, and in what sense the *Fountain of Life*, but as he was *essentially God*? No comparison can be instituted between finite being, however exalted, and Infinite. It has been truly said, that all finite beings are infinitely more destitute of life than they are possessed of it; and this will be the case forever. Standing by the grave that entombs the soul dead in sin, *Essential Life* exclaims—"*I am the Resurrection and the Life—Come forth!*" and in a moment the soul is quickened, and rises to *newness of life*. What but *Deity* could accomplish this? Take off your shoes from your feet, for you stand upon holy ground! *Jesus is the True God*, and *Essential Life*. The smallest seed, the most loathsome insect, the lowest creature on earth, and the mightiest angel, and the brightest saint in heaven, draw their life from Christ. All life—vegetable, animal, rational, spiritual—emanates from him, *the Fountain of Life* to all creatures. What a mighty and glorious Being, then, is the Son of God, the ceaseless energy of whose essence prevents each moment, every thing that has life from being destroyed, and from accomplishing its own destruction! Who would not believe in, who would not love, who would not serve such a Being? Who would not crown him *Lord of all*?

The spiritual life, then, of the believer is the life of Christ, or rather, "Christ who is our life" in the soul. The Scripture proof of this is overwhelming. *I in them*, are words declarative of this truth by the Savior himself. Again, in 2 Corinthians 13:5, the apostle thus exhorts—"Examine yourselves, whether you be in the faith; prove your own selves. Know you not your own selves, how that Jesus Christ is in you, except you be reprobates?" Alas! how is this precept overlooked! How few are they who rightly and honestly *examine themselves*! They can examine others, and speak of others, and hear for others, and judge of others; but *themselves* they examine not, and judge not, and condemn not. To the neglect of this precept may be traced, as one of its most fruitful causes, the relapse of the inner life of the Christian. Deterioration, and eventually destruction and ruin, must follow in the steps of willful and protracted neglect, be the object of that neglect what it may. The vineyard must become unfruitful, and the garden must lose its beauty, and the machinery must stand still, and the enterprise must fail of success, and the health must decline, if toilsome and incessant watchfulness and care has not its eye awake to every symptom of feebleness, and to every sign of decay. If the merchantman examine not his accounts, and if the husbandman examine not his field, and if the nobleman examine not his estate, and if the physician examine not his patient, what sagacity is needed to foresee, as the natural and inevitable result; confusion, ruin, and death? How infinitely more true is this of the soul! The lack of frequent, fearless, and thorough searching into the exact state of the heart, into the real condition of the soul, is before God, in the great matter of the inner life, reveals the grand secret of many a solemn case of declension, shipwreck, and apostasy. Therefore, the apostle earnestly exhorts, *Examine yourselves*; as if he would say, "Do not take the state of your soul for granted. Be not deceived by the too fond and partial opinion of others. Judge not yourselves by a human and a false standard, but examine yourselves, prove your own selves by the word; and rest not short of Christ dwelling in your hearts—your present life and your hope of glory."

But how does Christ dwell in the believer?—a most important question this. An ignorance with regard to the mode of Christ's indwelling at one time opened the door for the introduction into the church of one of the most fanatical errors that ever assailed its purity. We allude to the heresy of the personal, corporeal indwelling of Christ in the believer, which, being believed and asserted by many, they set themselves up as being themselves Christ, and thereby rushed into innumerable extravagant, blasphemous, and deadly sins. Thus has Satan ever sought to engraft the deadly nightshade of error, upon the life-giving Rose of Sharon, rendering the most spiritual and sanctifying truths of God's Word subservient to the basest and most unholy purposes. But by what mode does the Lord Jesus dwell in the truly regenerate? We answer—by his Spirit. Thus it is a spiritual and not a personal or corporeal indwelling of Christ. The Scripture testimony is most full and decisive on this point. "Know ye not that your body is the temple of the *Holy Spirit*." "If Christ be in you, the body is dead because of sin; but the Spirit is life because of righteousness. But if the Spirit of him that raised up Jesus from the dead dwell in you, he that raised Christ from the dead shall also quicken your mortal bodies by his Spirit that dwelleth in you." And that this inhabitation of Christ by the Spirit is not the indwelling of a mere grace of the Spirit, but the Spirit himself, is equally clear from another passage:—"Hope maketh not ashamed, because the love of God (here is a grace of the Spirit) is shed abroad in our hearts by the Holy Spirit which he hath given us"—(here is the possession of the Spirit himself). This is the fountain of all the spiritual grace dwelling in the soul of the truly regenerate, and at times so blessedly flowing forth in refreshing and sanctifying streams. "He that believeth on me, as the scripture has said, out of his belly shall flow rivers of living water. *But this spake he of the Spirit*" (John 7:38–39). Thus, then, is it most clear that by the indwelling of the Holy Spirit, Christ has his dwelling in the hearts of all true believers. Christian reader, what a solemn truth is this! What an unfolding of true Christianity! What a view of real, vital, saving religion, does this truth present! How do all religious rites, and forms, and ceremonies, dwindle into insignificance, before this all-important, all-essential, all-commanding doctrine of the inhabitation of Christ in the soul by the Holy Spirit of God! Apart from the experience of this truth, every other is a *false religion.*

But there is one view of our subject too interesting and important to be overlooked. "Christ *liveth* in me," says the apostle. It is a *living* Christ dwelling in a *living* soul. It implies permanency. The religion of some is a religion of the moment. Like the gourd of the prophet, it appears in a night, and it withers in a night. It is the religion of impulse and of feeling. It comes by fits and starts. It is convulsive and periodical. *It is easily assumed, and as easily laid aside.* But here is the grand characteristic of a truly converted man. Christ lives in him, and lives in him never to die. He has entered his heart, never to retire. He has enthroned himself, never to abdicate. And although the fact of his permanent indwelling may not always appear with equal clearness and certainty to the mind of the believer himself, nevertheless Christ is really there by his Spirit. It is his home, his dwelling-place, his kingdom. He lives there, to maintain his government, to sway his scepter, and to enforce, by the mild constraint of his love, obedience to his laws. He lives there, to guard and nourish his own work—shielding it when it is assailed, strengthening it when it is feeble, reviving it when it droops, restoring it when it decays; thus protecting the "lily among the thorns," preserving the spark in the ocean, and keeping, amid opposing influences, the life of God that it die not. Truly is the believer in Jesus a living soul; and all are dead who cannot say, "Christ *liveth* in me."

But let us briefly contemplate some of the characteristics of the inner spiritual life of the soul, as more fully illustrating its character, and as supplying evidences by which we may test the question of its personal possession.

The first characteristic which we notice is its *self-renouncing* tendency. "*I live, yet not I.*" The life of Christ and the life of self cannot co-exist in the same heart. If the one lives, the other dies. The sentence of death is written upon a man's self when the Spirit of Christ enters his heart and quickens his soul with the life of God. "I live," he exclaims, "*yet not I.*" What a striking and beautiful example of this have we in the life and labors of the apostle Paul. Does he speak of his *ministry?*—what a renunciation of self appears! Lost in the greatness and grandeur of his theme, he exclaims—"We preach *not ourselves,* but Christ Jesus the Lord." Again—"*Unto me, who am less than the least* of all saints, is this grace given, that I should preach among the Gentiles the unsearchable riches of Christ." Does he refer to his *office?*—what

self-crucifixion! "I magnify my office." In what way? Was it by vaunting proc-
lamations of its grandeur and legitimacy, its divine institution, or its solemn
functions? Did he challenge for it, otherwise than as it was connected with
miraculous endowments, the unquestioning and instant submission of men's
hearts and consciences, as to an oracle that must not be disputed—or their
subserviency in the conduct of life, as to a law that was death to disobey?
Did he ever exalt its possessors to a height of unintelligible and mystical
sacredness, above the condition of humanity and the common feelings and
infirmities of nature, which might demand the prostration of others at their
feet, as if separated from them by an impassable, though invisible chasm—
an abyss which it was sacrilege to traverse even in imagination, and which
still divided the priest, the bishop, or the pastor, from the man? Never! But
he magnified his office, by diminishing himself and exalting his Master. He
was nothing—ay, and even his office itself was comparatively nothing—that
"Christ might be all and in all." Does he speak of his *gifts* and *labors*? what
absence of self! "I am the least of the apostles, that am not meet to be called
an apostle, because I persecuted the church of God. But, by the grace of God,
I am what I am; and his grace, which was bestowed upon me, was not in vain,
but I labored more abundantly than they all: yet, *not* I, but the grace of God
which was with me." Such was the religion of Paul. His Christianity was a
self-denying, self-crucifying, self-renouncing Christianity. "I live, *yet not* I. I
laboured more abundantly than they all, yet *not* I." O what self-denying spirit
was his! "But where," asks somewhat quaintly a writer of olden time [Wil-
liam Bridge],—and how appropriate the inquiry to our own!—"where is this
self-denying power of heart now to be found among us? how does this *I*, this
same self, creep into all our speeches, and into all our doings! If it please the
Lord to use a minister in his service, what an *I-ing* is there! I converted such a
man, and I comforted such a man; and it was *my* prescription, and it was *my*
receipt, and I did it. And if a Christian do but pray, or perform a duty, Thus
and thus *I* said, and these words *I* spoke! did not *I* tell you so? *I* told you what
would come to pass. O what an *I-ing* is there among the people! How does
this I and self creep into all our speeches, and into all our doings!"

But every truly spiritual man is a self-renouncing man. In the discipline
of his own heart, beneath the cross of Jesus, and in the school of trial and
temptation, he has been taught in some degree, that if he lives, it is not he that
lives, but that it is Christ who lives in him. Upon all his own righteousness, his
duties, and doings, he tramples as to the great matter of justification; while,
as fruits of the Spirit, as evidences of faith, as pulsations of the inner spiritual

life, as, in a word, tending to authenticate and advance his sanctification, he desires to be "careful to maintain good works," that *God* in all things might be glorified. This thought suggests another of much importance. We should be always careful to distinguish between the denial of self and the denial of the life of God within us. The most entire renunciation of ourselves, the most humiliating acknowledgment of our personal unworthiness, may comport with the strongest assurance and profession of Christ living in us. Self-denial does not necessarily involve grace-denial. It is the profoundest act of humility in a Christian man to acknowledge the grace of God in his soul. Never is there so real a crucifixion, never so entire a renunciation of self as when the heart, in its lowly but deep and grateful throbbings, acknowledges its indebtedness to sovereign grace, and in the fervor of its adoring love, summons the whole church to listen to its recital of the great things God has done for it—"Come, all you that fear the Lord, and I will tell you what he has done for my soul." O yes! it is a self-denying life. Listen to Job—"I abhor myself, and repent in dust and ashes." Listen to Isaiah—"Woe is me! for I am undone; because I am a man of unclean lips, and I dwell in the midst of a people of unclean lips: for my eyes have seen the King, the Lord of hosts." Listen to the penitent publican—"God be merciful to me a sinner!" Listen again to Paul—"I live, yet not I." Thus does a sense of sin, and a believing sight of Christ, lay the soul low before God in self-renunciation and self-abhorrence. Judge your spiritual condition, dear reader, by this characteristic of the inner life. Is it yours? Has there been this renunciation of your sinful self, and of your righteous self? Has the Spirit of God emptied you? has the grace of God humbled you? has the life of God crucified you? Are you as one in whom Christ lives, walking humbly with God? O, it is the essence of vital godliness, it is the very life of true religion. If Christ is living in you, you are a humble soul. Pride never existed in the heart of Christ. His whole life was one act of the profoundest self-abasement. In the truest and in the fullest sense of the emphatic declaration, "he humbled himself." It is impossible, then, that he who was thus "meek and lowly in heart" can dwell in one whom "pride compasses as a chain." "I live, yet *not* I," are two states of the renewed soul as inseparable as any cause and effect. A humble and a self-denying Christ dwells only with a humble and a self-denying soul. If your gifts inflate you, if your position exalts you, if your usefulness engenders pride, if the honor and distinction which God or man has placed upon you have turned you aside from the simplicity of your walk, and set you upon the work of self-seeking, self-advancing, so that you are not meek and gentle, child-like and

Christ-like in spirit, be sure of this—you are either not a partaker of the life of Christ, or else that life is at a low ebb in your soul. Which of the two, do you think, is your real state? And have the self-denying, the self-renouncing, no reward? O yes! their reward is great. They are such as the King delights to honor. When John the Baptist declared, "He must increase, but I must decrease," and on another occasion, "Whose shoe-latchet I am not worthy to unloose," Christ pronounced him "the greatest born of women." When the centurion sent to say, "Lord, I am not worthy that you should come under my roof," our Lord places this crown upon his faith, "I tell you I have not found so great faith, no not in Israel." When the publican exclaimed, "God be merciful to me a sinner!" he descended from the temple justified, rather than the self-vaunting Pharisee. Yes, "when men are cast down then there is lifting up." There is a present reward of grace to the humble. Christ exalts them. "Humble yourselves under the hand of the Lord, and he will exalt you in due time." And what tongue can describe the inward peace, satisfaction, and contentment of that soul in whom this self-denying life of Christ dwells! Such an one hath *a continual feast*. He may be deeply tried, sorely tempted, heavily afflicted, severely chastened, but his meek and submissive spirit exclaims, "It is the Lord, let him do as seemeth good in his sight."

Another characteristic of this life is—it is a Christ-honoring, Christ-advancing life. A self-denying life, proceeding from a gospel principle, must be a Christ-exalting life. The Lord Jesus can only erect and carry forward his kingdom in the soul upon the ruins of self and as this kingdom of grace is perpetual in its growth, so the demolition of self is a work of gradual advancement. "He must increase," says the lowly-molded Baptist. As the inner life grows, Christ grows more lovely to the eye, more precious to the heart. His blood is more valued, his righteousness is more relied on, his grace is more lived upon, his cross is more gloried in, his yoke is more cheerfully borne, his commands are more implicitly obeyed. In all things Christ is advanced, and the soul by all means advances in its knowledge of, and in its resemblance to, Christ. Reader, is Christ advanced by you? Is his kingdom widened, is his truth disseminated, is his fame spread, is his person exalted, is his honor vindicated, is his glory promoted by the life which you are living? O name not the name of Christ if it do not be to perfume the air with its fragrance, and to fill the earth with its renown. We must group the remaining characteristics of the inner life. It is a *conflicting* life. It always wears the harness, and is ever clothed with the armor. Opposed by indwelling sin, assailed by Satan, and impeded by the world, every step in advance is only secured by a battle fought and a victory achieved. It is a *holy* life—springing from the indwelling of the Holy Spirit, it must necessarily be so. All its actings are holy, all its breathings are holy, all its fruits are holy; and without *holiness* no man hath this life, or can be an inheritor of that life to come, of which this is the seedling and the germ, the foretaste and the pledge. "The water that I shall give him," says Christ, alluding to the spiritual life, "shall be in him a well of water springing up into everlasting life." Need I add that *happiness, progression,* and *deathlessness,* are equally its characteristics? Happiness is but a phantom and a name, where Christ dwells not in the heart. Progression is but an advance towards eternal woe, where the love of God is not in the soul. And death is an eternal, lingering despair, the soul and body ever dying, yet never ceasing to exist—where the Spirit of life has not quickened the inner man, creating all things new.

Such, reader, is the life, the inner, spiritual, and deathless life, the relapse and recovery of which, the pages that follow will unfold. No imagination can fully depict, nor language adequately describe, the importance of this life, the grandeur of its nature and destiny, and the necessity of its progression and its manifestations. Reader, the world without you teems with sentient existence. All is life, activity, and progress. There is vegetable life, and animal life, and rational life. The flower that scents the air with its perfume, the insect that renders it vocal with its music, and man who fills and beautifies the earth with monuments of his greatness and creative genius, testify to the possession of a life of amazing power, activity, and progression. To this may be added a species of moral life, maintained by many, developed and embodied in religious forms, observances, and sacrifices. But there is a life as infinitely superior to all these as the life of him whose mind conceived the towering pyramid, is to that of the little insect that flutters its brief hour in the sunbeam and then vanishes forever. It is *the life of God in the soul of man.* Deep planted in the center of his spiritual nature, lodged within the hidden recesses of his deathless mind, diffusing its mysterious but all-pervading and renovating influence through the judgment, the will, the affections, and linking his being with a future of glory, "which eye hath not seen, nor ear heard, neither hath entered into the heart of man to conceive;" the world rushes on, and knows not its existence, and sees not its glories, and heeds not its joy—so deeply veiled from human eye, ay, and so far removed from human power, is the inner spiritual life "hidden with Christ in God." Reader, there is a religion towering as far above your religion of *merit,* and of *works,* and of *forms,* as the heavens are above the earth, even as the spiritual life of God is above the sensual life of man. It is the religion of a renewed mind, of a renovated heart, of a conquered will, of a soul—all whose sanctified faculties are consecrated to the glory of God here, and are destined to the enjoyment of God hereafter. Illustrious as may be your position in the church, luminous as may be your profession of Christianity, splendid as your gifts, and rich as your endowments, and costly as your offerings, and apostolic as your zeal, and unwearied as your labors may be, bear with me while with all solemnity I remind you, that you still may live, and toil, and die, a stranger to the *inner life*. Deeper and loftier and more momentous than all these is the great truth upon which we are expatiating—*"Christ liveth in Me."* Its foundation is in the soul, its summit is in heaven. I enunciate to you a great mystery—the mystery of Christ and his church, of the soul of man and the life of God—both spiritually and indissolubly one. Have *you* thus "passed from death unto life?" Has the great transformation taken place? Has the destroyer, entrenched within, in all the plenitude of undisputed power, been dispossessed? Have the avenues of the heart, closed and barred against the admission of Christ, been thrown open? Has the fearful alienation, and the withering curse, and the deep guilt, which portrays to you God as an enemy, and which arms all the powers of your soul against him as his foe, been revealed, felt, and deplored? Has the captive spirit been disenthralled, the prey taken from the mighty, the power of the destroyer broken, and the soul awakened from its deep slumber to listen to its Creator speaking in tones of mercy, and in thoughts of love? Has light, emanating from the abodes of glory—invisible to others—dawned upon the midnight of your spiritual desolation? has a voice, speaking from the throne of heaven—unheard by others—startled your spirit in its deep trance, and dispelled its floating dreams? has a hand, mighty and unseen, riven the chain, thrown open the dungeon, and led you forth to liberty and joy, to life and immortality? In a word—and this is the sum and consummation of all—has another and a Diviner life, a new and a superior nature, descending from God, and begotten within you by the Spirit, and unfolding to your view a heaven of brightness, full of purity and fragrance and song, been communicated to your soul, thus creating you a *new creature*, and constituting you an "heir of God, and a joint heir with Christ Jesus?" If so, then you may adopt the language of Paul, and exultingly exclaim, "I live, yet not I, but Christ lives in me." O deem not this a vain thing, for *it is your life!* But I will suppose your honest reply to these searching interrogatives decides the case against your claims to a possession of spiritual life; then let me beseech you, with a knowledge of this alarming fact, rest not where you are. What is your natural life but a vapor that is soon dissolved, a dream that vanishes away? And what are your present pursuits but things unworthy of your rational existence, and inappropriate to your approaching destiny? O what egregious folly, O what moral insanity, to merge all consideration of your future existence in the present brief space graciously allotted you for its study and its preparation! You are all life, all nerve, all animation, all ardor, all activity, all excitement, all hope, to whatever is noble, and intellectual, and refined, and enterprising, of earth; but all death, all insensibility, all indifferent, all languor, all hopeless, to every thought and feeling and consideration of the great things that relate to your state beyond the grave. Is this wise, is this rational, is this sane? Your studies of literature, your pleasures of taste, your pursuit of gain, your toil of ambition—those splendid impertinence, those cruel mockeries, those heartless soul-murderers of the present time; stifle in your heart all feeling, and annihilate in your mind all thought that you are an accountable steward, a moral agent, a deathless being; and that soon, yes, in *one moment*, your soul may be in eternity—standing agitated, trembling and speechless, before the tribunal of God! Yearning for your salvation, let me with the tenderest affection and the deepest solemnity plead with you *for your life*. Reflect for a moment what your present careless, unbelieving and impenitent state really is. It is nothing less than to challenge the vengeance of the Most High God, to defy his power, to disdain his clemency, to refuse his compassion, to reject his pardon, to insult his majesty, and to expose yourself to the fierceness of his eternal wrath. It is to be without the regeneration of his Spirit, to have no part in the propitiation of his Son, to have all your sins uncancelled, and to stand before the throne of eternal justice, a culprit and a criminal, upon whom the righteous judgment of God must pronounce and execute its withering sentence of an unchanging destiny, and an inexorable doom. Where, then, can you flee to hide from the dark storm that gathers over you, from the thick clouds, and treasured-up lightning, and embosomed bolt, and desolating winds that wait but the signal of God's uplifted hand to rush forth upon you in all their unchecked, unmitigated fury? Whither can you *flee*? You have "made a covenant with death, and are at an agreement with hell." You are fascinated with the world, and are enamored with yourself, and are satisfied to have no other portion. You reject the Rock of Ages, refuse the sheltering pavilion of the Savior's cross, and despise the offers of his grace,—whither, then, when the tempest leaps forth in all its maddening fury, will you flee? Yet how calmly you tread upon the very brink of ruin, how sportively you sail along the very edge of the vortex, how content and happy to course your way to the bar of a holy and a just God, through a world of disease and casualty and death, without one anxious thought to obtain deliverance, or one earnest struggle to escape your doom! Listen to a fact of recent occurrence, for the truth of which, in all its awful particulars, my personal knowledge of the parties can safely vouch. The conversation of a group of gentlemen, after dinner, turned upon the doctrine of a future state. Each one gave his opinion. It came to the turn of an elderly gentleman, a man of high legal attainments, of considerable wealth, and general esteem. He remarked that, "as it regarded himself, this life was good enough for him; that he desired no better, and would be willing to enter into an agreement to live in this world forever." The words had scarcely passed his lips when his hand relaxed its hold upon the glass it was grasping, his countenance changed, his head drooped, and he was borne insensible to a sofa. A vein was opened, restoratives were used, and every effort made that skill could devise; but life was extinct—his spirit had fled to the God who gave it! Reader, I leave this appalling fact to make its own impression. May that impression be deep, permanent, and saving!

But I turn to the living. I address those in whose souls are the deep, holy, deathless throbbings of an inner, spiritual life. Blissful day, Christian reader, that witnessed your resurrection from the grave of sin to walk in *newness of life!* Happy hour when you left your soul's shroud in the tomb, exchanging it for the robe of a glorious deathlessness,—when your enmity was conquered, and your hostility was subdued, and you were led in willing and joyous captivity, amid the triumphs of your Lord, to the altar where he bled—self-consecrated to his service. O memorable moment, when Jesus, by the resistless but gentle power of his grace, broke down every barrier, entered your heart, and planted there the germ of a life as divine, as holy, and as immortal as his own! Ever keep in mind your deep indebtedness to sovereign grace, your solemn obligation to divine love, and the touching motives that urge you to "walk worthy of the vocation with which you are called." Welcome all the dealings of God, whatever the character of those dealings may be, designed as they are but to animate, to nourish, and to carry forward this precious life in your soul. The *north wind* of sharp trial, and the *south wind* of covenant mercy, are made to breathe their blended gales over this beautiful garden, that the fruits and flowers of holiness may abound—that the actings of a living faith and love and hope may evidence to yourself, to the church, and to the world, that you are indeed "risen with Christ," a partaker of his new resurrection-life. It is perhaps a question of deep anxiety with you—"Oh, that I knew I were in reality a possessor of this inner spiritual life! My heart is so hard, my affections are so cold, my spirit is so sluggish, in everything that is spiritual, holy, and divine." Permit me to ask you—Can a stone feel its hardness, or a corpse its insensibility? Impossible! You affirm that you feel your hardness, and that you are sensible of your coldness. From where does this spring but from *life?* Could you weep, or mourn, or deplore, were the spiritual state of your soul that of absolute death! Again I say, Impossible! But rest not here—*go to Jesus.* What you really need is a fresh view of, a renewed application to, the Lord Jesus Christ. Sit not brooding over your mournful condition, in fruitless lamentation, but rise, and *go to Jesus.* Take to him the stone-like heart, the corpse-like soul. Tell him that you want to feel more, and to weep more, and to love more, and to pray more, and to live more. Go, and pour out your heart, with all its tremblings, and doubts, and fears, and needs, upon the bleeding, loving bosom of your Lord, until from that bosom, life more abundant has darted its quickening energy, vibrating and thrilling through your whole soul. "I have come," says Jesus, "that they might have life, and that they might have it *more abundantly.*"

You are, perhaps, a severely tried, a sorely tempted, a deeply afflicted believer. But cheer up! You have Christ living in you, and why should you yield to despondency or to fear? Christ will never vacate his throne, nor relinquish his dwelling. You have a suffering Christ, a humbled Christ, a crucified Christ, a dying Christ, a risen Christ, a living Christ, a triumphant Christ, a glorified Christ, a full Christ, dwelling in you by his Spirit. Yes! and you have, too, a human Christ, a feeling Christ, a sympathizing Christ, a tender, loving, gentle Christ, spiritually and eternally reposing in your heart—why, then, should you fear the pressure of any need, or the assault of any foe, or the issue of any trial, since such a Christ is in you? "Fear not!" They are his own familiar and blessed words—"It is I, do not be afraid." You cannot lack for any good, since you have the fountain of all good dwelling in you. You cannot be finally overcome of any spiritual evil, since you have the Conqueror of sin and Satan and the world enthroned upon your affections. Your life—the inner, divine and spiritual life—can never die, since Christ, *essential life,* lives and abides in you. Like him, and for him, you may be opposed, but like him and by him you shall triumph. The persecution which you meet, and the trials which you endure, and the difficulties with which you cope, shall but further your well being, by bringing you into a closer communion with Jesus, and by introducing you more fully into the enviable state of the apostles—"Always bearing about in the body the dying of the Lord Jesus, that the life also of Jesus might be made manifest in our body.... For which cause we faint not: but though our outward man perish, yet the inward man is renewed day by day. For our light affliction, which is but for a moment, worketh for us a far more exceeding and eternal weight of glory."

Soon the portals of glory will expand their gates, and receive you into the beatific life—the life which is eternal. You are, perhaps, mourning the loss of those who sleep in Jesus, or you are the occupant of a sick chamber, or, ecstatic thought!—it may be you are poised upon the wing for heaven, waiting only the signal for your upward flight. Whether it be the sorrow of bereavement, or the languishing bed of sickness, or the immediate prospect of eternity, *how appropriate, and animating, and soothing, the contemplation of the life which is before you!* How exceeding great and precious are the promises which refer to the security and assured enjoyment of that life: "My sheep hear my voice, and I know them, and they follow me; and I give unto them eternal life: and they shall never perish, neither shall any man pluck them out of my hand. My Father, who gave them to me, is greater than all: and no one is able to pluck them out of my Father's hand." Listen to his words of indescribable sweetness and overwhelming grandeur, breathed over the grave of one whom he loved: "I am the resurrection and the life; he that believeth in me, though he were dead, yet shall he live; and whoever believes in me shall never die." "Enough, dear Lord," may you exclaim. "You have spoken words of soothing and of hope to this bleeding, sorrowing heart of mine, and I am comforted. You have dried my tears, bound up my wounds, and calmed my spirit, healing, and hushing it to rest upon your own gentle, loving bosom—once stricken with a sorrow infinitely deeper, and keener, and bitterer than mine."

Are you, my reader, a searcher of this life? Are you breathing for it, panting after it, seeking it? Then, be it known to you, that he who inspired that desire is himself the Life for which you seek. That heaving of your heart, that yearning of your spirit, that "feeling after God, if haply you may find him," is the first gentle pulsation of a life that shall never die. Feeble and fluctuating, faint and fluttering, as its throbbings may be, it is yet the life of God, the life of Christ, the life of glory in your soul. It is the seedling, the germ of an immortal flower. It is the sunshine dawn of an eternal day. The announcement with which we meet your case—and it is the only one that can meet it—is, "*this man receives sinners.*" O joyful tidings! O blessed words! Yes, he receives sinners—the vilest, the lowest, the most despised! It was for this he relinquished the abodes of heavenly purity and bliss, to mingle amid the sinful and humiliating scenes of earth. For this he abandoned his Father's bosom, for a cross. For this he lived and labored, suffered and died. "He receiveth sinners!" He receives them, of every name and condition—of every stature, and character, and climate. There is no limit to his ability to pardon, as there is none to the sufficiency of his atonement, or to the melting pity of his heart. Flee, then, to Jesus the crucified. To him repair with your sins, as scarlet and as crimson, and his blood will wash you whiter than snow. What though they may be as clouds for darkness, or as the sand on the sea-shore for multitude—His grace can take them all away. Come with the accusations and tortures of a guilty conscience, come with the sorrow and relentings of a broken heart, come with the grief of the backslider, and with the confession of the prodigal—Jesus still meets you with the hope-inspiring words—"Him that cometh unto me, I will in no wise cast out." Then, "return unto the Lord, and he will have mercy upon you; and to our God, for he will abundantly pardon."

Such, reader, in conclusion, is the nature, and such the manifestations of the inner spiritual life, whose relapse and recovery, whose declensions and revivings, we are about to consider. Alas! that a life so heavenly and divine, so holy and so happy, should ever fluctuate and change—should ever droop and decay. Alas! that in its onward progress to the paradise of God, it should have its autumn and its winter—the seared leaf and the congealed current—and not be always clothed with the perpetual verdure of spring, and be ever laden with the ripe fruit of summer. But such is the fallen nature in which it dwells, and such the hostile influences by which it is surrounded and assailed, the utmost vigilance is demanded to maintain the heavenly spark alive and glowing in the soul. Ere, beloved reader, we pass to a more minute examination of our important subject, together let us solemnly "bow our knees unto the Father of our Lord Jesus Christ," praying "that he would grant us, according to the riches of his glory, to be strengthened with might by his Spirit in the inner man: that Christ may dwell in our hearts by faith: that we, being rooted and grounded in love, may be able to comprehend with all saints what is the breadth, and length, and depth, and height; and to know the love of Christ, which passeth knowledge, that we might be filled with all the fullness of God. *Now unto him that is able to do exceeding abundantly above all that we ask or think, according to the power that worketh in us, unto him be glory in the church, by Christ Jesus, throughout all ages, world without end. Amen.*"

ANNOTATED SELECTED BIBLIOGRAPHY OF
OCTAVIUS WINSLOW'S WORKS

Born Again, or, From Grace to Glory. London: John F. Shaw, 1864.

In this book, Winslow articulates his doctrine of regeneration. Amid the swirling controversy over baptismal regeneration (which Winslow clearly denounced), Winslow feared that the doctrine was handled with "levity" by those who lost sight of its doctrinal and experimental importance. One of his key arguments throughout the work is that "the Holy Spirit must be [the] Divine and sole Author [of salvation], from its commencement in grace to its consummation in glory" (vi). He first sets forth what does not constitute real conversion. He then explains the true characteristics of regeneration. The evidences and fruits of regeneration are also considered, followed by various aspects of sanctification that are related to the believer's conversion. Some of those include assurance of conversion, anxiety about conversion, and the believer's final transition from a state of grace to a state of glory. Concerning grace in the soul he wrote, "The grace of God in the soul was the pledge of its coming glory. It is indeed more than the pledge, it is essentially and undeniably a part of the glory itself. Present grace is to future glory what the outline is to the picture, the seed to the flower, the twilight to the day. He who has the smallest degree of grace in his soul has the first beginnings of glory" (116–17e). In this way, he provides a holistic picture of the doctrine.

Christ and the Christian in Temptation: Counsel and Consolation for the Tempted. London, 1878.

In Puritan fashion, this book serves as a meditation on Hebrews 4:15. Winslow explained, "Acceding—as we are bound—to the inspired declaration that our Lord was 'tempted in all points like as we are,' it follows that there must exist a corresponding coincidence in the collision of Christ with Satan, and the spiritual conflict in which every good man is engaged of the same nature and with the same foe" (1). Throughout the first six chapters, Winslow unpacks Hebrews 4:15 by giving an exposition of Christ's temptation in the wilderness (Luke 4). He looks at how Christ was and the Christian is tempted to (1) distrust divine providence; (2) self-destruction; (3) false and idolatrous worship; and (4) worldly grandeur and possession. He then turns to Hebrews 2 and encourages the reader with the sympathy of Christ in our temptation. Finally, Winslow closes his book with a triumphant tone as he describes the final overthrow of the Tempter and his works by Jesus.

Christ Is Ever with You: Illustrated by Experiences Drawn from the Prayer-Meeting, and Field and Hospital Life. London: John F. Shaw, 1864.

This short book is unique in that it is made up of one of Winslow's New Year's sermons, but taken by some editors in the United States to add various spiritual experiences that would make it more suitable for children, families, and even soldiers. In the preface, the editor notes that "the writings of Rev. Octavius Winslow, D.D., are known and appreciated over the whole Christian world.... [This] little work was published at the beginning of this year, and in the first quarter of the year thirty-five thousand copies had been printed and circulated" (i).

Christ, The Theme of the Home Missionary: An Argument for Home Missions. New York: John S. Taylor, 1838.

Christ, The Theme of the Home Missionary was one of Winslow's first publications. The substance of this short book was originally delivered from the pulpit. It was subsequently sent to the press for publication at the request of some who heard Winslow's sermon. Winslow took Paul's words in Philippians 1:18 as his sermon text: "Christ is preached; and therein I do rejoice, yea, and will rejoice." Winslow outlines his message in four sections. First, he argues that the design of the home mission enterprise aims at the salvation of men. Second, he declares that the grand instrument of home mission success is the preaching of Christ. Third, he provides arguments by which churches should support home missions. Finally, he addresses the motives that might move churches to give to the Home Mission Society. This work reveals the importance Winslow placed on mission work in his ministry.

Consider Jesus: Thoughts for Daily Duty, Service, and Suffering. London: John F. Shaw, 1870.

Consider Jesus is a book comprised of thirty short chapters which focus the reader on various aspects of the person and work of Christ. Each chapter serves as a meditation on a particular facet of Christ's life. Examples of some chapter titles include "Consider Jesus—in Lowliness of Birth"; "Consider Jesus—the Object of Popular Hate"; "Consider Jesus—Without Deceit"; "Consider Jesus—as Receiving Sinners"; and "Consider Jesus—in His Atoning Blood." As typical of Winslow's writings, he demonstrates how each truth concerning Jesus matters for the life of the believer.

Divine Realities, or, Spiritual Reflections for the Saint and Sinner. London: John F. Shaw, 1860.

Divine Realities is a compilation of some previously published writings of Winslow that were penned for the beginning of a new year. The eight chapters are divided equally between four Old Testament meditations and four New Testament meditations, revealing Winslow's balanced exposition of the whole counsel of God. Two of his previously published tracts included are "My Times in God's Hands," which highlights the sovereignty and loving protection of God throughout all of life, and "Go and Tell Jesus," which exhorts readers in their communion with Christ.

Eminent Holiness: Essential to an Efficient Ministry. London: Houlston & Stoneman, 1843.

This work expanded an address delivered by Winslow at the opening session of Stepney College, the school he attended in London. Speaking to those preparing for ministry, Winslow provides much instruction concerning the pastoral assignment. While he covers other related matters, his focus is on encouraging ministerial holiness. In the spirit of Baxter's *Reformed Pastor,* Winslow discusses the character of the pastoral office, the temptations ministers must resist, and their pursuit of personal holiness. More than any other work by Winslow, *Eminent Holiness* provides readers with his view of pastoral ministry.

Emmanuel, or, Titles of Christ: Their Teaching and Consolations. London: John F. Shaw, 1869.

Emmanuel, or Titles of Christ, is yet another Christ-centered work from Winslow. Each chapter of the work takes up a different name of Christ. Some of those include Emmanuel; Christ, the Counselor; Christ, the Prince of Peace; Christ, the Man of Sorrow; and the Resurrection and the Life. He wrote of his purpose: "Each title embodies a distinct meaning and illustrates a particular truth, the significance and preciousness of which the Holy Spirit can alone unfold and the believing heart alone appreciate. Like His twofold nature, the titles of our Lord are wonderful, and, like His infinite resources, they are exhaustless. The present volume is an attempt to explore, in a limited degree, this costly treasure" (1e).

Evening Thoughts, or, Daily Walking with God: A Portion for Each Evening in the Year. London: John F. Shaw, 1859. Reprint, edited by Joel R. Beeke and Kate DeVries. Grand Rapids: Reformation Heritage Books, 2005.

Roughly a year after he published his *Morning Thoughts,* Winslow published his companion volume, *Evening Thoughts.* He believed that it was just as important to turn one's heart toward God at the close of the day as it is at the beginning.

He hoped that his work would "suggest to the mind 'pleasant thoughts' of God, of Christ, of the Spirit, and of heaven; and so, pillowing the soul upon these precious truths, which whether sleeping or waking, are the joy and the rejoicing of his heart, compose the body to rest" (viii).

The Foot of the Cross and the Blessings Found There. New York: Robert Carter, 1868. Reprinted as *Atonement and the Cross.* Stoke-on-Trent, U.K.: Tentmaker, 2008.

Winslow offers this meditation to the church on a theme that he believed "all vital, saving truth centres in, and all sanctifying and comforting blessing springs from" (3). He calls the cross of Christ "a theme which the combined intellect of heaven could not fully unfold, nor the study and contemplation of eternity utterly exhaust" (3). He covers a range of topics related to the believer living under the shadow of the cross of Christ. Those topics include personal holiness, prayer, love, forgiveness, conviction of truth, the unity of the church, and the believer's own crucifixion with Christ at the cross. One of the most intriguing chapters addresses "The Cross of Christ, the Christian's Weapon." Winslow refers to the blood of Jesus as the weapon that "is to vanquish and overcome all the spiritual opposition by which our path to heaven is intercepted" (144). This book is yet another volume in Winslow's library that displays the work of his gospel-centered and Christ-exalting pen.

Glimpses of the Truth As It Is in Jesus. Philadelphia: Lindsay & Blakiston, 1856.

Glimpses of the Truth As It Is in Jesus is a series of sermons that Winslow delivered on a trip to Scotland. He wrote in the preface, "It is proper briefly to allude to the history of this work. Scotland is its birth-place. It contains the substance of a few discourses which the author delivered from the pulpit of different Christian denominations, during a recent visit to that magnificent and interesting land" (v). These sermons cover a range of topics but have several sections that specifically address the Christian minister. His sermons on "The Pastor's Request for Prayer" and "Voice of the Charmer" serve as great examples. Moreover, his sermon from Jeremiah 2:13 on "Broken Cisterns" is an excellent account of the satisfaction that is found in Christ alone in comparison with the worthlessness of idolatry. These sermons are very devotional and practical in nature but do not neglect deep theological reflection on the doctrinal content of the text under consideration.

The Glory of the Redeemer. 8th ed. London: John F. Shaw, 1865. Reprint, Pittsburgh: Soli Deo Gloria, 1997.

Winslow wrote this treatise to present "in an experimental and practical light, a view of the personal and official glory of the Redeemer" (vii). He spoke of his purpose when he wrote, "To aid the spiritual mind in its endeavors to obtain an occasional sight of the Redeemer's glory, in the vale of darkness and of tears, is the simple design of this work" (ix). Ten chapters comprise this lengthy work covering a wide range of topics. Winslow opens the work by unfolding the pre-existent glory of Christ and how Christ reveals the Father's glory. His Christ-tocentric hermeneutic surfaces throughout the work, particularly in chapters 3 and 4, where he addresses the typical and prophetical glory of Christ. He also covers some of the major events of the life of Christ, devoting chapters to his humiliation, resurrection, and ascension and exaltation. The final three chapters declare Christ's glory in His people, the Holy Spirit's glorifying the Redeemer, and the second coming of Christ.

Heaven Opened: A Selection from the Correspondence of Mrs. Mary Winslow. London: John F. Shaw, 1864. Reprint, Grand Rapids: Reformation Heritage Books, 2001.

In *Heaven Opened,* Winslow compiled some personal correspondence of his mother, Mary. One of her gifts was encouraging and instructing through the many letters that she wrote to friends and those who needed her special care. In the preface, Winslow spoke of his mother: "*Heavenly*-mindedness,—the highest order of *spiritual*-mindedness—seemed to individualise Mrs. Winslow's Christianity" (v). These letters could be read as daily devotionals.

Hidden Life: Memorials of John Whitmore Winslow. London: John F. Shaw, 1872.

Winslow first penned this book shortly after his son Whitmore accidentally drowned while bathing at sea in 1856. He described his son's death as a "sudden shock and convulsed agony" (vi). Winslow includes many journal extracts from Whitmore and describes his short life of twenty-one years. Whitmore was a believer. In fact, he was converted under his father's ministry and had planned to go into the ministry after college.

Hymns: Selected and Arranged for the Use of Emmanuel Church, Brighton. London: W. Hunt, 1868.

Winslow selected and compiled these hymns for use at his new pastorate, Emmanuel Church in Brighton.

The Inner Life: Its Nature, Relapse, and Recovery. London: John F. Shaw, 1850.

Winslow was a pastor who was deeply concerned about the spirituality of the church. He described the impetus for writing in one of the most extensive explanations found in any of his works. He wrote,

The subject of this work suggested itself to the author's mind during a visit to the metropolis. His close communion, at that time, with what is called the 'religious world,' forced upon his mind the painful conviction, that while religious profession was greatly on the increase—and never more so in the higher classes of society than at the present—vital godliness was in proportion on the decline; that while—to speak commercially— the quantity of religion was increasing, its quality was deteriorating. The vast number whose Christian profession was avowed—whose religious character was recognized—whose theological creed was sound—whose conversation was pious—whose sacred observances were rigid—whose benevolence was applauded—whose zeal was admired—who prided themselves upon their eloquent preacher, and their favorite religious author; but who yet were living in the world, and living as the world, and living to the world—deeply and painfully saddened him. The question frequently arose in his mind—"Where is the salt? Where are the really living souls? Where are those who know what true conversion is? Who are following Christ, and are living for God? Where are the possessors of the true spiritual life?" Alas! the world has become so like the Church, and the Church so closely resembles the world; the one so religious, and the other so carnal; an unskilled eye may be deceived in searching for the essential points of difference. Nor this alone. Even among those in whose souls it would be wrong, no, impossible, to deny the existence of spiritual life, how few are found who really seem for themselves to know it! On his return to his flock, the author—in his usual extemporary mode of address—unburdened his mind from the pulpit. The result, in a calmly written and greatly amplified form, is now, with lowliness and prayer, presented to the public (1–2).

Thus, Winslow set out to unfold the nature, relapse, and recovery of the spiritual life in the soul of the believer.

The Inquirer Directed to an Experimental and Practical View of the Atonement. London: John F. Shaw, 1839. Reprinted as *Atonement and the Cross.* Stoke-on-Trent, U.K.: Tentmaker, 1998.

The Inquirer Directed to an Experimental and Practical View of the Atonement was Winslow's first major publication, the first in a series of three that fell under the general title "The Inquirer Directed to an Experimental and Practical View of Divine Truth" (7). He subsequently published *The Inquirer Directed to an Experimental and Practical View of the Holy Spirit* and *The Glory of the Redeemer in His Person and Work.* These works demonstrate Winslow's belief that mere intellectual assent to God's truth profits nothing. He wrote, "The religion of the Lord Jesus is valuable only as its power is experienced in the heart" (7). Winslow chose to write on the atonement first because he believed "the doctrine of the

Atonement of Christ [is] the central truth of the Bible, on which all others are based, and around which they all entwine" (9). Winslow opened the work with a chapter on the use of reason in the investigation of truth. After discussing matters of theological method, he addressed the relation of the atonement to the deity of Christ, the design of the atonement, the freeness of the atonement, and the sympathy of the atonement. He finished the book with a warning concerning "The Fearful Alternative of Rejecting the Atonement."

The Inquirer Directed to an Experimental and Practical View of the Holy Spirit. London: John F. Shaw, 1840. Reprinted as *The Work of the Holy Spirit: An Experimental and Practical View.* Edinburgh: Banner of Truth, 2003.

Winslow was ever interested in theology that touches life. He believed that doctrine matters for everyday living. He was after experimental religion. This writing on the Holy Spirit supplies a striking example of his aim as a pastor and writer. He explained, "To impress the mind more deeply with the glory of His person and with the necessity and value of His work, and to awaken a more ardent desire and more earnest and constant prayer for a greater manifestation of His influence, and a more undoubted evidence of His glory and power in the church and in the believer, are the object of the writer in the following treatise" (6). After arguing for the deity of the Spirit in chapter 1, Winslow spends the next two chapters on the regenerating work of the Spirit. He moves on to cover the indwelling of the Spirit, the Spirit's work of sanctification, and the sealing and witness of the Spirit. He concludes his work by examining the Spirit as the author of prayer and as a comforter. Winslow relies on Scripture to make his case throughout the work, and he accomplishes his purpose of providing an experimental and practical view of the Spirit's work.

Instant Glory: A Reflection for the Year 1867 with a Short Biographical Notice of the Late Mrs. Winslow. London: John F. Shaw, 1867.

Winslow delivered this New Year's address roughly two months after his wife Hannah Ann died suddenly at their home. After providing a lengthy doctrinal exposition of 1 Thessalonians 5:17, he offers a short biographical sketch of his wife. This is valuable for studies on Winslow because so little is known about Hannah Ann. He tells the story of her conversion and of the final moments he was able to spend with her. Winslow also takes this opportunity to praise God for His work in her life and through her personal ministry to him, the family, and others in the church and community.

"Is the Spirit of the Lord Straitened?" A Plea for a National Baptism of the Holy Ghost with Incidents of American Revival. London: John F. Shaw, 1858.

This work constitutes a plea for revival among British churches. Winslow makes a clear call for seeking the Spirit's divine blessing for the church's witness. It reveals his passion for souls and his deep convictions concerning the person and work of the Holy Spirit. His goal in writing was revealed when he wrote: "There being, then, no straitness in the Spirit, other than that which His own sovereign will imposes, why should we not look for such an extensive Revival of Religion, such a National Baptism of the Spirit, as that which at this moment prevails in the United States?" (26–27). After unpacking a practical theology of the Holy Spirit, he then went on to give his readers extensive examples of how revival was breaking out in the United States.

Jesus and John, or, The Loving and the Loved: A Tribute to the Memory of the Late Rev. William Marsh, D.D. London: James Nisbet & Co., 1859.

Winslow delivered this sermon as a tribute to one of his Anglican brothers, Rev. William Marsh, who had recently passed away. He memorializes his life by meditating on the beloved disciple John. Winslow explained, "In searching for a Scripture portrait illustrative of the character of my departed friend, not one struck me as presenting so true and perfect a resemblance as that of 'the disciple whom Jesus loved'" (9–10). After explaining the love of Christ, Winslow reflects on the character, convictions, and ministerial influence that Rev. Marsh exercised throughout his life. This sermon provides an example of the friendship Winslow enjoyed with other ministers.

Life in Jesus: A Memoir of Mrs. Mary Winslow Arranged from Her Correspondence, Diary, and Thoughts. London: John F. Shaw, 1890. Reprint, Grand Rapids: Reformation Heritage Books, 2013.

Life in Jesus was written by a son who desired to bless the church with a memoir of his godly mother. Octavius believed it would be a disservice to neglect perpetuating the legacy of his mother, Mary Winslow, whose life was "too interesting and instructive to be altogether lost" (viii). This memoir traces her life as chronologically as possible from birth to death by relying on her personal correspondence and journal entries. The book not only tells of this godly woman who dedicated her life and family to the Lord, but also provides insight into the life of Octavius. This work is particularly important for researchers of Winslow since he never had a biographer in his day.

The Lights and Shadows of Spiritual Life. London: John F. Shaw, 1876. Reprint, *Spiritual Life: Soul-Depths and Soul-Heights* and *Lights and Shadows of Spiritual Life.* Stoke-on-Trent, U.K.: Tentmaker, 1998.

In *Lights and Shadows of Spiritual Life,* Winslow expounds "the life of God in the soul of man" (8). The work begins with an exposition of Galatians 2:20 concerning the nature and source of spiritual life. Winslow takes up different aspects of the spiritual life including service, solitude, and holiness. He also considers some of the various means that God uses to grow His saints, such as sickness and bereavement. He concludes by reflecting on the second coming of Christ, which is "the crown and consummation of spiritual life" (85).

The Lord's Prayer: Its Spirit and Its Teaching. London: John F. Shaw, 1866. Reprint, Stoke-on-Trent, U.K.: Tentmaker, 2003.

Winslow penned *The Lord's Prayer,* which he would prefer to call "The Disciples' Prayer," in order to set forth the spirit of the prayer. Thus, in each of the twelve chapters of this book, he takes a word or phrase of the prayer and expounds its meaning and significance. He unpacks the filial ("Father"), the catholic ("our"), the celestial ("which art in heaven"), the reverential ("hallowed be thy name"), the prophetical ("thy kingdom come"), the submissive ("thy will be done on earth as it is done in heaven"), the dependent ("give us this day our daily bread"), the penitential ("forgive us our debts"), the forgiving ("as we forgive our debtors"), the watchful ("lead us not into temptation"), the devotional ("but deliver us from evil"), and the adoring ("for thine is the kingdom, and the power, and the glory, for ever and ever. Amen.") spirit of the prayer.

The Man of God, or, Spiritual Religion Explained and Enforced. London: John F. Shaw, 1865.

Winslow observed that it is difficult for the church to grow both wide and deep. He penned *The Man of God* in order to set forth the deep spirituality that should be present in maturing disciples of Christ. He said that his work seeks "to portray the man of God in some of the essential and prominent features of his holy character, and to trace a few of the stages of his Christian experience; making the Lord Jesus Christ—the Divine Man—the central object of the picture" (1–2e). Throughout the twenty chapters of the work, Winslow explains various aspects and fruit of sanctification, such as the believer's joy, confessing and forsaking sin, awaiting the Lord's return, and integrity.

Midnight Harmonies, or, Thoughts for the Season of Solitude and Sorrow. New York: Robert Carter & Brothers, 1853.

The origin of this work was the "sudden and alarming illness of a beloved relative" (v). The dedication reveals that the beloved relative was his sister. Winslow explained his distress, writing, "A period of much anxiety ensued, during which the idea and the themes of this little volume suggested themselves to his mind" (v). He composed *Midnight Harmonies* "at intervals between a sick chamber and the study" for "those who may be passing through a season of anxiety and trial" (vi). Written with the goal of comforting those in trial, the chapters highlight God's sovereignty in trials and the help that He gives to His children. In typical fashion, Winslow's work is very Christ-centered, with chapters titled "Jesus Veiling His Dealings," "A Look from Christ," "Looking Unto Jesus," and "Jesus Only."

The Minister's Final Charge: A Discourse, Delivered on Relinquishing the Pastoral Care, of the Central Baptist Church, New York, December 20, 1835. New York: Leavitt, Lord, & Co., 1836.

This rare work records Winslow's farewell sermon to the first church he pastored, Central Baptist Church in New York, New York. The overarching purpose of this message was to review the most important doctrines he "set distinctly and prominently before" them throughout his ministry (4). He expounds the doctrines of the original fall and universal depravity of all mankind; the sinner's justification through the imputed righteousness of the Lord Jesus Christ; the expiatory nature of the sufferings and death of Christ; the distinct office of the Holy Spirit in the work of regeneration; the coming Savior; and the holiness of the gospel. He also speaks of different ministry endeavors Central Baptist engaged in under his leadership, such as domestic and foreign missions, Sabbath school instruction, ministerial education, the Bible Society, and the Tract Society (31). Winslow displays a warm, pastoral tone in this his final charge to the saints at Central Baptist.

The Ministry of Home, or, Brief Expository Lectures on Divine Truth Designed Especially for Family and Private Reading. London: William Hunt & Co., 1868.

Winslow wrote this book for a specific audience and purpose, as the title indicates. He said, "The object is to supply simple and brief Expositions of Divine Truth, suitable for domestic instruction and closet meditation; thus aiding the 'priest over his closet meditation' and the 'priest over his own house' in conducting family worship, and in other ways training his children and his household for God and eternity" (v). Twenty chapters make up this lengthy work. As always, Winslow explains, "It has been the earnest aim of the author to make Christ the substance of each reading and the centre of the entire work; that, viewing the subject from any standpoint, He may be seen as the one Object around whom all Divine honour clusters, from whom all saving truth emanates, and towards whom all Christian experience and practical godliness should converge" (vi).

Morning Thoughts, or, Daily Walking with God: A Portion for Each Day in the Year. London: John F. Shaw, 1858. Reprint, edited by Joel R. Beeke and Kate DeVries. Grand Rapids: Reformation Heritage Books, 2003.

With the opening words of the preface, Winslow explained the origin of *Morning Thoughts*. He wrote, "In compliance with frequent requests from various quarters that the author would allow selections from some of his published works to appear in the form of Daily Readings, he ventures to offer to the Christian church the following pages" (vii). What follows are 366 devotional readings for each morning of the year. Winslow viewed one's devotional life as vital to his overall life as a Christ follower. He said, "To begin the day with God is the great secret of walking through the day with God" (vi–viii).

The Nightingale Song of David: A Spiritual and Practical Exposition of the Twenty-Third Psalm. London: John F. Shaw, 1876.

Winslow opened this work with a defense of the inspiration of Scripture and more specifically, the Psalter by pointing to 2 Samuel 23:1–2, which tells of the Spirit speaking through David. This is important due to the intense skepticism and attack on the inspiration of Scripture during the latter days of Winslow's life. He called the Twenty–Third Psalm "the divinest, richest, and most musical of all the songs which breathed from David's inspired harp" (1e). Winslow believed that Psalm 23 "begins with Christ and ends with heaven" (1e) The eleven chapters of exposition work phrase by phrase through the psalm and uncover the various doctrinal and practical themes.

No Condemnation in Christ Jesus: As Unfolded in the Eighth Chapter of the Epistle to the Romans. London: John F. Shaw, 1853. Reprint, Edinburgh: Banner of Truth, 1991.

No Condemnation in Christ Jesus is a compilation of Winslow's sermons on Romans 8. The preface reveals that he abridged these messages, which were "originally delivered by the Author in the course of his stated ministrations, and in his usual extemporaneous mode of address" (v). Winslow called Romans 8 "a mine of sacred wealth, as inexhaustible in its resources, as those resources are indescribable in their beauty, and in their excellence and worth, priceless" (v). He went on to say, "It would, perhaps, be impossible to select from the Bible a single chapter in which were crowded so much sublime, evangelical, and sanctifying truth as this eighth of Romans. It is not only all gospel, but it may be said to contain the whole gospel" (v). Each of the chapters unveiled the doctrinal truth contained in Romans 8 verse by verse and phrase by phrase. Winslow was careful throughout to show the experimental relevance of the truth for the daily lives of his readers.

None Like Christ. New York: A. D. F. Randolph, 1863.

Winslow wrote *None Like Christ* as a reflection for the New Year in 1860. This short booklet is the length of one of his sermons and is a meditation on Song of Solomon 5:9, "How is your beloved better than others?" His purpose in writing is to present Christ "as worthy of your undivided affection, supreme confidence, and unreserved service, infinitely distancing and eclipsing all other beings and all other objects brought in competition with him" (5–6). After considering some of the rivals of Christ in the heart of man (self, the world, the creature), Winslow expounds the worth of Christ in light of His glory, beauty, love, as our Savior, teacher, friend, and servant. He concludes with a few practical exhortations to stand firm, to be faithful to His Word, and to be spiritually minded.

Our God. London: John F. Shaw, 1870. Reprint, Grand Rapids: Reformation Heritage Books, 2007.

Our God is Winslow's devotional treatment of some of the moral perfections of God. In the preface to the work, he encouraged his readers to personally apply the doctrines, precepts, and promises of God's Word. He wrote, "The design of these pages is to raise the believer to this elevated and proper standard in his personal religion" (ix). The ten chapters address such themes as God's love, patience, comfort, grace, holiness, and peace. His insights concerning the relationship between the patience of God and the mercy of God help demonstrate how all of God's moral perfections unfold the beauty of the gospel. He explained, "The patience of God seems like a central link in this golden chain of attributes. Mercy would have no room to act if patience did not prepare the way, and His truth and goodness in the promise of the Redeemer would not have been made manifest to the world if He had shot His arrows as soon as men committed these sins and deserved His punishment" (39). Throughout the work Winslow demonstrated how the character of God should influence the daily life of His people.

A Pastoral Letter Addressed to the Church and Congregation Assembling in the Warwick-Street Chapel, Leamington. London: Houlston & Stoneman, 1852.

Winslow penned this letter to his congregation in Leamington after he came down with an illness while on vacation to continental Europe in the summer of 1852. He took opportunity to share his love for them, remind them of the gospel, and even provide some candid instruction concerning their corporate worship. His statement regarding the aim of his ministry reveals his heart for ministry.

He wrote, "It has been the distinctive aim, and the sincere desire of my ministry amongst you, to make known and to endear the Saviour to your hearts.... And may I, as from a languid couch, still press the Saviour's claims to your regard? Oh, how worthy is he of your most exalted conceptions,—of your most implicit confidence,—of your most self-denying service,—of your most fervent love. When he could give you no more—and the fathomless depths of his love, and the boundless resources of his grace, would not be satisfied by giving you less— he gave you *himself.* Robed in your nature, laden with your curse, oppressed with your sorrows, wounded for your transgressions, and slain for your sins, he gave his entire self for you.... You cannot in your drafts upon Christ's fullness be too coveteous, nor in your expectations of supply be too extravagant. You may fail, as, alas! the most of us do, in making too little of Christ,—you cannot fail, in making too much of him" (6–7).

Patriarchal Shadows of Christ and His Church: As Exhibited in Passages Drawn from the History of Joseph and His Brethren. London: John F. Shaw, 1863. Reprint, Grand Rapids: Sovereign Grace Treasures, 2005.

Patriarchal Shadows is a compilation of sermons delivered extemporaneously by Winslow which were recorded by a stenographer. In this series of expositions from Genesis, he unpacks the narrative detailing the lives of Joseph and his brothers. While Winslow does not totally disregard the original context of the narrative, his main purpose is to unfold the shadows of Christ in the narrative. The opening words of his first sermon reveal his Christocentric hermeneutic: "The Word of God is as a garden of fruit and flowers—luscious with the sweet- ness, penciled with the beauty, and fragrant with the perfume of—Christ. All its shadows, types, and prophecies, all its doctrines, precepts, and promises testify of Him. Search the Scriptures in whatever part, or view them from whatever standpoint you may, of Christ they speak and to Christ they lead" (3). He faith- fully employs typological interpretation in many cases, but at times crosses over into spiritualizing the text as he presents Christ as our "true" and "spiri- tual" Joseph.

Personal Declension and Revival of Religion in the Soul. London: John F. Shaw, 1841. Reprint, Edinburgh: Banner of Truth, 2000.

This work addresses the life of God in the soul of man. His concern is the church's progress in sanctification. The key question Winslow puts before his readers is this: "What is the present spiritual state of my soul before God"? He examines how the believer's devotion to Christ often declines and what he can do to seek its revival. Specifically, he addresses the believer's love, faith, prayer, and doctrinal precision. He also has chapters on grieving the Spirit, the fruitless and fruitful professor, and the Lord as the restorer and keeper of His people.

In each chapter, Winslow explains various causes of declension and prescribes remedies as to how one can be restored. His prescriptions are always God-centered and deal much with the atoning work of Christ on the cross. This work highlights the need for self-examination and grace-motivated obedience. His chapter on doctrinal error is well done, speaking to the inextricable relation-ship between one's doctrine and life. This book provides the church with a great resource on discipleship.

Pisgah Views, or, The Negative Aspects of Heaven. London: John F. Shaw, 1873.

Winslow stated the purpose of *Pisgah Views* in the preface when he wrote, "The design of this little work is to serve a twofold, soul-animating, purpose—as a staff, aiding faith's ascent of the glorious height of Pisgah; and then, from its summit—as a telescope, bringing nearer to its sanctifying and comforting view those sublime beauties and winning attractions of the 'land which is very far off,' and which, in our present imperfect state, are best understood and felt in their shadowy and negative forms" (ix). When Winslow spoke of the negative forms or views of heaven, he meant the negative descriptions of what heaven is like given in Scripture. His chapters address truths such as the abolition of the curse, hunger, pain, tears, and death.

The Precious Things of God. London: James Nisbet & Co., 1860. Reprint, Ligonier, Pa.: Soli Deo Gloria, 1993.

Winslow composed *The Precious Things of God* with the hope that it might be used devotionally as a means of edifying his readers toward a deeper knowledge of God's covenant mercies. His aim was what he termed "experimental Chris-tianity." He wrote, "These pages address themselves pointedly and strongly to that essential principle of vital religion—the experimental. We really know as much of the gospel of Christ, and of the Christ of the gospel, as by the power of the Holy Spirit we have the experience of it in our souls. All other acquain-tance with Divine truth must be regarded as merely intellectual, theoretical, speculative, and of little worth" (iv). The subjects he addressed were most often those explicitly referred to as "precious" in Scripture. Some of those include the preciousness of Christ, the preciousness of faith, the preciousness of trial, the preciousness of God's thoughts, and the preciousness of God's Word. An excerpt from his opening chapter on the "Preciousness of Christ" serves as a sample of the quality of Winslow's work. He wrote, "Now, the only spiritual faculty that discerns Christ, and in discerning Christ realizes His preciousness, is faith. Faith is the optical faculty of the regenerate, it is the spiritual eye of the soul! Faith sees Christ, and as Christ is seen His excellence is recognized; and as His excellence unfolds, so He becomes an object of endearment to the heart! Oh, how lovely and how glorious is Jesus to the clear, far-seeing eye of faith!

Faith beholds Him the matchless, peerless One; His beauty eclipsing, His glory outshining, all other beings! Faith sees majesty in His lowliness, dignity in His condescension, honor in His humiliation, beauty in His tears, transcendent, surpassing glory in His cross!" (18).

The Silver Trumpet, or, The Church Guided and Warned in Perilous Times. London: John F. Shaw, 1844.

In a book dedicated to his congregation, Winslow provides an exposition of the gospel with implications for the life of the church. He unfolds the truth of the gospel by unpacking a spiritualized or typological reading of Numbers 10:1–2, 5. His purpose is observed when he wrote, "From the various uses of the trumpet among the Jews, we have selected a single one, as affording an illustration, if not a type, of the 'glorious Gospel of the blessed God,' deeply significant and instructive" (3). After expounding the gospel, Winslow carefully and gently exposes many errors among the Plymouth Brethren and Tractarianism (40–74). Winslow's grief over false doctrine is evident. He decried, "Oh, it is an awful and a fearful thing to pervert the gospel of Christ! A single error may prove fatal to thousands of souls" (68). He closes with some practical exhortations to the church concerning the perils of false doctrine and their love for the gospel.

Soul-Depths & Soul-Heights: Sermons on Psalm 130. London: John F. Shaw, 1874. Reprint, Edinburgh: Banner of Truth, 2006.

Soul-Depths & Soul-Heights is a series of expositions on Psalm 130 delivered during his weekly pulpit ministry. Winslow calls Psalm 130 a "Christ-unfolding Psalm" (vii). He takes the chapter verse by verse and expounds the doctrine of the verse in each sermon. He preaches Christ in various ways, sometimes in the instruction of the text, sometimes in the application, and sometimes as the theological fulfillment of the text. In addition to the Christ-centered nature of his exposition, two other qualities stand out. First, the exhortative nature of his preaching is interspersed throughout. He consistently encourages his hearers to put the truth into practice. Another prominent feature of his preaching involves how he concludes most of his sermons with an eschatological thrust. No matter what topic his sermon expounded, he almost always demonstrated how it should be viewed in its cosmic scope and with a view to our future hope with Christ in the new creation. This feature is representative of the biblical theology that pervades his preaching and writing ministry.

Thus Saith the Lord, or, Words of Divine Love. London: John F. Shaw, 1872.

This work provides its readers with thirty–one devotional reflections from God's Word. Winslow penned the purpose of the work when he wrote, "It is intended to be a faint echo of God's words of divine love addressed from time to time to His people, amid the varied experiences, duties, and trials of their Christian course" (n.p.). The title of this work is even more significant when one understands the cultural and ecclesiastical context in which Winslow ministered. He explained, "Never was there a period when we had greater need to keep close to the, 'Thus saith the Lord,' than the present! The Word of God is assailed by avowed foe and by sworn friend. Its most subtle and dangerous enemies are among its professed and sworn friends" (n.p.). Winslow's meditation on scriptural truth demonstrates his conviction that adherence to God's Word makes Christians and nations great.

The Sympathy of Christ with Man: Its Teaching and Its Consolation. New York: Robert Carter & Brothers, 1863. Reprint, Harrisonburg, Va.: Sprinkle, 1994.

The Sympathy of Christ with Man provides another example of Winslow's commitment to experimental Christianity. Winslow's purpose is observed when he wrote, "One, and the chief, design of this volume is to exhibit and illustrate the *practical* character of our Lord's emotional nature—thus linking Him in closer and personal actuality with our circumstances" (iii). This work emphasizes the humanity of Christ while not neglecting His divinity. It covers topics such as the tears of Christ, His anger, His love, His sensitivity to suffering, and His sympathy with temptation. Throughout Winslow exposes the relevance of Christology for the Christian life.

The Tree of Life: Its Shade, Fruit, and Repose. London: John F. Shaw, 1868.

The Tree of Life is yet another book centered on the person of Christ. More specifically, this work emphasizes several incidents from his life demonstrating how it "was pre-eminently a practical life" (1e). A few of the events examined include the episode of Jesus as a child in the temple, His tears at the grave of Lazarus, the washing of the disciples' feet, His crucifixion and resurrection, and His appearing to Paul on the Damascus road. The book serves as an example of Winslow's dual purpose of edifying believers while not neglecting his responsibilities as an evangelist. Of the latter he wrote, "It has been the aim of the author of the present volume so to unfold the 'way of life' that each chapter should contain an epitome of the gospel plan of salvation. It may thus be found an appropriate work to place in the hands of those alas! how countless the number!—who are living in blinded ignorance or in criminal neglect of the claims of God, the interests of their soul, and the solemnities of eternity" (2e). This work supplies a rich depository of christological truth.

Words Addressed to an Anxious Soul on the Borders of Eternity. London: John F. Shaw, 1858.

This short letter was a response to a letter sent by an anxious man who was alarmed because he was "on the brink of eternity" and not ready to die. In this letter, Winslow encouraged him to look to Christ and His atoning work for sinners. He spoke directly to him saying, "Again, I repeat, your eye of faith must now be directed entirely out of, and from yourself, to Jesus" (6–7). This letter provides an example of how Winslow pled with individuals to be reconciled to God.

BIBLIOGRAPHY

Primary Sources

Winslow, Octavius. "Additional Reasons for Preferring the English Bible As It Is." In *Objections to a Baptist Version of the New Testament*, 52–66. By William T. Brantly. New York: J. P. Callender, 1837.

———. *Born Again, or, From Grace to Glory*. London: John F. Shaw, 1864.

———. *Christ and the Christian in Temptation: Counsel and Consolation for the Tempted*. London, 1878.

———. *Christ Is Ever with You: Illustrated by Experiences Drawn from the Prayer-Meeting, and Field and Hospital Life*. London: John F. Shaw, 1864.

———. *Christ, The Theme of the Home Missionary: An Argument for Home Missions*. New York: John S. Taylor, 1838.

———. *Consider Jesus: Thoughts for Daily Duty, Service, and Suffering*. London: John F. Shaw, 1870.

———. "The Deepening of the Spiritual Life: Its Hindrances and Helps among Clergy and People." *Authorized Report of the Church Congress Held at Nottingham October 10, 11, 12, & 13*, 437–41. By Church Congress. London: Wells Gardner, 1871.

———. *Divine Realities, or, Spiritual Reflections for the Saint and Sinner*. London: John F. Shaw, 1860.

———. *Eminent Holiness: Essential to an Efficient Ministry*. London: Houlston & Stoneman, 1843.

———. *Emmanuel, or, Titles of Christ: Their Teaching and Consolations*. London: John F. Shaw, 1869.

———. *Evening Thoughts, or, Daily Walking with God: A Portion for Each Evening in the Year*. London: John F. Shaw, 1859. Reprint, edited by Joel R. Beeke and Kate DeVries. Grand Rapids: Reformation Heritage Books, 2005.

———. *The Foot of the Cross and the Blessings Found There*. New York: Robert Carter, 1868. Reprinted as *Atonement and the Cross*. Stoke-on-Trent, U.K.: Tentmaker, 2008.

———. *Glimpses of the Truth As It Is in Jesus*. Philadelphia: Lindsay & Blakiston, 1856.

———. *The Glory of the Redeemer in His Person and Work.* 8th ed. London: John F. Shaw, 1865. Reprint, Pittsburgh: Soli Deo Gloria, 1997.

———. "Going Home." In *Living Unto God, or, Chapters in Aid of the Christian Life,* 248–55. London: Elliot Stock, 1867.

———. *Grace and Truth.* London: John F. Shaw, 1849.

———. *Heaven Opened: A Selection from the Correspondence of Mrs. Mary Winslow.* London: John F. Shaw, 1864. Reprint, Grand Rapids: Reformation Heritage Books, 2001.

———. *Help Heavenward: Guidance and Strength for the Christian's Life-Journey.* London: James Nisbet, 1869. Reprint, Edinburgh: Banner of Truth, 2007.

———. *Hidden Life: Memorials of John Whitmore Winslow.* London: John F. Shaw, 1872.

———. *Human Sympathy, A Medium of Divine Comfort: An Incident in the Life of David.* London: John F. Shaw, 1854.

———. *Hymns: Selected and Arranged for the Use of Emmanuel Church, Brighton.* London: W. Hunt, 1868.

———. *The Inner Life: Its Nature, Relapse, and Recovery.* London: John F. Shaw, 1850.

———. *The Inquirer Directed to an Experimental and Practical View of the Atonement.* New York: M. W. Dodd, 1838.

———. *The Inquirer Directed to an Experimental and Practical View of the Atonement.* London: John F. Shaw, 1839. Reprinted as *Atonement and the Cross.* Stoke-on-Trent, U.K.: Tentmaker, 1998.

———. *The Inquirer Directed to an Experimental and Practical View of the Holy Spirit.* London: John F. Shaw, 1840. Reprinted as *The Work of the Holy Spirit: An Experimental and Practical View.* Edinburgh: Banner of Truth, 2003.

———. *Instant Glory: A Reflection for the Year 1867 with a Short Biographical Notice of the Late Mrs. Winslow.* London: John F. Shaw, 1867.

———. Introduction to *A Short Memoir of the Rev. John Finley, Late Ministerial Trustee of the Countess of Huntington's Connexion…with a Brief Account of His Two Sons.* By Harriet Finley. London: James Nisbet & Co., 1856.

———. Introductory preface to *Sermons on the First Epistle of Peter,* by Hermann Friedrich Kohlbrügge. London: Patridge & Oakley, 1853.

———. Introductory preface to *The Spirit of Holiness.* By James Harington Evans. New York: J. S. Taylor, 1837.

———. "Is the Spirit of the Lord Straitened?" *A Plea for a National Baptism of the Holy Ghost with Incidents of American Revival.* London: John F. Shaw, 1858.

———. *Jesus and John, or, The Loving and the Loved: A Tribute to the Memory of the Late Rev. William Marsh, D.D.* London: James Nisbet & Co., 1859.

———. "Jesus Veiling His Dealings." In *The Bow in the Cloud: Springs of Comfort in Times of Deep Affliction,* 77–87. Edited by William Bacon Stevens.

Philadelphia: Hubbard Brothers, 1871. Reprint, Birmingham, Ala.: Solid Ground Christian Books, 2007.

———. "A Letter Addressed to a Religiously Speculative Mind." In *The Christian Treasury*, 325–29. London: John Johnstone, 1858.

———. *Life in Jesus: A Memoir of Mrs. Mary Winslow Arranged from Her Correspondence, Diary, and Thoughts*. London: John F. Shaw, 1890. Reprint, Grand Rapids: Reformation Heritage Books, 2013.

———. *The Lights and Shadows of Spiritual Life*. London: John F. Shaw, 1876. Reprint, Stoke-on-Trent, U.K.: Tentmaker, 1998.

———. *The Lord My Portion*. London, 1870.

———. *The Lord's Prayer: Its Spirit and Its Teaching*. London: John F. Shaw, 1866. Reprint, Stoke-on-Trent, U.K.: Tentmaker Publications, 2003.

———. *The Man of God, or, Spiritual Religion Explained and Enforced*. London: John F. Shaw, 1865.

———. *Midnight Harmonies, or, Thoughts for the Season of Solitude and Sorrow*. New York: Robert Carter & Brothers, 1853. Reprint, Grand Rapids: Ebenezer Publications, 2002.

———. *The Minister's Final Charge: A Discourse, Delivered on Relinquishing the Pastoral Care, of the Central Baptist Church, New York, December 20, 1835*. New York: Leavitt, Lord, & Co., 1836.

———. *The Ministry of Home, or, Brief Expository Lectures on Divine Truth Designed Especially for Family and Private Reading*. London: William Hunt & Co., 1868.

———. *Morning Thoughts, or, Daily Walking with God: A Portion for Each Day in the Year*. London: John F. Shaw, 1858. Reprint, edited by Joel R. Beeke and Kate DeVries. Grand Rapids: Reformation Heritage Books, 2003.

———. *The Nightingale Song of David: A Spiritual and Practical Exposition of the Twenty-Third Psalm*. London: John F. Shaw, 1876.

———. *No Condemnation in Christ Jesus: As Unfolded in the Eighth Chapter of the Epistle to the Romans*. London: John F. Shaw, 1853. Reprint, Edinburgh: Banner of Truth, 1991.

———. *None Like Christ*. New York: A. D. F. Randolph, 1863.

———. *Our God*. London: John F. Shaw, 1870. Reprint, Grand Rapids: Reformation Heritage Books, 2007.

———. *A Pastoral Letter Addressed to the Church and Congregation Assembling in the Warwick-Street Chapel, Leamington*. London: Houlston & Stoneman, 1852.

———. *Patriarchal Shadows of Christ and His Church: As Exhibited in Passages Drawn from the History of Joseph and His Brethren*. London: John F. Shaw, 1863. Reprint, Grand Rapids: Sovereign Grace Treasures, 2005.

———. *Personal Declension and Revival of Religion in the Soul*. London: John F. Shaw, 1841. Reprint, Edinburgh: Banner of Truth, 2000.

———. *Pisgah Views, or, The Negative Aspects of Heaven*. London: John F. Shaw, 1873.

———. *Practical Suggestions Appropriate to the Present Religious Crisis*. London: William Hunt & Co., 1868.

———. *The Precious Things of God*. London: James Nisbet & Co., 1860. Reprint, Ligonier, Pa.: Soli Deo Gloria, 1993.

———. Preface to *The Nature and Evidences of Regeneration*. By George Townshend Fox. London: William Hunt, 1872.

———. "The Saints in Light." In *In Heaven: Glimpses of the Life and Happiness of the Glorified*, 117–28. London: W. Kent & Co., 1865.

———. *The Silver Trumpet; or, The Church Guided and Warned in Perilous Times*. London: John F. Shaw, 1844.

———. *Soul-Depths & Soul-Heights: Sermons on Psalm 130*. London: John F. Shaw, 1874. Reprint, Edinburgh: Banner of Truth, 2006.

———. "The Spiritual Life: Discussion. In *The Authorised Report of the Church Congress Held at Brighton October 6, 7, 8, & 9*, 467–68. By Church Congress. London: William Wells Gardner, 1874.

———. *The Sympathy of Christ with Man: Its Teaching and Its Consolation*. New York: Robert Carter & Brothers, 1863. Reprint, Harrisonburg, Va.: Sprinkle, 1994.

———. *Thus Saith the Lord, or, Words of Divine Love*. London: John F. Shaw, 1872.

———. *The Tree of Life: Its Shade, Fruit, and Repose*. London: John F. Shaw, 1868.

———. "The Weaned Child. In *The Bow in the Cloud: Springs of Comfort in Times of Deep Affliction*, 140–53. Edited by William Bacon Stevens. Philadelphia: Hubbard Brothers, 1871. Reprint, Birmingham, Ala.: Solid Ground Christian Books, 2007.

———. *Words Addressed to an Anxious Soul on the Borders of Eternity*. London: John F. Shaw, 1858.

———. *Words of Divine Comfort*. London: John F. Shaw, 1872.

Secondary Sources

Adam, Peter. *Speaking God's Words: A Practical Theology of Expository Preaching*. Downers Grove, Ill.: IVP, 1996.

Agnus, M. E. *Henry Dunckley M.A., LL.D.* Manchester, U.K., 1896. Reprint, Charleston, S.C.: BiblioBazaar, 2009.

Akin, Daniel. "Axioms for a Great Commission Resurgence." In *The Great Commission Resurgence: Fulfilling God's Mandate in Our Time*. Edited by Chuck Lawless and Adam W. Greenway. Nashville: B&H Academic, 2010.

The American and Foreign Christian Union. "Book Notices." *Christian World: A Magazine of the American and Foreign Christian Union* 14 (March 1863): 94–95.

American Tract Society. "Tract Meeting in New York." *The American Tract Magazine for the Year 1830* 5, no. 12 (December 1830): 157.

Annual Register, or, A View of the History and Politics of the Year 1854. London: F. & J. Rivington, 1855.

Arndt, William, Frederick Danker, and Walter Bauer. *A Greek-English Lexicon of the New Testament and Other Early Christian Literature.* 3rd ed. Chicago: University of Chicago Press, 2001.

Azurdia, Arturo. *Spirit Empowered Preaching: Involving the Holy Spirit in Your Ministry.* Ross-shire, U.K.: Mentor, 2007.

Baptist Missionary Society. "Anniversary Services." *The Baptist Magazine* 41 (April 1849): 248.

———. "Brief Notices." *The Baptist Magazine* 55 (1863): 517–19.

———. "Recognition and Ordination Services." *The Baptist Magazine* 49 (1857): 503–4.

Beecher, Henry Ward. *Life Thoughts Gathered from the Extemporaneous Discourses of Henry Ward Beecher.* Edited by Edna Dean Proctor. Boston: Phillips, Sampson, & Co., 1858.

Beeke, Joel. "Experiential Preaching." In *Feed My Sheep: A Passionate Plea for Preaching,* 53–70. 2nd ed. Lake Mary, Fla.: Reformation Trust, 2008.

———. Foreword to *Morning Thoughts.* By Octavius Winslow. London: John F. Shaw, 1857. Reprint, Grand Rapids: Reformation Heritage Books, 2003.

———. Foreword to *Our God.* By Octavius Winslow. London: John F. Shaw, 1870. Reprint, Grand Rapids: Reformation Heritage Books, 2007.

———. *Living for God's Glory: An Introduction to Calvinism.* Lake Mary, Fla.: Reformation Trust, 2008.

———. *The Quest for Full Assurance: The Legacy of Calvin and His Successors.* Edinburgh: Banner of Truth, 2000.

Begg, James. *The Baptist Church, Warwick Street, Lamington Spa: A Short History.* [Leamington?]: n.p., 1980.

Bickel, Bruce. *Light and Heat: The Puritan View of the Pulpit.* Morgan, Pa.: Soli Deo Gloria, 1999.

Black, Adam, and Charles Black. *Black's Guide to Leamington and Its Environs: Including Warwick, Stratford-on-Avon, & Kenilworth.* Edinburgh: Adam & Charles Black, 1883.

Breed, Geoffrey R. *Calvinism and Communion in Victorian England: Studies in Nineteenth-Century Strict-Communion Baptist Ecclesiology Comprising the Minutes of the London Association of Strict Baptist Ministers and Churches, 1846–1855 and the Ramsgate Chapel Case, 1862.* Springfield, Mo.: Particular Baptist Press, 2008.

———. *Particular Baptists in Victorian England and Their Strict Communion Organizations.* Didcot, U.K.: Baptist Historical Society, 2003.

Bridges, Charles. *The Christian Ministry with an Inquiry into the Causes of Its Inefficiency.* London: R. B. Seely & W. Burnside, 1830. Reprint, Edinburgh: Banner of Truth, 2006.

Briggs, Asa. *Victorian People: Some Reassessments of People, Institutions, Ideas, and Events, 1851–1867.* London: Odhams Press, 1954.

Briggs, J. H. Y. "Winslow, Octavius." In *The Blackwell Dictionary of Evangelical Biography,* 1213. Edited by Donald M. Lewis. Oxford: Blackwell Publishers, 1995.

Broadus, John. *A Treatise on the Preparation and Delivery of Sermons.* New York: A. C. Armstrong, 1887.

Bunyan, John. *Differences in Judgment about Water Baptism, No Bar to Communion.* In *The Works of Bunyan.* Vol. 2. Edited by George Offor. Glasgow, U.K.: W. G. Blackie & Son. Reprint, Edinburgh: Banner of Truth, 1991.

Buttrick, David. *Homiletic: Moves and Structures.* Philadelphia: Fortress, 1987.

Campbell, John, ed. "Church News of the Month." *The Christian's Penny Magazine and Friend of the People* 4 (1868): 303–8.

———. "Notices of New Books." *The Christian Witness and Congregation Magazine* 6 (1970): 478–79.

Carrick, John. *The Imperative of Preaching: A Theology of Sacred Rhetoric.* Edinburgh: Banner of Truth, 2002.

Cave, Lyndon F. *Royal Leamington Spa: Its History and Development.* Chichester, U.K.: Phillimore & Co., 1988.

Chadwick, Owen. *The Victorian Church: An Ecclesiastical History of England, Part I.* New York: Oxford University Press, 1966.

Chapell, Bryan. *Christ-Centered Preaching: Redeeming the Expository Sermon.* Grand Rapids: Baker, 1994.

———. *Using Illustrations to Preach with Power.* Rev. ed. Wheaton, Ill.: Crossway, 2001.

Christmas, Henry. *Preachers and Preaching.* London: William Lay, 1858.

Church Congress. *The Authorized Report of the Church Congress Held at Leeds: October 8th, 9th, 10th, & 11th, 1872* (London: John Hodges, 1872), 213.

———. *Authorized Report of the Church Congress Held at Nottingham October 10, 11, 12, & 13.* London: Wells Gardner, 1871.

Clark, David. *To Know and Love God: Method for Theology.* Wheaton, Ill.: Crossway, 2003.

Clowney, Edmund. *Preaching Christ in All of Scripture.* Wheaton, Ill.: Crossway, 2003.

Cole, George. *Euthanasia: Sermons and Poems in Memory of Departed Friends.* London: William MacIntosh, 1868.

Cole, Graham. *He Who Gives Life: The Doctrine of the Holy Spirit.* Wheaton, Ill.: Crossway, 2007.

Cooper, R. E. *From Stepney to St. Giles: The Story of Regent's Park College 1810–1960.* London: Carey Kingsgate Press, 1960.

Craddock, Fred. *As One without Authority.* Nashville: Abingdon, 1979.

"Critical Notices." *Southern Presbyterian Review: Conducted by an Association of Ministers in Columbia, S.C.* 1 (December 1847): 153–64.

Dale, A. W. W. *The Life of R. W. Dale of Birmingham.* 6th ed. London: Hodder & Stoughton, 1905.

Dargan, Edwin Charles. *A History of Preaching.* 2 vols. New York: Hodder & Stoughton, 1905. Reprint, Birmingham, Ala.: Solid Ground Christian Books, 2003.

Davies, Horton. *The Worship of the English Puritans.* Westminster, U.K.: Dacre Press, 1948.

"Death of the Rev. Dr. Winslow." *Brighton Gazette.* March 7, 1878.

Deetz, James, and Patricia Scott Deetz. *The Times of Their Lives: Life, Love, and Death in Plymouth Colony.* New York: W. H. Freeman, 2000.

De Witt, Thomas. Recommendation for *Personal Declension and Revival of Religion in the Soul.* By Octavius Winslow. New York: Robert Carter, 1847.

Doddridge, Philip. "Extracts from Doddridge's Lectures on Preaching." In *The Preacher's Manual,* 133–40. Edited by Sheva. London: Richard Baynes, 1820.

Driscoll, Mark. *Confessions of a Reformission Rev.* Grand Rapids: Zondervan, 2006.

Drummond, Lewis. *Spurgeon: Prince of Preachers.* Grand Rapids: Kregel, 1992.

Dudley, T. B. *From Chaos to the Charter: A Complete History of Royal Leamington Spa.* Royal Leamington Spa, U.K.: P. & W. E. Linaker, 1901.

Edwards, O. C. *A History of Preaching.* Nashville: Abingdon, 2004.

Ellison, Robert. *The Victorian Pulpit: Spoken and Written Sermons in Nineteenth-Century Britain.* London: Associate University Presses, 1998.

Ensor, Robert Charles Kirkwood. *England, 1870–1914.* Oxford, U.K.: The Clarendon Press, 1936.

Evangelical Alliance. "Evangelical Alliance: The Bath Conference." *Evangelical Christendom: A Monthly Chronicle of the Churches* 7 (November 1866): 551–60.

———. "Evangelical Alliance." *Evangelical Christendom; A Monthly Chronicle of the Churches Conducted by Members of the Evangelical Alliance* 7 (October 1866): 519–20.

———. *Evangelical Alliance: Report of the Proceedings of the Conference, Held at Freemasons' Hall, London, From August 19th to September 2nd Inclusive, 1846.* London: Partridge & Oakey, 1847.

———. "Home Intelligence: The Late Dr. Winslow." *Evangelical Christendom, Christian Work, and The News of the Churches: Also a Monthly Record of the Transactions of the Evangelical Alliance* 19 (April 1878): 120.

———. "Home Intelligence: Mr. Spurgeon and Charity." *Evangelical Christendom: A Monthly Chronicle of the Churches* 5 (October 1864): 511–13.

———. "Monthly Retrospect: Home." *Evangelical Christendom: A Monthly Chronicle of the Churches* 9 (October 1868): 399–400.

———. "Public Meeting." *Evangelical Christendom: Its State and Prospects* 3 (November 1862): 567–68.

Fant, Clyde E., and William M. Pinson Jr. *A Treasury of Great Preaching.* 12 vols. Dallas: Word, 1995.

Ferguson, Sinclair. Foreword to *The Art of Prophesying with The Calling of Ministry.* By William Perkins. N.p.: n.p., 1606. Rev. ed. Edinburgh: Banner of Truth, 2002.

Forsyth, P. T. *Positive Preaching and the Modern Mind.* London: Independent Press, 1907.

Fosdick, Harry Emerson. "Preaching as Personal Counseling." In *The Company of Preachers: Wisdom on Preaching, Augustine to the Present.* Edited by Richard Lischer. Grand Rapids: Eerdmans, 2002.

Fuller, Andrew. *The Complete Works of Andrew Fuller.* Vol. 1. Philadelphia: American Baptist Publication Society, 1845.

Goldsworthy, Graeme. *Preaching the Whole Bible as Christian Scripture: The Application of Biblical Theology to Expository Preaching.* Grand Rapids: Eerdmans, 2000.

Greenleaf, Jonathan. *A History of the Churches, of All Denominations, in the City of New York, from the First Settlement to the Year 1846.* New York: E. French, 1846.

Greidanus, Sidney. *Preaching Christ from the Old Testament: A Contemporary Hermeneutical Method.* Grand Rapids: Eerdmans, 1999.

———. *Sola Scriptura: Problems and Principles in Preaching Historical Texts.* Toronto: Wedge Publishing Foundation, 1970. Reprint, Eugene, Ore.: Wipf & Stock Publishers, 2001.

Grudem, Wayne. *Systematic Theology.* Grand Rapids: Zondervan, 1994.

Hamilton, James M. "Was Joseph a Type of the Messiah? Tracing the Typological Identification between Joseph, David, and Jesus." *The Southern Baptist Journal of Theology* 12, no. 4 (Winter 2008): 52–77.

Heisler, Greg. *Spirit-Led Preaching: The Holy Spirit's Role in Sermon Preparation and Delivery.* Nashville: B&H Academic, 2007.

Hendrix, John D. *Nothing Never Happens: Experiential Learning and the Church.* Macon, Ga.: Smith & Helwys, 2004.

Henry, Robert T. *The Golden Age of Preaching: Men Who Moved the Masses.* New York: iUniverse, 2005.

Herrick, Lucy Kendall. *Voyage to California Written at Sea, 1852.* Edited by Amy Requa Russell, Marcia Russell Good, and Mary Good Lindgren. San Marino, Calif.: Huntington Library, 1998.

Hughes, Jack. *Expository Preaching with Word Pictures with Illustrations from the Sermons of Thomas Watson.* Ross-Shire, U.K.: Christian Focus Publications, 2001.

Hughes, Robert G., and Robert Kysar, *Preaching Doctrine for the Twenty-First Century.* Minneapolis: Fortress, 1997.

Irving, Joseph. *The Annals of Our Time: A Diurnal of Events, Social and Political, Home and Foreign, from the Accession of Queen Victoria, June 20, 1837.* London: MacMillan & Co., 1871.

Jennings, John. "Of Particular and Experimental Preaching." In *The Christian Pastor's Manual: A Selection of Tracts on the Duties, Difficulties, and Encouragements of the Christian Ministry*, 49–65. By John Brown. Edinburgh: David Brown, 1826. Reprint, edited by Don Kistler. Morgan, Pa.: Soli Deo Gloria, 2003.

Johnson, Dennis. *Him We Proclaim: Preaching Christ from All the Scriptures*. Phillipsburg, N.J.: P&R, 2007.

Kaiser, Walter C. *The Majesty of God in the Old Testament: A Guide for Preaching and Teaching*. Grand Rapids: Baker, 2007.

———. *Toward an Exegetical Theology*. Grand Rapids: Baker, 1981.

Keller, Tim. "Advancing the Gospel into the 21st Century: Acts 13–19." *City Reaching* (blog). Accessed December 5, 2013. http://cityreaching.com/floating154.php.

———. *Center Church: Doing Balanced, Gospel-Centered Ministry in Your City*. Grand Rapids: Zondervan, 2012.

———. "Preaching the Gospel." *Resurgence* (blog). Accessed December 5, 2013. http://theresurgence.com/2006/07/11/preaching-the-gospel.

Keller, Tim, and J. Allen Thompson. *Redeemer Church Planting Manual*. New York: Redeemer Church Planting Center, 2002.

Kidder, Daniel P. *A Treatise on Homiletics: Designed to Illustrate the True Theory and Practice of Preaching the Gospel*. New York: Carlton & Porter, 1864.

Killinger, John, ed. *Experimental Preaching*. Nashville: Abingdon, 1973.

———. "Experimental Preaching." In *Concise Encyclopedia of Preaching*, 128–29. Edited by William H. Willimon and Richard Lischer. Louisville: Westminster John Knox, 1995.

Larsen, David L. *The Company of the Preachers*. 2 vols. Grand Rapids: Kregel, 1998.

Letham, Robert. *The Holy Trinity: In Scripture, History, Theology, and Worship*. Phillipsburg, N.J.: P&R, 2004.

Lints, Richard. *The Fabric of Theology: A Prolegomenon to Evangelical Theology*. Grand Rapids: Eerdmans, 1993.

"Literary Notices." *The Boston Review: Devoted to Theology and Literature* 3 (May 1863): 319–33.

Lloyd-Jones, D. Martyn. *Preaching and Preachers*. Grand Rapids: Zondervan, 1971.

———. *The Puritans: Their Origins and Successors*. Edinburgh: Banner of Truth, 1987.

Lowry, Eugene. *The Homiletical Plot: The Sermon as Narrative Art Form*. Atlanta: John Knox, 1980.

Luther, Martin. *Martin Luther's Basic Theological Writings*. Edited by Timothy F. Lull. Minneapolis: Augsburg Fortress, 1989.

MacArthur, John. *Rediscovering Expository Preaching*. Dallas: Word, 1992.

———. "Why Doesn't John MacArthur Add Much Application to His Sermons?" *Grace to You Blog*. Accessed December 5, 2013. http://www.gty.org/Resources/Sermons/GTY117.

Machen, J. Gresham. *Christianity and Liberalism*. Grand Rapids: Eerdmans, 1977.

Marsh, Catherine. *The Life of the Rev. William Marsh, D.D.* London: James Nisbet & Co., 1867.

Methodist Episcopal Church. "Critical Notices." *The Methodist Quarterly Review* 28 (October 1846): 625–34.

Middleton, Judy. *The Encyclopaedia of Hove and Portslade D to E.* Vol. 4. N.p.: n.p., 2002.

Miller, Mark. *Experiential Storytelling: (Re)Discovering Narrative to Communicate God's Message.* Grand Rapids: Zondervan, 2003.

Mitchell, Henry. *Celebration and Experience in Preaching.* Rev. ed. Nashville: Abingdon, 2008.

"Monthly Retrospect: Home Affairs." *The United Presbyterian Magazine* 15 (1871): 94–96.

"Monthly Retrospect: Rev. Mr. Spurgeon and Baptismal Regeneration." *The United Presbyterian Magazine* 8 (October 1864): 476–78.

Moore, Daniel. *Thoughts on Preaching, Specially in Relation to the Requirements of the Age.* London: Hatchard & Co., 1861.

Morgan, G. Campbell. *Preaching.* New York: Fleming H. Revell, 1937.

New York University Alumni Association. *Biographical Catalogue of the Chancellors, Professors and Graduates of the Department of Arts and Science of the University of the City of New York.* New York: Alumni Association, 1894.

"Notices of Books." *The Christian Observer and Advocate Conducted by Members of the Church of England for the Year 1875* (February 1875): 154–58.

Old, Hughes Oliphant. *The Reading and Preaching of the Scriptures in the Worship of the Christian Church.* Grand Rapids: Eerdmans, 1998–2010.

"Ordinations." *The Baptist Magazine* 25 (November 1833): 516–19.

"Ordinations." *The Ecclesiastical Gazette, or, Monthly Register of the Affairs of the Church of England and of Its Religious Societies and Institutions* 33 (July 12, 1870): 20–21.

"Our Memorial Record: The Rev. Octavius Winslow." *The Sunday Magazine for Family Reading* 1 (1878): 503–4.

Owen, John. *The Works of John Owen.* Edited by William H. Goold. 24 vols. Edinburgh: Johnstone & Hunter, 1850–1855. Reprint, Edinburgh: Banner of Truth, 1991.

Packer, J. I. *Keep in Step with the Spirit: Finding Fullness in Our Walk with God.* Grand Rapids: Baker, 2005.

———. *A Quest for Godliness: The Puritan Vision of the Christian Life.* Wheaton, Ill.: Crossway, 1990.

———. "Why Preaching?" In *The Preacher and Preaching: Reviving the Art in the Twentieth Century,* 1–29. Edited by Samuel T. Logan Jr. Phillipsburg, N.J.: P&R, 1986.

Pagitt, Doug. *Preaching Re-Imagined.* Grand Rapids: Zondervan, 2005.

Pederson, Randall J. "The Life and Writings of Octavius Winslow." In *Midnight Harmonies, or, Thoughts for the Season of Solitude and Sorrow*. By Octavius Winslow. London: John F. Shaw, 1851. Reprint, Grand Rapids: Ebenezer Publications, 2002.

Perkins, William. *The Art of Prophesying with the Calling of Ministry*. N.p.: n.p., 1606. Rev. ed. Edinburgh: Banner of Truth, 2002.

Phillips, Alfred. "The Coventry District." In *Records of an Old Association: Being a Memorial Volume of the 250th Anniversary of the Midland, Now the West Midland, Baptist Association, Formed in Warwick, May 3rd, 1655*. Edited by J. M. Gwynne Owen. Birmingham, U.K.: Press of Allday, 1905.

Pipa Jr., Joseph. "William Perkins and the Development of Puritan Preaching." PhD diss., Westminster Theological Seminary, 1985.

Piper, John. "Preaching As Expository Exultation for the Glory of God." In *Preaching the Cross*, 103–15. By Mark Dever, J. Ligon Duncan III, R. Albert Mohler Jr., et al. Wheaton, Ill.: Crossway, 2007.

Piper, John, Alex Chediak, and Tom Stellar. "Baptism and Church Membership at Bethlehem Baptist Church: Eight Recommendations for Constitutional Revision." *Desiring God Resource Library*. August 9, 2005. http://www.desiringgod.org/resource-library/articles/baptism-and-church-membership-eight-recommendations-for-constitutional-revision.

Prime, Nathaniel. *History of Long Island: From Its First Settlement by Europeans to the Year 1845 with Special Reference to its Ecclesiastical Concerns*. New York: Robert Carter, 1845.

Reed, Parker M. *The Bench and Bar of Wisconsin: History and Biography, with Portrait Illustrations*. Milwaukee: P. M. Reed, 1882.

"Review." *The General Baptist Repository and Missionary Observer* 4 (1842): 18–21.

Richard, Ramesh. *Preparing Expository Sermons: A Seven-Step Method for Biblical Preaching*. Grand Rapids: Baker, 2001.

"The Robert Forbes Family Bible." Winslow Genealogy. Accessed January 16, 2010. http://winslowtree.com/robert.htm.

Robinson, Haddon. *Biblical Preaching*. 2nd ed. Grand Rapids: Baker, 2001.

Rummage, Stephen. *Planning Your Preaching: A Step-by-Step Guide for Developing a One-Year Preaching Calendar*. Grand Rapids: Kregel, 2002.

Scharf, J. Thomas. *History of Westchester County, New York including Morrisania, Kings Bridge and West Farms Which Have Been Annexed to New York City*. Vol. 1, Part 2. Philadelphia: L. E. Preston & Co., 1886.

Schindehette, Susan. "'The Smiling Preacher.'" *People.com*. June 6, 2005. http://www.people.com/people/archive/article/0,,20147762,00.html.

Shaddix, Jim, and Jerry Vines. *Power in the Pulpit: How to Prepare and Deliver Expository Sermons*. Chicago: Moody, 1999.

Sherwood, J. Manning. "Bible Preacher." *The American National Preacher* 27 (September 1853): 206–15.

Smith, Henry B. and J. M. Sherwood, eds."Criticism on Books: Practical Religion." *The American Presbyterian and Theological Review* 1 (July 1863): 518.

Smith, Lucius E., ed. "Editorial Notices." *The Baptist Quarterly* 1 (1867): 354–83.

Smith, Robert. *The Quiet Thoughts of a Quiet Thinker.* London: Oliphant Anderson & Ferrier, 1896.

Spurgeon, Charles H. *The Metropolitan Tabernacle Pulpit.* Vol. 7. Pasadena, Tex.: Pilgrim Publications, 1986.

Stanton Street Baptist Church. *A History of Stanton Street Baptist Church in the City of New York; With a Sketch of Its Pastors, and a Register of the Entire Membership.* New York: Sheldon & Co., 1860.

Stephens, William Richard Wood. *A Memoir of Richard Durnford, D.D., Sometime Bishop of Chichester: With Selections from His Correspondence.* London: John Murray, 1899.

Stott, John. *Between Two Worlds: The Art of Preaching in the Twentieth Century.* Grand Rapids: Eerdmans, 1996.

Suddards, W. *The British Pulpit: Consisting of Discourses by the Most Eminent Living Divines, in England, Scotland, and Ireland.* Vol. 2. New York: Robert Carter, 1845.

Summers, W. H. *History of the Congregational Churches in the Berks, South Oxon and South Bucks Association with Notes on the Earlier Nonconformist History of the District.* Newbury, U.K.: W. J. Blacket, 1905.

Taylor, John. *Autobiography of a Lancashire Lawyer, Being the Life and Recollections of John Taylor, Attorney-at-Law, and First Coroner of the Borough of Bolton, with Notice of Many Persons and Things Met During a Life of Seventy-Two Years Lived in and about Bolton.* Edited by James Clegg. Bolton, U.K.: The Daily Chronicle Office, 1883.

Tripp, Paul. *Instruments in the Redeemer's Hands: People in Need of Change Helping People in Need of Change.* Phillipsburg, N.J.: P&R, 2002.

Urban, Sylvanus, ed. "Deaths." *The Gentleman's Magazine July–December 1866.* Vol. 221 (1866): 695–708.

Warren, Rick. "A Primer on Preaching Like Jesus, Part One." *CBN.com.* Accessed December 5, 2013. http://www.cbn.com/spirituallife/churchandministry/warren_preach_like_jesusa.aspx.

Wayland, Francis. *Notes on the Principles and Practices of Baptist Churches.* New York: Sheldon, Blakeman, & Co., 1857.

Webber, F. W. *A History of Preaching in Britain and America: Including Many of the Biographies of Many Princes of the Pulpit and the Men Who Influenced Them.* 3 vols. Milwaukee: Northwestern Publishing House, 1952.

Wells, David. *God in the Wasteland: The Reality of Truth in a World of Fading Dreams.* Grand Rapids: Eerdmans, 1994.

———. *No Place for Truth, or, Whatever Happened to Evangelical Theology?* Grand Rapids: Eerdmans, 1993.

————. "The Theologian's Craft." In *Doing Theology in Today's World*, 171–94. Edited by John Woodbridge and Thomas McComiskey. Grand Rapids: Eerdmans, 1991.

Whittington-Egan, Molly. *Doctor Forbes Winslow: Defender of the Insane.* Foley Terrace, U.K.: Cappella Archive, 2000.

Winks, Joseph Foulkes, ed. "Deaths." *The Baptist Reporter and Missionary Intelligencer* 22, no. 264 (August 1848): 328.

————. "Intelligence: Baptist." *The Baptist Reporter and Missionary Intelligencer* 25 (November 1851): 431–33.

Winslow, Douglas Kenelm. *Mayflower Heritage: A Family Record of the Growth of Anglo-American Partnership.* New York: Funk & Wagnalls Co., 1957.

York, Hershael, and Bert Decker. *Preaching with Bold Assurance: A Solid and Enduring Approach to Engaging Exposition.* Nashville: Broadman & Holman, 2003.